Knitting
Fashion, Industry, Craft

Knitting
Fashion, Industry, Craft

SANDY BLACK

V&A PUBLISHING

First published by V&A Publishing, 2012
Victoria and Albert Museum
South Kensington
London SW7 2RL
www.vandabooks.com

Distributed in North America by Harry N. Abrams Inc., New York
© The Board of Trustees of the Victoria and Albert Museum, 2012

ISBN 978 1 85177 559 0

Library of Congress Control Number 2011923011

10 9 8 7 6 5 4 3 2 1
2016 2015 2014 2013 2012

Front jacket illustration: Elsa Schiaparelli, *trompe l'oeil* sweater (see page 91).
Back jacket illustration: Sandra Backlund, dress (see page 210).
Frontispiece: *Woman at her Toilet* (detail), Jan Steen, *c.*1661. Rijksmuseum Amsterdam.
Title page illustration: Liturgical gloves (see pages 16 and 17).

Designer: Nigel Soper
Copy-editor: Philippa Baker
Index: Hilary Bird

New photography by Richard Davis, V&A Photographic Studio

Printed in China

V&A Publishing
Supporting the world's leading
museum of art and design,
the Victoria and Albert
Museum, London

Contents

History, Tradition and Mythology:

from the Third Century to the Late Nineteenth Century

'Hand-knitting…like spinning on the wheel was pursued through every rank of female society from the palace to the cottage.'

W. FELKIN, *History of the Machine-Wrought Hosiery and Lace Manufactures*

KNITTING IS AN ANCIENT CRAFT but its origins are still unclear and its early history may never be definitively established. Some early fragments of constructed woollen fabric dating from the second and third centuries CE bear a resemblance to knitting but were in fact produced by related but different techniques.[1] Archaeological finds from burial grounds, particularly in Egypt and parts of Europe and Scandinavia, suggest that knitting may have originated in several parts of the world independently.[2] The Victoria and Albert Museum contains a number of outstanding pieces of virtuoso knitting, and this chapter traces the evolution of knitting using examples from the museum dating from about the third century through to the end of the nineteenth century.

The etymology of the words used for knitting is often confusing: no word specifically for this craft existed in Greek or Latin, and, until the Renaissance period, several languages borrowed words from the more ancient crafts of weaving and netting. Contemporary words such as *la maille* in French and *punto* in Spanish are derived from the words for mesh or stitch. There may be similarities with knotting and netting, but one notable characteristic of most knitted fabric is that it can be easily unravelled from a final single loop (as can crochet).

Knitting is commonly understood to be the creation of a fabric from a single thread, formed into horizontal rows of individual loops that intermesh with each successive row of loops. Knitted items were originally made using a range of simple hand tools that were gradually refined from hand-carved sticks of wood, bone, quill or ivory, which in some parts of Europe had hooked ends, to metal wires and the fine steel knitting needles that became commonplace in the nineteenth century. It can be speculated that primitive looped fabric was made on the fingers of the hands, since it was certainly later made on both circular and straight peg frames.[3] In contrast, woven construction utilizes two sets of threads, warp and weft, which interlace each other in horizontal and vertical directions; warp-knitting, which emerged during the Industrial Revolution, combines elements of knitting and weaving.[4] Unlike weft-knitting, warp-knitted fabric is not easily unravelled and is usually cut and sewn.

Plain knitting can be produced 'in the round' (also known as circular or tubular knitting), using a set of four or five needles to create a continuous seamless spiral formation that can be shaped three-dimensionally, particularly when knitting caps, stockings, gloves and body garments. Alternatively, hand-knitting can be made flat by working in rows with two knitting needles, turning the work from front to back each row, using the purl loop as the reverse of the plain knitted loop. Both techniques developed according to regional practice and the functional requirements of the knitting itself, and some garments used both techniques (see p.31), but the flat-knitting technique gradually became dominant in hand-knitting. This corresponded with the rise of literacy, as patterns were no longer handed down

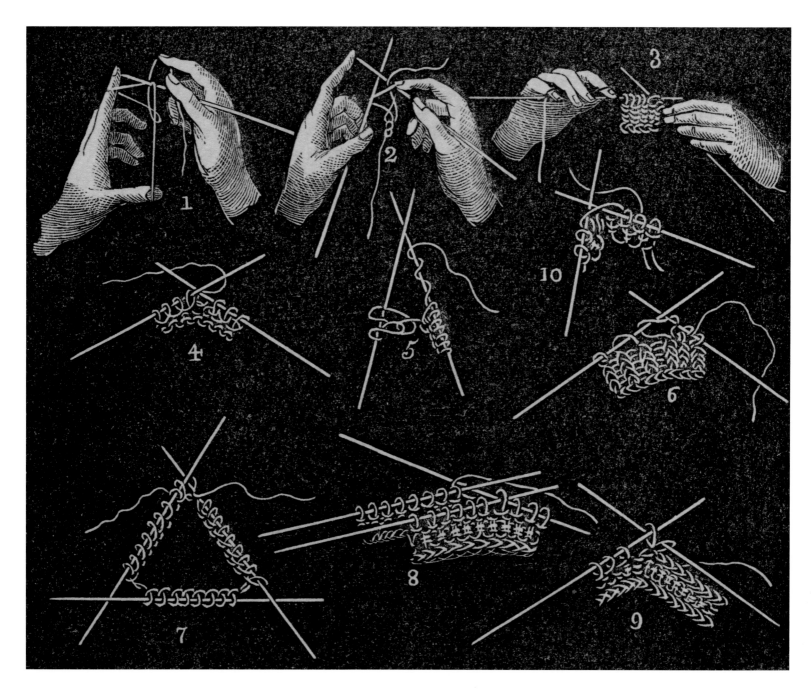

orally but spread by the use of printed instructions and charts for more decorative work (plate 1). The circular method was less suited to such representations, depending instead on tacit skills and knowledge and the invention of each knitter. A parallel transition from hand- to machine- production methods took place from the late sixteenth century. In machine knitting, the rows of loops were constructed on pegs or hooked metal needles constrained within a frame.

Knitting remains today both an industrial and a domestic activity, each completely separate spheres. Recent knitted artefacts from Europe, the British Isles,

Scandinavia and South America demonstrate a range of techniques and practices that have spread and developed distinctive regional characteristics.

Subtle differences in technique between eastern and western knitting methods include crossing or twisting the stitches by knitting into the back of the loop rather than the front.[5] Crossed-loop fabrics can be clearly seen in the earliest examples of socks from third- to fifth-century Egypt, as well as in many twentieth-century knitted socks from Turkey or Greece (see V&A: T.94&A–1990). The methods by which knitting needles and yarn are held and the yarn thrown over the needles also vary, with significant differences within Continental Europe, the Americas and Britain. For example, in English knitting the yarns are held in the right hand; Continental knitting technique uses the left hand to throw the yarn; Shetland knitters work with two colours, one held in each hand; and South American knitters pass the yarn around their necks for tension. Colourful geometric patterning is a strong knitting tradition worldwide, from the earliest Islamic Egyptian socks to bold Norwegian and Macedonian patterns, the subtle natural shades of Fair Isle Shetland knitting and the extremely fine circular-knitted multicoloured hats of Bolivia and Peru. The constraints of the fundamental unit structure of the knitted stitch mean that many similar geometric patterns and stitches can be found in different knitting traditions. At the same time, patterns, perhaps inspired by embroidered or woven fabrics and interpreted into unique local stitches, may have been spread via trade and shipping routes. The spread of knitting – a highly portable technique requiring minimal tools – was certainly accelerated through international trade and British, Spanish, Portuguese and Dutch imperialism.

Regardless of regional variations, the fundamental loop construction of all weft-knitted fabrics is the same – knit and purl loop formations – and all forms of knitting have much in common, including origins, techniques and fabric structures. Similar knitted fabrics are produced worldwide and have been for centuries.

Heads, hands and feet

The earliest finds from burial grounds give only tantalizing glimpses into the origins of knitting. The oldest fragments that exist in museums were found preserved in the dry earth of Egypt or Syria during Edwardian-era expeditions. The easily biodegradable textile materials available to early peoples – linen, hemp, wool and later cotton – would have perished long before remains of stone, bone, wood or metal. And, although wool was widely available in many countries and may have been preferred for its natural softness and warmth, it is much less resistant to wear and tear than cellulose-based hemp, linen and cotton. Some early knitted fragments are today known only through written records, or are too fragile to be examined for any further information on the origins of knitting.

From the remains found in excavations, it appears that the practice of knitting began with items made to protect the extremities: coverings for heads, hands and feet that combined warmth and flexibility. Caps, stockings and gloves were important as both everyday clothing and to denote status, and such garments predate knitted coverings for the upper body. Most of the earliest artefacts that have survived to the present day are, as would be expected, examples of items made for royalty or aristocracy rather than the well-worn clothing of the lower classes.

The oldest 'knitted' artefacts in the V&A collection are seamless foot coverings with divided toes, suitable for wearing with sandals (plates 2 and 3). Known as Coptic socks and dating from the second to the fifth centuries, these were excavated from Egyptian tombs in the 'Romano-Egyptian period'.[6] Four key examples, all made in wool – one pair in red and individual socks in purple and brown – show the crossed-loop technique and split toe, but with different features such as ribbing and lacing. Another sock striped ochre and red is much smaller in size and therefore said to be a child's sock; the division of the toe section here is almost in the centre of the foot, which may have been somewhat difficult to wear. The construction of these seamless socks, with stitches worked in different directions and three-dimensional

1 *Treasures in Needlework*, Mrs Warren and Mrs Pullan, 1855, London
This diagram shows techniques for casting on (1, 2), plain knitting (3), purling (4), making stitches (5), decreasing (6), circular knitting (7), knitting to join together (8), casting off (9), and knitting three together (10). The accuracy of the diagrams is sometimes wanting.

shaping, was initially believed to indicate what is now accepted as a 'true knitting' technique on straight needles.[7] However, reconstruction has revealed that the method was consistent with the single-needle looping method, known as nalbinding or knotless netting, practised in Scandinavia since prehistoric times using short lengths of yarn or other materials and sometimes the fingers of one hand as a foundation.[8] This theory is supported by the particular methods of increasing and decreasing loops, which could not be replicated in knitting, and the fact that no suitable tools for knitting have been found in these areas, though several large-eyed needles that could be used for sewing with yarn were present.

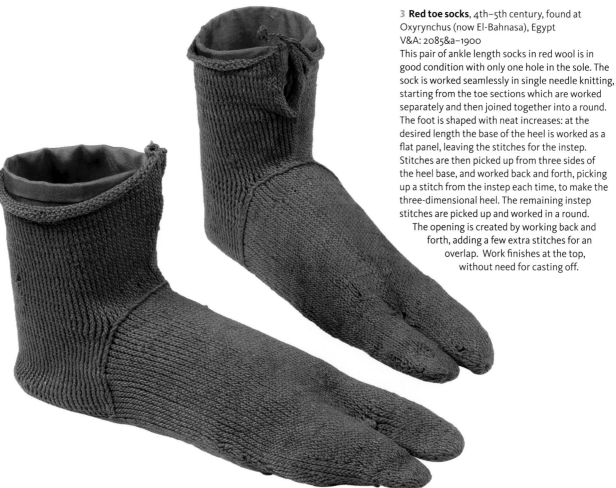

2 Brown toe sock, 5th–6th century, Found at Oxyrynchus (now El-Bahnasa), Egypt
V&A: 1243–1904
This single sock is of similar design to the socks in plate 3. Now faded brown in colour, it is mended with several patches on the heel, sole and top of the foot, made using the same single-needle knitting technique.

3 Red toe socks, 4th–5th century, found at Oxyrynchus (now El-Bahnasa), Egypt
V&A: 2085&a–1900
This pair of ankle length socks in red wool is in good condition with only one hole in the sole. The sock is worked seamlessly in single needle knitting, starting from the toe sections which are worked separately and then joined together into a round. The foot is shaped with neat increases: at the desired length the base of the heel is worked as a flat panel, leaving the stitches for the instep. Stitches are then picked up from three sides of the heel base, and worked back and forth, picking up a stitch from the instep each time, to make the three-dimensional heel. The remaining instep stitches are picked up and worked in a round.
     The opening is created by working back and forth, adding a few extra stitches for an overlap. Work finishes at the top, without need for casting off.

The pair of red foot coverings was, like the other socks of this date, constructed in the round, working from the toes upwards (see diagram in Glossary), in the opposite direction to later European stockings. A fragment in the V&A collection, originally described when found in 1896 as a 'doll's cap' (V&A: 1939A–1897), has

exactly the same asymmetrical triangular shape as the outer toe section of the pair of red socks and is probably an unfinished piece or a replacement part for a sock. All the socks, particularly the purple one, are well worn on the soles, encrusted with dirt and mended; the brown sock has patches that have been worked over the top, which is easily accomplished in the nalbinding technique. It is possible that these foot coverings were worn directly on the ground as well as with sandals. A roundel and small bag at the V&A, also found in Egypt, provide further examples of nalbinding. All other items classed as 'knitted' in the V&A collections are of true knitting made either on needles, manual knitting frames or industrial knitting machines.

Medieval knitting

From the first few centuries until early medieval times, the historical trail is barren. No true knitted artefacts dating from the sixth to the eleventh centuries appear to exist in any public collections internationally.[9]

Two very different fragments in the V&A are both from Egyptian burial grounds of the Fatimid period. The first is part of a blue-and-cream patterned cotton stocking – one of a number of similar items in museum collections around the world.[10] Close examination of the V&A's fragment (plate 4) shows clearly that, although now flat, it was knitted in the round. The spiral construction is evident from the typical mismatch of knitting courses that occurs when this technique is employed, creating an invisible 'seamline' marking the beginning of each round, most evident when stripes or patterns are knitted. The remains of an inserted heel appear at either side of the fragment.[11] Unusually for the majority of socks and stockings but typical of Egyptian examples, the fragment was knitted from the foot upwards. It has a chain cast-off edge at the top and measures approximately 50 cm in length. An interesting element of its construction relates to the shaping of the stocking to fit the leg: to solve a common knitting problem – that is, to maintain the pattern repeat while still shaping the stocking – the knitting gauge (tension) changes gradually from bottom to top, being tighter at

Socks from around the world

KNITTED SOCKS AND LEGGINGS appear in a range of cultures as part of the folk tradition of costume, for example in Central Europe and Asia. A variety of localized knitting techniques has resulted in a strong identity within specific regions. The joy of pattern and vitality of vernacular design is demonstrated in these artefacts, expressed in medium- and heavy-weight wools or in finer silks, all in geometric pattern and colour combinations. Some socks take a simple pointed shaping for toes and heels, others have more rounded forms. All find a way to turn a corner in the basic tubular construction of a shaped cylindrical form. Embroidered decoration can be profuse or subtly blended in, but the woven-together strands of coloured knitting create both layers of warmth and visual decoration. Shown are socks from Greece, Albania, Hungary, Turkey, Armenia, Bulgaria and Iraq.

TOP, LEFT TO RIGHT:

Leggings,
1960s, Greece
V&A: T.86&A–1990
These leggings are knitted as tubes, in three colours of tightly spun wool and cotton. The size of the diamond motif is precisely calculated to fit the number of stitches and work perfectly in the round. The leggings were worn by Sarakatsani women.

Socks,
19th century, Albania
V&A: T.106&A–1934
These heavy woollen socks are knitted on a cream ground in stranded colour knitting in black and red, with pattern highlights in yellow, purple and pale green. Both the foot and heel are shaped to a point. They were probably part of a man's winter costume.

Sock,
19th century, Hungary
V&A: 901–1883
This thick woollen sock is knitted in black, red and cream, with knitted gores surrounded by thick floral embroidery at each side, adding yellow, blue and green highlights. The design is reminiscent of the fine silk stockings of previous centuries.

Socks,
1960s, Turkey
V&A: T.94&A–1990
The striped pouch-shaped heels of these woollen socks form a bullseye pattern. They have pointed toes and are knitted in crossed stocking stitch. The pink, brown and turquoise colours contrast with the cream and purple ground, with highlights in yellow.

BOTTOM, LEFT TO RIGHT:
Socks,
1960s, Armenia
V&A: T.85&A–1990
These socks in cream wool with eyelet diagonal patterning on the cuffs and top of the foot are decorated with finely detailed banded patterns and single-stitch colour motifs on the fronts only, worked in bright contrast colours.

Socks,
19th century, Bulgaria
V&A: T.19&A–1937
These tightly knitted woollen sock-boots use both plain and crossed-stitch techniques, in red with bands of pattern in brown. There are side openings finished with knitted edgings in gold metallic yarn, and twisted woollen cords for fastening.

Silk socks,
1930s, Iraq
V&A: T.4&A–1968
These socks are finely knitted in stocking stitch in strong, bright colours including black, yellow, turquoise, pink, orange and cream. The patterning is small scale and highly intricate, with a border design outlining the foot, creating a jewelled effect.

5 Fragment,
14th–15th century, Egypt
V&A: T.87–1937
Highly complex in technique, this
fragment is a mix of stranded
knitting in the ground colours of
navy and chestnut, and intarsia
technique (worked in blocks of
colour similar to tapestry; see
Glossary), with each lozenge
introducing new colours knitted
only over that area.

the ankle. Hence two diamond repeats (12 sts and 14 rows) are 5.2 cm long and 3.5 cm wide at the top, 4.7 cm long and 3.1 cm wide in the middle band, and 4.2 cm long and 3 cm wide at the bottom (foot). This variation could most easily have been achieved by changing the thickness of the knitting implements used or, with more difficulty, by knitting more loosely as the work progressed. Little is known of the context in which these stockings were worn, but remarkably similar

stockings and socks can be found in twentieth-century cultures around the world (see pp.12–13).

The second intriguing fragment is a piece of intricate knitting in wools of five colours, which now appear as chestnut brown, camel, cream and light grey–green on a ground of navy and chestnut (plate 5). There are no clues as to the fragment's context but, even though it is badly damaged with many holes, the rich patterning and technique is clear. Reminiscent of traditional knotted carpet designs, the pattern features individual lozenge motifs of abstract design, together with various crosses, and includes a stylized animal, which may be a bird, camel or lion. The yarn is a tightly twisted two-ply and the knitting is extremely fine, at a gauge of 70 sts to 10 cm. Four of the five colours are used in several lozenges, stranded across.[12] This piece is unlikely to have been knitted in the round and has been described as one of 'possibly the oldest known pieces of flat knitting'.[13]

The fragment demonstrates the high level of skill employed in medieval knitting – an occupation that was regulated in Continental Europe by hand-knitting guilds. These were established in Paris as early as the fourteenth century, and by the mid-sixteenth century in centres such as Strasbourg, Prague and Vienna. Combined techniques of stranded and intarsia knitting such as those used in this fragment would have been familiar to the skilled knitters making intricate 'masterpiece' carpets (even if these were made on peg frames).

The two fragments described above begin to indicate the extensive range of knitted goods produced throughout this period of history, from articles made for the everyday use of the lower social classes, of which little physical evidence remains, to items used by the aristocracy or clergy, which are well represented in museums and demonstrate remarkable intricacy and craftsmanship of construction and design.[14] This is not to say that the commonplace items such as stockings are not worthy of note: on the contrary, elaborate three-dimensional shaping is much in evidence in all early examples (see p.24). The same knitters might have made higher-quality goods for sale as well as knitting basic items for personal and family use.

Two cushions from royal tombs at Las Huelgas Monastery in Spain also date from the late thirteenth century and demonstrate a high level of knitting skill, with insignia from Islamic, French and German traditions such as fleur-de-lis, rosettes and castles.[15] After this, though, there are few extant knitted artefacts until the sixteenth century.[16] There is, however, visual evidence for knitting in several fourteenth-century religious paintings from Italy and Germany. One of the most well known among these is the Buxtehude Altar by Master Bertram of Minden, in which the Madonna is clearly shown knitting the neckline of a body garment in the round mounted on four pins (plate 6). This indicates knitting was a familiar activity to the painter, but little else: 'The artists could have known of knitting because it was done elsewhere. It may have been done

6 *Visit of the Angel*, from the right wing of the Buxtehude Altar, Master Bertram of Minden, *c.*1390s
Tempera on panel
Hamburger Kunsthalle, Germany

often or rarely, by the wealthy or the poor, by house-wives or by nuns.'[17] Such is the little-known early history of knitting.

Sixteenth-century knitting

Two important types of garment from the six-teenth century demonstrate the extremes of everyday and ceremonial knitting: on the one hand, liturgical gloves from Spain represent the high church, while on the other knitted medieval caps found in London represent the English vernacular.[18]

Far more than a simple covering for the hand, gloves in the Middle Ages were 'a symbol of power, dignity, grace and feeling'.[19] Two pairs of liturgical gloves in the V&A, both said to be of Spanish origin and dated to the 1500s, demonstrate different but equally sophisticated techniques of production. These gloves would have been worn by bishops to perform symbolic rituals and ceremonies and are therefore well preserved. Their use dates back to the eleventh and twelfth centuries, when papal bulls specified that gloves must be close fitting with five elongated fingers, a long knit-ted cuff and the back of the hand decorated with a sacred symbol. Both pairs are of a similar shape, with gauntlet cuff, and use similar yarns, but they are rather differently constructed, and one of the pairs is richly patterned with all-over decoration.

The comparatively plain gloves (plate 7) are finely knitted in red silk, at a gauge of approximately 20 sts and 20 rows to 2.5 cm, with areas of patterning worked in silver-gilt yarn (yellow silk yarn wrapped with silver metallic thread – an expensive material that appears gold). The shaped gauntlet, thumb and fingers are all knitted in the round, with neat three-way decreasings giving rounded fingertips. However, there appears to be a partial edge-to-edge seam (or perhaps reinforce-ment) at the outer edge of the palm, where the ends of a separate silk thread and overstitches are clearly visi-ble. The octagonal cartouches therefore seem to have been worked in flat knitting, probably from a chart. The thumb is knitted into the front of the palm, picked up from a group of stitches that has simply been divided

horizontally to form its base. The glove is subse-quently rejoined into a circle and each finger completed seamlessly. Without the mono-gram patterning on the back, it would have been usual to complete the entire glove seamlessly. The reversal of the IHS motif on the left hand suggests something of both the method of work-ing, which is consistent with flat knitting, and the literacy of the knitter. It could be that the only way the knitter could achieve the left–right mirror symmetry of the hand was to reverse everything, including the motif. If such a pattern were worked from a chart, both the shaping and the letters would be reversed.[20]

The second pair of liturgical gloves is rather more intricately constructed and decorated and extremely finely knitted, to a gauge of 25 sts and 20 rows to 2.5 cm (plate 8). Worked in two-coloured patterned knitting

7 Liturgical gloves,
16th century, Spain
V&A: 876&a–1897
The gloves bear a
monogrammed octagonal
cartouche of leaves and
crosses on the back of each
hand; the gauntlet cuffs are
patterned with bands of
rosettes and geometric motifs
and finished with an ornate
tassel at the outer cuff. They
are partially lined in yellow silk
over the patterned areas,
which would prevent fingers
catching in the stranded yarns
on the back of the fabric. The
cartouche on the right hand
shows the letters IHS – a
symbol for Jesus much used in
the Middle Ages. The left-hand
motif shows these letters in
reverse.

8 Liturgical gloves,
16th century, Spain
V&A: 437–1892
The all-over patterned back and
palm of the hand includes cross
and heart motifs, together with
geometric patterning on the
gauntlet cuffs. Gussets between
each finger are decorated with
stripes and a wave pattern and a
serpent-wrapped sword or crook
motif. The gored thumb is
knitted plain and positioned at
the outer side seam of each
hand in contrast to the gloves
with IHS monogram. Bobbin lace
edging decorates the cuffs and
thumbs, with a heart-shaped
motif at the base of each
thumb. A meandering
chain stitch line is
embroidered around
the thumb in gilt thread.

throughout the palms, backs, cuffs and fingers, these gloves feature religious symbols such as a cross and heart. They are unlined, but the insides of the gloves are very neat, using the technique of 'weaving in' the floats of colour not in use, thus avoiding long strands that could catch. Perhaps because of the complexity of the all-over design, the gloves are knitted in the round for the main part of the hand and the fingers, three of which are knitted to a shaped point (the middle finger is seamed at the top for a rounder shape). The fingers have then been cut to insert gussets (forchettes) made of separately knitted cut-up pieces of different patterns and symbols, following the typical construction method of a pair of gloves made from woven fabric. All

seams are decorated in gilt-thread braid, and the gloves are finished with the application of narrow bobbin lace worked in the same thread. Save for a hole in the left wrist, the gloves show little sign of wear and represent highly skilful execution, befitting their purpose and high status. Such items provide strong evidence that knitting was already well established as a craft industry in Europe by the sixteenth century, reflecting the wealth of its patrons.

Contemporary with the Spanish liturgical gloves are English pieces distinguished not by exclusivity but by their commonplace usage. Knitted caps were worn by men and boys under English sumptuary laws in the latter part of the sixteenth century.[21] Several illustrations

Iohn More Sᵗ Thomas Mores Son.

9 *John More the Younger*,
Hans Holbein the Younger,
*c.*1526–7, Britain
Black and coloured chalk
on paper
The Royal Collections
The caps seen in the Holbein
images have a split brim with
two overlapping sections and
are comparable with several in
the V&A collection which are
knitted all in one piece to create
a firm double-layered brim.

and paintings depict this headwear: for example, Hans Holbein the Younger's paintings and sketches of Thomas More's son of about 1526–7 (plate 9). Such caps were generally dyed red (with madder) or black, which was an especially difficult colour to dye and was therefore sought after. They were often decorated with velvet ribbons and feathers, as were their more expensive woven velvet counterparts. Those seen in museums vary now from shades of russet red to reddish brown and dark brown because of the degradation of the dyes and their archaeological condition, many having been found in Thames mud.

Cap-making was a significant industry in medieval England, and their manufacture and price was regulated by Parliament. The cappers' guilds, making caps from woven cloth, were among the oldest in England, dating from the mid-thirteenth century. The term 'capknytters' was recorded in 1422 in York. Fragments showing shapings that could be for a cap were found in late fourteenth-century London deposits, and reference to knitted caps as a common article of clothing is found in a statute of 1488, which fixed the price at 2 shillings and 8 pence.[22]

By Tudor times, caps had become highly fashionable. The Puritan Philip Stubbes, inveighing against current fashions in the 1580s in his *Anatomie of Abuses*, observed that a man was 'of no account or estimation amongst men' if he did not own a cap of velvet or taffeta; hence woollen caps were for 'common' people.[23] The Cappers Act of 1571 identified 15 distinct 'callings' in cap knitting, including carding and spinning of fleece, knitting, fulling (light felting), dyeing, dressing (raising of the nap), shearing (trimming the raised surface) and lining. The act appears to have been a protectionist response to the growth of the stocking-knitting trade. This sumptuary law stated that every English resident over the age of six, except 'maids, ladies, gentlewomen, noble personages and every Lord, Knight and gentle-man of 20 marks land', should wear on Sundays and holidays 'a cap of wool, thicked and dressed in England, made within this realm and only dressed and finished by some of the trade of cappers, upon pain to forfeit for every day of not wearing 3s 4d'.[24] Although this statute was resented, ridiculed and not easily enforced, many contemporary paintings, for example by Pieter Brueghel the Elder, indicate the extent to which caps of this type were common everyday wear in the Low Countries as well as in Britain. The Cappers Act was eventually repealed in 1597.

Significant finds of caps have been made during building excavations in the City of London on the probable site of cap-making workshops, confirming that London was a major centre for the capping trade. Three were also recovered in 1982 from the ship *Mary Rose*, which sank suddenly with its crew and cargo in 1545.

Each cap is knitted slightly differently, but following similar general principles, that would have been learnt by apprentices from master craftsmen. They are generally made all in one piece in the round, with a flat circular crown and several different styles of single or double brim which were divided into overlapping sections and sometimes slashed in fashionable style when felted and finished (see p.21). This circular construction method, worked either from the brim to the crown or more usually by increasing from a central small loop of stitches to create a flat circle, is easily created in hand-knitting (and also familiar in crochet) and has continued to be used for hats and berets to the present day.[25] The same construction can still be seen in hand-knitted Scottish tam-o'-shanter-style berets, often worked in Fair Isle patterning, common in the early and mid-twentieth century. Caps and berets continue to cycle in and out of fashion: at the start of the twenty-first century knitted caps and hats became popular again, being produced by high-street fashion stores such as Topshop and taken up by hip hop musicians.

Tudor cap knitting in the round

For any Cap, what ere it bee
Is still the sign of some degree

ELIZABETHAN BALLAD

THE GROUP OF TUDOR knitted caps in the V&A collection comprises 24 caps or parts of caps. The caps were knitted more coarsely than they now appear, and degradation of the nap of the felted surfaces often reveals the construction beneath and the stitch shapings placed randomly over the crown. The caps were generally made in one piece in the round, usually starting from the centre crown and increasing to the required size, then decreasing again to the desired head circumference.

Apprentices would have learnt from long experience the size to knit and the amount of shrinkage to expect. The caps were knitted on wooden or metal multiple needles or even goose quills. (Metal needles were expensive and prized possessions until the introduction of water-powered wire-drawing into Britain in 1566, which transformed many aspects of the textile industry). After knitting, fulling by hand or foot closed up and thickened the fabric teasels so the cap would protect its wearer from wind and weather. The resulting felted fabric could be cut to shape without unravelling. Finally the cap was raised by brushing with teasels, creating a smooth velvety surface that mimicked the more expensive woven velvet caps. Knitted-on linings, turned in and cut to size after felting, are a feature of several caps. Finished edges, either cast on or cast off, can be seen on others. Although there are common elements, there are no common patterns and each cap is individual in its construction, depending on many variable factors: the knitting tension, the size of the needles and the type of fleece used, the spinning of the yarn, the twisting of the plies and the depth of fulling.

Knitted caps,
16th century, London
(clockwise from top left):
V&A: 1571–1901, 1565–1901,
741–1904, 1570–1901
Governed by the prevailing sumptuary laws, which strictly limited dress according to class and occupation, caps in Tudor times were a clear indicator of status, 'a sign of some degree'. Black velvet caps, made from woven fabrics, were worn by the fashionable upper classes of society, whereas cheaper knitted caps were worn mainly by the lower classes as everyday wear.

The V&A's collection of caps features a number of general types. The simplest model is a head hugging coif shape in single-thickness knitting throughout, with or without lappets, which could be worn down as earflaps or tied up over the crown. One has separately knitted shaped lappets, which are also knitted in the round (see V&A: T.190–1958). Some finished edges are visible on the coif cap shown bottom left. Caps with double-thickness brims, split into overlapping sections (see plate 9), form the majority, although three have a single-layer brim with cast off edge (see top right). There are several caps with a double brim at the front and flap at the back of the neck, which could be worn up or down and might be fashionably slashed into sections after felting, as in the cap bottom right. A cap with a double-layer brim extending halfway round the circumference has the appearance of a modern-day peaked cap (top left). Almost all the caps have a separately knitted crown as a lining, which would have improved the warmth and protection. A single coif cap is intriguingly different from all the others with a textured surface visible in concentric purl-stitch pattern bands on a plain-knit ground. However, nothing is known about its provenance (see V&A: 936–1902).

Stocking knitting and fashion

The use of the name 'stocking stitch' to denote the fundamental structure of hand and machine knitting indicates the pivotal role of knitted stockings in the development of the hosiery and knitting industry. It is clear from records from the sixteenth century onwards, including inventories, wills and port accounts, that stockings were both an everyday necessity for the population of Britain and Europe and highly fashionable garments, particularly in male fashions. The ability to create fine knitting was given impetus in Britain after the introduction of water-powered metal-wire drawing mills in 1566 facilitated the making of finer metal needles. Stocking knitting developed into a thriving domestic and export trade in the sixteenth and seventeenth centuries: it is estimated that between 90,000 and 110,000 knitters were working in the domestic trade in England in 1595, based on the assumption that each citizen would have consumed at least two pairs of stockings per year.[26]

The origins of stockings lie in sixteenth-century 'hose' – a combination of short breeches with attached leg coverings made from woven fabrics cut on the cross. Until the early seventeenth century, these were separated into trunk hose – or 'upper stocks' – and 'nether stocks'. The latter became stockings, held in place by garters above or below the knee. By the mid-to-late eighteenth century, men could also wear all-in-one close-fitting garments, also called hose or pantaloons and similar to present-day tights but cut from woven cloth (see p.69).[27] Referring to such stockings or socks (known originally as 'half hose'), the term hose gave its name to the hosiery industry. But 'hosiery' became a catch-all term for any type of knitted garment until the twentieth century, when the term 'knitwear' came into use and hosiery came to refer largely to legwear and lingerie.

By the mid-sixteenth century, stimulated by changes in male fashions, elaborately decorated knitted silk stockings were worn by the fashionable men of the Spanish court, high-quality knitting in silk having been available in Spain since the thirteenth century. This expensive attire was highly prized and much admired by members of the English court, and silk stockings were imported into England to be worn by royalty and nobility (plate 12), including Henry VIII and Edward VI. The London Port Book of 1567–8 records 12 pairs of silk stockings imported from Malaga at a recorded cost of nearly £4.[28] This can be compared with a top servant's wage of £5 per year. By the 1560s, copies were being made in London, marking the beginnings of a thriving luxury fashion and export trade, especially with Spain. Stockings became a key part of the Tudor nobleman's ornate clothing and, beneath short breeches, the legs were clad in bold-coloured hose, dyed to match the outfit, with rich embroidery embellishing the outer and inner ankle region, known as the 'clocks'. As the desire for these stockings spread, Philip Stubbes, writing in his *Anatomie of Abuses* in 1585,

10 and **11** **Blue stocking**, late 18th/early 19th century, Spain; **Green stocking**, mid-18th century, Britain
V&A: T.77–1957; V&A: T.199–1958
Elaborately embroidered frame-knitted stockings were worn by both men and women, knitted flat and shaped for the calf, with a seam at the back. The Spanish-made blue silk stocking features exquisite silk embroidered clocks, but has relatively crudely stitched seams. The English-made green silk stocking is more skilfully knitted and finished, with fashioned toe and gored clocks, and metallic thread embroidery that incorporates a crown, denoting high status.

expressed his outrage at their extravagance: 'The very knitting of them is worth a noble [6 shillings and 8 pence] or a royal [11 shillings and 3 pence]…The time might have been when one might have clothed all his body well, from top to toe, for less than a pair of these [silk] nether stockes will cost.'[29]

Fine silk-knitted stockings proved far superior to those of cloth, owing to their extensibility and close fit, which reduced unsightly wrinkles. Importantly, hand-knitted stockings could be made seamlessly for comfort

12 Portrait miniature of Richard Sackville, 3rd Earl of Dorset, (detail) by Oliver Isaac, 1616, British V&A: 721–1882
Portraits of Tudor noblemen were designed to show off their powerful status through the symbolism of their fashionably elaborate clothing and related artefacts. Richard Sackville, pictured in this miniature with his armour, is shown wearing richly embroidered stockings dyed exactly to match his doublet. Such display stimulated a major industry in stocking knitting.

because they could be knitted in the round, while the flexibility of the construction could be used to shape the calf, turn the heel and neatly close the foot. Decoration was incorporated in the form of knitted-in textured or coloured patterns, which often mimicked the 'seam' of a woven stocking. The focal point of male stocking fashion remained the clocks, which were elaborately over-embroidered in metal or silk threads (plates 10, 11).

Similarly decorated stockings were also worn by women. Although female legs remained hidden beneath voluminous skirts and petticoats, movement and small changes in the fashionable length of skirts might tantalizingly reveal the ankle or instep in public. What was revealed in private or by dancers and prostitutes was clearly also a design consideration for clever entrepreneurs with an eye for business (see frontispiece).

When William Lee invented the stocking knitting frame in the late sixteenth century, the hand-knitted stocking trade was then booming. This revolutionary machine at first produced coarse fabric but was eventually refined to enable fine silk stockings to be manufactured many times faster than by hand. However, the machine could make only flat fabric, requiring stockings once again to be constructed with a seam, as their woven predecessors were. By the early seventeenth century, knitted stockings had replaced woven hose completely in all strata of society with the exception of the army, who continued to wear cloth hose until the end of the century.[30]

Seventeenth-century boot hose

The earliest pair of English stockings in the V&A collection, dated to the 1640s, is hand-knitted seamlessly in medium-weight cream lustrous wool with dark-blue wool patterning. Known as 'boot hose', they illustrate a particular era in male fashions (plate 13). The spectacularly large tops were designed to sit inside the fashionable cavalier boots of the period, which could be worn turned down or left up. Although intended to protect finer silk stockings beneath, the boot hose were themselves intricately knitted and embroidered, designed to be seen. This pair was evidently highly valued as the hose are darned and mended throughout in mismatched assorted wools. The stockings are knitted from the top edge down (the common method) in a pattern of blue stripes with self-coloured purl-stitch diamond-and-cross decoration between, worked to a gauge of 11 sts and 21 rows to 2.5 cm.[31] The ankle and foot are shaped, as in certain hose of woven cloth, by means of a triangular gore worked seamlessly by knitting up stitches to change direction. A small purl-stitch diamond pattern is worked at the inner and outer ankle gores. It is over-embroidered in blue chain stitch, which outlines the gores and meets under the heel.

The creation of knitted gores enhanced the three-dimensional shaping and fit of stockings, and they were often made in a contrasting colour, providing a focal point for further decoration, which sometimes rose up to calf level. Gores gradually diminished in size as fashions and decoration generally became simplified. By the latter part of the nineteenth century, this detail had been replaced by narrow lines of hand embroidery with a final decorative flourish, known as 'chevening' – a style that continued well into the twentieth century (see p.63).

Eighteenth- and nineteenth-century stockings

The V&A collection includes many examples of fashionable knitted silk stockings, for both men and women from the eighteenth and nineteenth centuries, both hand-knitted on needles and manually made on the knitting frame, which continued to be a major means of production during nineteenth-century developments in powered machinery (see Timeline). A pair of nineteenth-century hand-knitted salmon-pink silk stockings (V&A: T.22H/I–1928) demonstrates the classic seamless construction in the round, with shaping at the calf and a square Dutch heel (see Glossary), the foot finished

13 **Boot hose**, 1640s, Britain
V&A: T.63&a–1910
The width of the tops is greatly reduced by decreasing stitches across one row, immediately before the change to ribbing. Perhaps in reference to woven hose, but also as a means of controlling the calf shaping and providing a guide for decoration, a knitted-in 'seamline' effect is worked from top to bottom using alternately knitted and slipped stitches. The mock seamline is a familiar device in hand-knitted stockings and other garments worked in the round. Within the leg section, either side of this seamline, purl stitches are worked in chevrons, which served as guide stitches for striking chain-stitch embroidery in a feather pattern, which is thus perfectly even down the back of each leg. The shaping of the calf by increasing and then decreasing stitches is symmetrically placed outside these chevron marks.

with a neatly fashioned toe shaped by two lines of decreasing. However, the majority of the V&A's eighteenth- and nineteenth-century stockings are frame-knitted. These are easily identified because they are constructed as flat pieces knitted to shape and size with finished selvedges and have, of necessity, seams at the back of the leg and also in the foot. To form the foot, the central section of the flat leg length was continued to form the top of the foot and toe, and shorter lengths at each side were joined to form the heel, with a separate sole section joined to the top foot.[32]

Many early examples of frame-knitting are beautifully patterned and shaped or 'wrought'. As demand grew from all classes of society for a less expensive product, stockings were more roughly constructed, being cut out from a rectangle of knitted fabric and entirely sewn to shape – an inferior production. These notorious 'cut-ups' undermined the skilled work of the frame-work knitters and helped spark the Luddite uprising of 1811–12 (see p.63) but were also the precursor of the cut-and-sewn knitwear industry so ubiquitous a century later (see p.68–9, 77).

The decorative intricacy and workmanship of early legwear can be astounding compared with modern-day examples of everyday industrially made stockings. Indicative of this is a striking pair of eighteenth-century Spanish silk stockings, frame-knitted in green and pink silk (plate 14). The stockings are in good condition, though, as is often the case, the sewing of the seams appears slovenly in comparison with the execution of the intricate knitting and embroidery. (This is not so surprising when the low piecework rates are taken into account.)

A later single stocking of English origin (plate 15) dated to the early nineteenth century, though of different construction, provides evidence for the practice of copying imported Spanish stockings. The two colours (blue with ivory gore) used in this stocking have been joined together not by the intarsia technique but by seaming after the main embroidered designs have

been applied to the gore and stocking sections separately – a much more practical solution. As a result, the embroidered border is not worked over the seam, but outside it. The quality of the embroidery is high, being comparable to the Spanish stockings with near identical design, and the sewing slightly more skilful.

By this time, English-made stockings had a high reputation and were exported to Europe, Scandinavia and the United States. Notable for the different style of embroidery are some pink-silk frame-knitted stockings from the same period, either English or French (plate 17). Here, the dark-green gored clocks are outlined in a simple but striking stylized floral design in the same colour, which gives the appearance of having been knitted rather than hand-embroidered. This could have been painstakingly made using a technique of plated

14 Stocking, 18th century, Spain
V&A: T.156/A–1971
The green and pink silk are knitted together using the intarsia technique for the pink gore clock, which reaches high up the calf. The knitting serves solely as a background for the most complex hand embroidery, based on counted stitches. A border pattern covers the join between the colours. The pink gore is covered with motifs of baskets and ferns, flanked by ornate peacocks, which reduce in size up the leg. The clock is topped with a fern-and-scroll motif with two more peacocks and a coronet.

15 Stocking, 1800–29, Britain
V&A: 666–1898
Blue and ivory silk stocking featuring similar embroidered decoration to the Spanish stocking (left). Variation is seen in the straight-edged border, the plant containers and the filling patterns. Compare the position of the border around the clock, outside the separately knitted ivory gore.

stitches or 'inlaid brocade' in which a second yarn was inserted manually in front of the first colour as knitting progressed on the handframe.[33] A possible alternative is a darning and reinforcing technique later known as Swiss or German darning, which mimics the knitted stitch, worked on top using similar yarn of matching or different colour.[34] However, the stockings' early date and the floats on the reverse of the pattern would seem to suggest the machine method was more likely.[35]

As expensive items, handmade silk stockings were often well worn and mended or stained with use. As spinning techniques improved, finer worsted and cotton stockings replaced silk stockings and, with changing fashions, decoration became simplified. There remained, however, a great diversity of types of stocking: by 1800, there were still 17 or 18 kinds of frame-knitted stockings worn as fashion.[36] Hand-knitted and frame-knitted stockings continued to exist side by side. Two white cotton stockings from Germany provide an example of practical heavier-gauge hand-knitted stockings made in the nineteenth century. Typically worn on festive occasions, stockings such as these featured damask patterns of knit-and-purl stitches and well-shaped heels and toes (plate 16). Another pair of sturdy, plain, white-cotton stockings with short ribbed tops are knitted in heavy cotton and monogrammed with BH in elaborate beaded letters (V&A: T.102&A–1973).

Although there is much evidence of knit-and-purl stitch combinations being used in damask-type textures in early knitting, there is surprisingly little sign of hand-knitted rib construction – a simple regular arrangement of knit and purl making an elastic fabric (see p. 24). This can partly be attributed to the technique of circular knitting, which can be made using just knit loops and employing purl loops only for decorative effect. There is no doubt, however, that hand-knitted ribbed stockings (plate 18) were better fitting than stocking-stitch ones.

Vertical lines of both colour and texture became fashionable for menswear in the late eighteenth century, achieved by the ingenious method of knitting the stockings sideways from seam to seam on wider stock-

ing frames (plate 19). Some pains were taken to replicate the visual effect, if not the elasticity, of hand-knitted ribs by using a fancy 'knotted' stitch.[37] Similar textural effects were made on later frames using the tuck presser, which could make 'silk stockings with the appearance of ribs, having a straight line of plain work down the stocking, and a very striking shaded appearance in parallel lines'.[38] For example, a pair of nineteenth-century light-brown silk stockings (V&A: T.1724&a–1913) made from a similar type of rib-effect fabric were roughly cut to shape and sewn up with a somewhat bulky seam that nevertheless creates an

16 Stockings, 1800s, Germany
V&A: 505&a–1899
Hand-knitted cotton seamless stockings, typically worn for festival occasions by peasant women from Vierlande, a district near Hamburg, Germany. Each stocking is from a different pair, featuring gored clocks, shaped toes and similar intricate decoration. Geometric purl-stitch heraldic patterns are worked on a plain ground with a narrower panel up the back of the leg and welts in garter stitch or a diagonal pattern to stabilize the edge.

17 Stocking, 1750–60,
Britain or France
V&A: T.34–1969
Pink and green silk gored
stocking featuring simple
border decoration topped by
rose and coronet, worked in
one colour using an inlay or
'plating' technique on the
manual knitting frame to
overlay the dark colour on
top of the lighter yarn.

18 Ribbed stockings,
early 19th century, Britain
V&A: T.439&A–1988
These hand-knitted ribbed
stockings are finely knitted in
the round in a wide (16sts) rib
stitch in marled silk formed by
twisting three colours together
(cream, lilac and green) to create
a speckled brown effect. The
construction features a mock
seamline at the back, shaping at
the calf and gored ankles, and a
chevron-patterned welt in purl
and plain stitches. The vertical
lines were fashionable in
menswear of the time.

19 Fashion plate from *Le
Magasin des Modes Nouvelles,
Francais et Anglaises*, 1787
The Metropolitan Museum of
Art, New York
A fashionable promenade suit,
formal wear for a gentleman,
shows a skirted coat, striped
waistcoat, knee-length breeches
and vertically striped stockings.
These are typical of stockings
machine-knitted sideways using
the wide stocking frames.

attractive chevron effect at the back of the calf from the converging lines. Vertically colour-striped stockings were created in a similar manner.[39]

Both men's and women's stockings were worn in many colours, including yellow and blue, dyed to match specific outfits, but by 1900 black stockings, both plain and embroidered, were ubiquitous, owing to improvements in dyeing technology and their practicality for daily wear in towns or for sports.[40] A 1902 price list from Dickens and Jones in London shows black lisle thread stockings with 'hand embroidered silk fronts, in great variety' costing between 2 shillings and 6 pence and 5 shillings and 11 pence a pair, and 'ladies black pure silk hose with silk clox' from 5 shillings and 11 pence to 18 shillings and 6 pence per pair.[41]

Men's fashions underwent a significant shift in the early nineteenth century towards the wearing of trousers that covered the lower leg, greatly reducing the demand for stockings but creating new demand for half hose or socks. Attention was therefore transferred to design for women's stockings. As industrial knitting technology developed, novelty patterns became popular, with companies offering designs that focused on the front of the shin, which would be revealed under skirts when dancing or walking.

The *fin de siècle* saw an upsurge in new decorative techniques (plate 21). The concept of intarsia, similar to tapestry weaving, enabled separate pattern blocks and detailed shapes of colour to be knitted and was often used as a basis for over-embroidery by hand (plates 20 and 22). Manufactured lace shapes were inserted into industrially knitted silk stockings by applying cut-out shapes to the stockings (butterflies or floral patterns for example), finely hand embroidering the joins, then cutting away the stocking and embroidering final flourishes to decorate (plate 23; V&A: T.45&a–1939). The cost of these intricate items was over five guineas (5 pounds and 5 shillings).[42] A fine example of the novelty genre, contemporaneous with the cancan era, is a French pair of plain black silk stockings dated around 1900 with a sequinned snake embroidered around each leg, exhibited in the Exposi-

20 Stocking (detail), 1869–99, Britain
V&A: T.46–1939
This stocking is boldly coloured in gold and blue, with a simple angled line dividing the two colours worked in intarsia and the pattern then embroidered in many colours.

21 Advertisement for Wm Morley & Gray stockings, in *Drapers Record*, 15 March 1902, London
Recalling the scandalous French entertainment style of the cancan, this advert promotes to the trade the many styles of black high lace ankle hose (lace-patterned stockings) available from Morley & Gray.

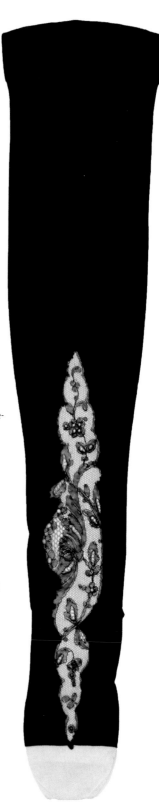

22 Stocking, 1890s, possibly France
V&A: T.18&A–1938
These stockings are frame-knitted in pink-and-black silk with three intarsia panels embroidered in black. The white-striped welts are marked with the initials A.B. in openwork.

23 Stocking with lace insertion, *c*.1898, France
V&A: T.76–1951
Many novelty treatments for ladies' legwear became popular in the 1890s, including this complex construction in which shapes were cut from manufactured lace and inserted into industrially knitted silk stockings. The work was highly skilled, as the knitted stocking could easily ladder.

tion Universelle, Paris, in 1900, at the height of the Art Nouveau movement (V&A: T.53/A–1962).

Industrial development continued through the eighteenth and nineteenth centuries, and William Lee's original invention was continually refined. His hand-operated stocking frame was eventually replaced by steam-powered frames, and stocking-frame knitting evolved into the fully industrialized hosiery trade (see pp.64–5). Stimulated by fashionable demand, patterning on the knitting frames, including intarsia and lacy openwork stitches became more and more inventive, requiring a high level of manual skill.

From the mid-eighteenth century, new improvements were made in frame-knitting to emulate hand-made embroidered laces. These had developed since the sixteenth century in centres across Europe as a high art and had come to symbolize wealth and elevated status. The fashion for lace details spread among the growing middle classes of the eighteenth and nineteenth centuries, and hand-knitting afforded a more accessible means to this fashionable end compared with laborious needle laces and bobbin lace. Needlework manuals show that lacy openwork stitches were being produced by hand-knitting by the 1840s, and no doubt well before then.[43] Machine-made versions of netting and knitted lace meshes were developed on the stocking handframe but the invention of the warp-knitting machine method in 1775 greatly increased the possibilities.[44]

Fine lace-knit stockings could be produced on the frame by the knitter painstakingly moving the loops to create patterns, aided by some simple hand tools. This laborious (and therefore costly) work was often confined to a part of the leg that might be seen. A pair of white-silk stockings from 1830–40 is very fine with delicate fronts in fancy lace (plate 24). Lace stockings were also worked in heavier silks in colours such as black and crimson, weighing around 4 oz (113 g), but fine stockings were as light as 1½ oz (43 g). Other examples are in linen thread, such as a pair of fine hand-knitted ankle socks (V&A: T.117&A–1927), or in heavy cotton. The most elaborate, dating from the late nineteenth century, are women's wedding stockings, finely frame-knitted in cream silk with intricate lace patterns over-embroidered in delicate floral motifs in coloured silks or all in white.

Hand-knitting and hand-frame knitting of stockings continued in parallel for more than 250 years after the frame's first invention, each with their different specialities and costs. For some considerable time,

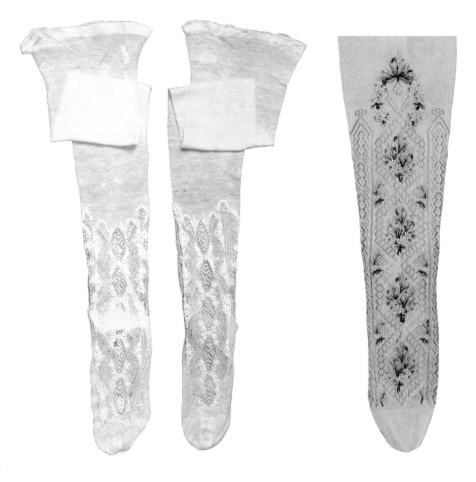

hand-knitting was of higher quality but wages were consistently lower than those for frame-knitting, partly because hand-knitting required no expensive equipment. An intriguing example of hybrid hand and machine production can be seen in several pairs of two-part stockings dating from the 1830s (V&A: T.205/206 – 1911). The foot and lower leg were hand-knitted seamlessly in lace patterns in either a delicate silk or heavy cotton, then joined to a top section of plain machine-knitted flat cotton fabric, which was seamed at the back. These stockings would have been a pragmatic means of meeting demand for fashionable women's lace stockings without wasting skill, time and costs in making openwork on areas not visible. During peak periods in demand for knitting it was common for work to be divided into different skill sets, known as 'leggers', 'footers' or 'toppers'.

24 **Stockings**, 1830–40, France
V&A: T.46&a–1909
Fine white cotton lace stocking with openwork lozenge-shaped patterns, embellished with embroidered flowers and knots in white cotton. Marked in openwork with initials A.U.C.O.C and address 4 rue de la Paix.

25 **Stocking**, c.1900, Britain
V&A: T.14–1956
Cream silk lace stocking from the wardrobe of H.M. Queen Alexandra. Knitted in openwork lace transfer patterning, enclosing plain sections embroidered with sprays of flowers and leaves. They represent some of the most prestigious and expensive stockings produced in the Edwardian era.

Body garments: early 'knitwear' from the seventeenth and eighteenth centuries

The earliest examples of knitting tend to be practical items for heads, hands and feet, some of which became articles of high fashion, but sixteenth-century records show the emergence of knitted garments worn on the torso (underwear and later outerwear). Now variously referred to as 'shirts', 'vests', 'jackets' or 'waistcoats', knitted body garments, with partial or complete front openings, may have been worn over a woven linen shirt in a complex system of elite clothing with both a practical and a fashionable purpose. Gradually these undergarments were revealed at the neckline or protruding through slashes in the outer clothing. A well-known early knitted example is a pale-blue silk garment with self-coloured textural patterning made from purl stitches, which may have been worn by Charles I at his execution in 1649 (plate 26).[45]

Such shirts were constructed in the round, knitted in one piece up to the armholes, where the stitches were divided for back and front. In some cases the shape is straight; in others, it flares from the armholes to the lower edge. The relatively simple shape of these garments – with wide, rounded necklines and sleeves knitted on at right angles to the body – can be traced right through the history of knitwear, from underwear, outerwear and sporting jerseys to the traditional guernsey or gansey of the nineteenth century and beyond to the simple T-shaped designer knits of the 1980s.

Seemingly simple seventeenth- and eighteenth-century garments made for children and adults in ecru (undyed) matt cotton seem to bridge indoor wear, underwear and modern-day outerwear. One infant's jacket in the V&A, dated between 1630 and 1685, is said to have been worn by Charles II as a baby, but there is only anecdotal evidence to support this claim (V&A: T.30–1932). A second jacket, dated to the eighteenth century, is almost identical, featuring a different decorative purl-stitch pattern but the same in all other design and construction details (plate 27). This type of simple T-shaped jacket remained fun-

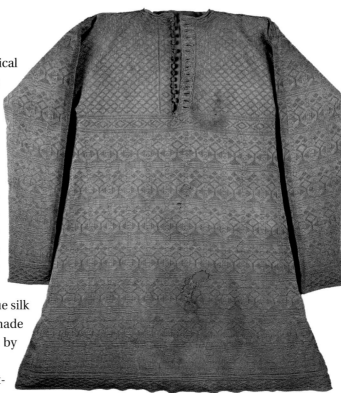

27 **Baby's jackets**, 17th and 18th century, Britain, V&A: T.5–2002 (top), Britain, V&A: T.30–1932 (bottom)
Two similar cotton jackets demonstrate continuity of design over a long period of time. The upper jacket, although British made, was discovered in New Zealand in 1986, part of its colonial history. The lower jacket was said to have been worn by Charles II as an infant, and its patterning matches the adult jacket in plate 28. Firmly knitted in stocking stitch at approximately 28 sts to 10 cm, the decorative borders in purl- and plain-stitch geometric motifs are used at the armholes, centre back and sleeves. The square neck shaping is edged with moss stitch or garter stitch.

damentally unchanged for infants' wear for more than two centuries and is still familiar today. Like the adult shirts, these jackets were often knitted in the round to the armholes, where the stitches were divided and the sleeves knitted up from each armhole edge and worked from shoulders to cuffs. The centre front was cut open below the armholes, and the edges turned and sewn back to create the front openings. The whole garment was therefore created seamlessly on the needles with just the centre front neatened by sewing.[46]

In comparison, an eighteenth-century adult's jacket (probably made for a woman, as its small chest circumference is 83.5 cm) is longer in proportion but created in exactly the same manner, with the special addition of triangular gored panels at either side, providing a more fashionable fit and room for movement at the hips (plate 28). In this jacket, the knitting tension is looser at 18 sts and 26 rows to 10 cm.[47]

There is no documentary evidence of how children or adults wore such garments, but they probably provided an extra layer for warmth.[48] The adult garment may have been worn in private while dressing, its appearance being relatively modest. But, cotton was a relatively new fibre, imported into England from the mid-seventeenth century and by the eighteenth century a fashion fabric, therefore its value at the time may belie the jacket's humble appearance today.[49] The jacket's similarity to the first infant's jacket described above, with identical subtle decorative patterning of purl stitches, suggests that the garment may have been part of a layette, and worn by new mothers.[50]

A man's long waistcoat, dated about 1780, develops the same concept of textural decoration on white cotton – the knitted equivalent of 'white-work' embroidery (white embroidery on white fabric) – but this time for fashionable clothing. Here, the fabric for the fronts is frame-knitted with hand-transfer lace patterns bordering the front edge and pocket flaps (plate 29). The construction is cut and sewn, with the back and lining of the waistcoat made from matching woven cotton twill fabric. The fronts may have been knitted to shape or made as a straight panel and cut. The lace pattern is

precisely engineered to follow the angle of the front opening, which suggests the former. Waistcoats in this style in sumptuous embroidered silks were worn as formal menswear for a long period. This waistcoat appears somewhat modest in comparison but represents technical novelty.

Brocade knitting in the seventeenth century

Of particular importance for the history of knitting are elaborately patterned seventeenth-century silk jackets. Now commonly termed 'brocade jackets' but termed 'waistcoats' at the time, a significant number of similar

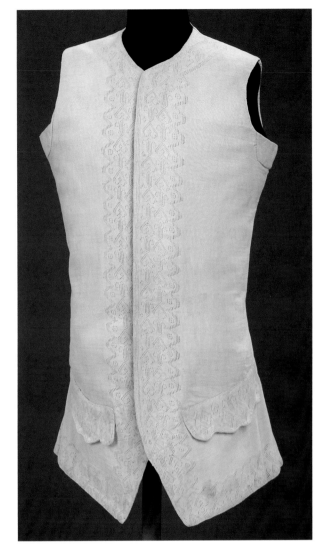

28 Adult jacket,
18th century, Britain
V&A: T.61–1939
Knitted in the round, this jacket
has purl stiches at the centre
front up to the armholes to
provide an edging when the
piece was cut. The cut edge was
then neatly bound with linen
fabric. In a similar manner to
stockings, the side gore panels
are outlined by stitch 'seamlines'
that continue all the way up the
sides. Border patterns also
extend around the armholes,
down the centre of the back and
along the length of the sleeves.

29 Waistcoat,
c.1780, Britain
V&A: T.135–1976
The fronts of this waistcoat were
frame-knitted and sewn onto a
back of woven cotton. Traces of
alteration can be seen in the
changed position of the false
pocket flaps. The fly fastening
conceals Dorset thread buttons.

these largely unstructured garments may have been informal wear, made in imitation of expensive woven garments. They may have been knitted in a centre in Italy such as Venice, where silk was easily available, and imported as panels and sewn together by or for the client, but there is no clear record of this, and they may have originated from different centres or been copied. Opinion is divided as to whether they are hand- or hand-frame knitted: there is evidence for both methods.

The jackets are typically knitted in repeating patterns of two- or three-coloured floral motifs over the upper body, outlined in smaller edging patterns and worked in separate shaped panels comprising back (in one or two panels), fronts and sleeves. All feature similar textural border patterns of purl and plain stitches, usually in basketweave or chevron patterns, and some have purl-stitch fillings within the flower patterns. The repeated stylized floral motifs were influenced by woven fabrics of the period, especially ornate French and Spanish silks patterned with gold and silver threads.[54]

Of three complete jackets in the V&A collection, two are similar in design, but of quite different quality of knitting and making up, and all date to the first half of the seventeenth century. The first (plate 30) is coral pink with gold silver-gilt yarn and elaborate stylized floral- and leaf-pattern motifs that reverse with each repeat. It is well constructed with a fine, even knitting tension. The second jacket (plate 31) is in emerald-green silk with gold silver-gilt yarn and is thought to have been knitted in Britain. This jacket is more loosely knitted, patterned with a simpler floral sprig motif and has similar basket-stitch edgings and tapered flat-knitted sleeves with straight tops set at right angles to the body. This jacket is unlined and the yarns are loosely stranded across the back, with no attempt at 'weaving in', perhaps because the jacket was intended to be lined. This stranded knitting has been taken by some scholars to be evidence of framework knitting but cannot be conclusive. Both jackets feature purl stitches infilling some parts of the flower shapes, creating a damask shaded effect. A similar green-silk and metallic-gold jacket is held in the Whitworth Collection in Manchester, dated to the seventeenth

pieces – long and short, open-fronted or with partial opening – in rich colours of plain and metal-wrapped silks are found in several museums across Europe and the United States, and many are thought to have originated in Britain.[51] Although no known portraits show such jackets, records such as wardrobe inventories indicate they were worn by both men and women, although this evidence is scant.[52] Textual references include a London newspaper of 1712, which reports the theft of 'a green silk-knit waistcoat with gold and silver flowers all over it and about fourteen yards of gold and silver lace thick upon it'.[53] Like the ecru jackets discussed above,

30 Jacket, 1625–50,
Britain or Italy
V&A: 807–1904
The cuffs and lower borders are in basket stitch, with the panels and openings at the waist and cuffs edged in garter stitch. The lining of blue woven linen shows traces of sewn-on fastenings. A slight flare at the hips narrows to the waist. Knitting tension 70s sts and 60 rows to 10 cm. (Back view shown)

32 Jacket, 1625–50(?), Britain
V&A: 473–1893
Three coloured yarns are here knitted together in a complex pattern arranged in vertical lines with stylized floral imagery. The gold yarn used as ground for the pattern comprises yellow silk wrapped with silver metal, both of which are exposed in the body of the jacket. The finish is high quality, with the neckline bound in blue-silk ribbon and the lower border of basketweave stitch turned under to create an even edge. Closely positioned *passementerie* thread buttons are made from the metallic yarn, and buttonholes are sewn into the front edges, which are bound with linen and blue silk.

31 Jacket,
no later than 1620, Britain
V&A: 106–1899
The front and back panels are knitted with a slight flare but added gussets create a more exaggerated shape, using knitted striped fabric, possibly from another garment. The neckline is unfinished, without edging, and some stitching of seams is crude. Knitting tension 30 sts and 56 rows to 10 cm. (Back view shown)

century (Museum no 8331), but its sleeves are tubular knitted, as are a number of others elsewhere.[55]

The fact that some jackets have tubular sleeves confirms their hand-knitted provenance.[56] However, technical developments to mimic handmade fancy stitches on the knitting frame were in progress from the late seventeenth century. One of the earliest was the making of 'turn stitches' – that is, purl stitches – using a manual tool.[57] Further support for the use of frame-knitting in these jackets is provided by an 1831 history of framework knitting, which states: 'The Spaniards invented a method of working flowered waistcoats and ornamenting the clocks of stockings on the frame by making inlays of gold, silver and coloured silks, which

tern, style and finish, hand-knitted in three-colour floral patterns throughout (plate 32). Unlike the others, this jacket is connected to Italy, as it was purchased in Paris with a consignment of Italian woven silks. The colour is now pale grey and gold but was originally pale blue as revealed by turned hems. The sleeves here are knitted in the round with a mock seam and are not tapered to the wrist but instead gathered into the separate gauntlet cuff, avoiding the need for shaping the tubular knit and interrupting the floral design.

A fourth brocade garment, knitted in purple and grey silks and silver-gilt yarns, was configured as a cape with added silk fringe when first acquired by the V&A in 1898 but was in fact fashioned from panels of a brocade jacket similar to those described above, with the bodice panels joined together, ignoring the armhole shaping, and the sleeve panels sewn to the outer edges (plate 33). These panels could more feasibly have been frame-knitted, as suggested by the evenness and consistency of the plain-knit texture, the presence and length of floats, the main pattern design – a relatively small symmetrical repeat with no reversals – and the use of basic stripes to change colour across the width of the entire panel, including the border pattern on the front panels.[59] This gives credence to the theory that such panels were imported and put together by the client.

had been imitated with success in England.'[58] The turning of the stitches to reverse stocking stitch within the detail of the pattern was, however, an added complication when frame-knitting, but could be easily produced in hand-knitting.

The third silk brocade jacket in the V&A collection, dated between 1625 and 1650, is far more ornate in pat-

Eighteenth- and nineteenth-century virtuoso hand-knitting

Virtuoso pieces from the eighteenth and nineteenth centuries represent the pinnacle of the hand-knitter's art in different eras. One such is an excellent example of the 'masterpiece' hangings or 'carpets' that were the most complex of the articles required to qualify as a master knitter in the hand-knitting guilds. A statute of 1605 for the guilds of the Alsace region stated that, to become a master knitter, a journeyman had to make a cap, a pair of gloves, a woollen waistcoat and a flower-patterned carpet (the only item of hand-knitting production at that time not made to be worn), all to be produced in 13 weeks at a recognized workshop. Later, fashionable garments could be substituted for the flowered carpet.[60] The 29 extant or recorded masterpiece carpets preserved in European museums suggest that the key centres of excellence were in Alsace and Silesia.[61] As squares or rectangles often measuring over 2 metres in length, the complexity, size and weight of these works makes it hard to envisage their being knitted on needles (although a series of separate consecutive needles is possible), and it is conjectured that they may have been knitted on a peg frame. Reminiscent of ornate pile carpets in their patterning and stylistic arrangements, they were commissioned by churches and nobles for wall, bed, table or floor coverings.

One example was knitted in 1781 in Strasbourg in Alsace and is approximately 163 cm square, knitted at an unusual square tension of 8 sts and 8 rows to 2.5 cm using many colours of wool stranded across the back. It features a frequently used religious figurative scene of the Dream of Jacob with a ladder to heaven and the Hebrew word for God, 'Jahve', in the clouds at the top. This scene is surrounded by a border of stylized chintz-like flowers and vines, with a small vignette in the bottom centre showing Adam and Eve with the serpent under a tree in the Garden of Eden (plate 34).[62] No general hand-knitting guilds were ever set up in Britain, because hand-knitters were more dispersed as a result of the putting-out system, whereby work was distributed to be done in the home. Nevertheless, many guilds

33 Jacket panels,
17th century,
possibly Britain or Italy
V&A: 346–1898
This all-over design on a purple ground uses two different colours alternately in broad stripes for the pattern; therefore only two yarns are used at any one time in contrast to the jacket in plate 32, in which three colours are worked together throughout the pattern areas. The yarns are complex, consisting of stranded purple silk floss, silver-gilt yarn, silver metallic yarn and silver silk floss. Knitting tension is 80 sts and 72 rows to 10 cm.

such as the drapers, mercers, dyers and feltmakers were established informally at the end of the twelfth century, and from the mid-fourteenth century were granted royal charters, together with the clothworkers, haberdashers and glovers. The cappers' companies (making caps of cloth and later by knitting), having first emerged in the thirteenth century, were well established in many towns by the late fifteenth century. As mechanized knitting developed during the following 150 years, the growing concentration of frame-work knitters based in London petitioned Oliver Cromwell in 1655 to grant a charter, and in 1657 they were incorporated as the Worshipful Company of Framework Knitters, which still survives today.

Another virtuoso piece is a probably unique woollen circular petticoat hand-knitted in the 1740s (plates 35, 36 and 37).[63] No documentary evidence exists pertaining to this petticoat, which is magnificent in its scale and design. Thought to be of English or Dutch origin, the piece is seamless, made in circular knitting in cream, smoothly spun, worsted cream wool. It is populated by a bestiary of animals of all kinds and one lone male figure running as if in pursuit of them. The animals and abundant foliage are perfectly 'drawn' in outline and texture, each executed with great detail and excellent proportions and delineated in purl and plain stitches on a stocking-stitch ground in a knitted equivalent of popular embroidered white work.[64] Some animals are domestic and familiar – the hare, the horse, the peacock; others, such as the rhinoceros, elephant and camel, are more exotic; and still others, such as the griffin, are fantastical and could have been copied from one of the numerous printed bestiaries.

Nothing is known about the method of construction of the petticoat, which comprises one very large seamless tube, measuring 3.4 metres in circumference. With approximately 2650 stitches and knitted at a tension of 21 sts and 34 rows to 10 cm, the whole piece seems too large for knitting on needles, and it is possible that a type of circular knitting peg frame was used and the stitches manually looped. In this case the reverse (purl) loops would have had to be turned individually to make the design motifs, which in many creatures include whimsical filling patterns of plain and purl to create different visual textures. The petticoat is likely to have been made to be worn under the wide, hooped pannier styles of mid-eighteenth-century fashionable dress, where the front of the petticoat would have been on view and the damask effect of the purl-stitch patterning would have shown best from a short distance (plate 38).

Could this be another masterpiece made to show consummate skill and obtain work? In order to achieve the precision in knitted execution of such a complex design, such as the meticulous positioning of an eyelet hole for a creature's eye, the animals would probably have been charted before knitting, in the same way that embroidery cross-stitch charts were used in the mid-eighteenth century and cartoons made for tapestry weaving. However, great skill was needed to keep the proportions of the creatures naturalistic while working in a 2:3 stitch-to-row ratio: that is, a square on an embroidery chart is not a square when knitted but

34 Carpet (detail),
1781, Alsace
V&A: T.375–1977
Detail of the lower part of the carpet showing Adam and Eve in the Garden of Eden with serpent, flanked by a lion and a stag. The symbols of shears and teasels, tools of the trade for finishing knitted fabric, are included in the lower border. Such motifs appear on other master carpets as guild emblems.

35, 36, 37 Petticoat, 1740s, Britain
or the Netherlands
V&A: T.177–1926
The entire surface of the petticoat
(approximately 3.4 m in
circumference) is covered with
animals, birds, insects, foliage and
flowers plus one human figure. Purl
stitches on a plain ground define the
outlines of the figures and leaves,
which are filled with repeating
patterns in different plain and purl
combinations, with eyes formed by
eyelet stitches. Many leaves are
given dimension by being knitted in
reverse stocking stitch. Shown in
close-up are the griffin under a palm-
like tree, birds, small rat-like
creatures, a flamingo and insects.

38 Mantua, 1740–45,
probably Britain
V&A: T.260–1969
Formal court dress based on
17th-century styles of mantua,
comprising outer robe and
decorative petticoat skirt. The
embroidered decoration here is
highly naturalistic, as it is in the
knitted petticoat in plate 35–7.

rather a rectangle. It is remarkable that no design motif is repeated around the entire work: although there are two lions, two elephants and three peacocks, all are different in design.

The growth of lace knitting

As has been seen, the skills and expertise of hand-knitting led the development of hand-powered machine knitting, which, since its inception in the sixteenth century, imitated whatever could be produced on knitting needles. From the 1760s, inventions to develop and emulate hand-knitted lace with manufactured processes were encouraged by competitions organized by the Society for the Encouragement of Arts, Manufacture and Commerce:

> It having been discovered that a very curious manufacture of Thread Lace has been made with knitting needles, the society offered a premium of thirty guineas to the person who shall produce the greatest quantity of clear, fine lace, of this sort, not less than six yards in length and two inches and a half in width.[65]

There remained, however, techniques that could not be mimicked exactly by machine: many fine examples of hand-knitted lace and beaded knitting from the eighteenth and nineteenth centuries illustrate this, their growth fuelled by the rapid rise of printed manuals containing 'recipes' (see p.122). An example is an exquisite child's christening dress in many different stitches of fine lace. This was awarded a medal at the Great Exhibition in London in 1851, which, although focused on industry, included needlecrafts such as hand-knitting. Knitted by Miss Sarah Ann Cunliffe from Saffron Waldon from 5770 metres of no. 100 sewing cotton thread, the piece took five months' full-time knitting to complete, and is calculated to have 1,464,859 stitches (V&A: T.45–1964).

During the nineteenth century the popularity of lace patterning flourished and was introduced to many other items, particularly shawls, babywear and fine mit-

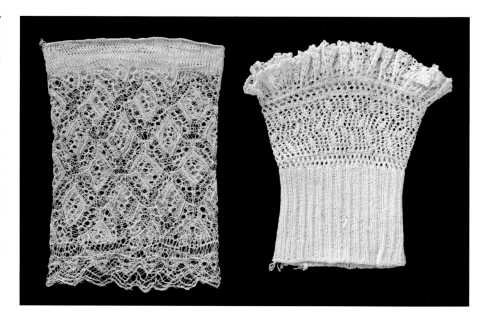

tens and gloves (plates 45 and 51). Etiquette decreed that gloves be worn by gentlemen and ladies at all times, delineating the difference between those who worked and those who did not. Kid-leather gloves were the pinnacle of taste, but cotton and silk were acceptable substitutes and glove-making became a staple of the hosiery industry.[66] Ladies' silk gloves (plate 42) and fingerless mittens in lace became highly fashionable in the mid-nineteenth century. An array of delicate cuffs – as well as long and short cotton mittens buttoned, fringed or ribbed, fingerless or with thumbs – shows a wide range of openwork patterns, most hand-knitted seamlessly in the round (plates 39 and 40). It is interesting to compare the long hand-knitted seamless mittens with a pair of nineteenth-century silk mittens with seams, made industrially by warp-knitting, which was well established at this time and provided a more economical alternative (plate 41).

A key item of a baby's layette was the bonnet, which throughout the late eighteenth and nineteenth centuries was often made from delicate hand-knitted lace and textured knitting, sometimes decorated with beads and bobbin lace. Bonnets and caps were typically constructed with a circular whorl- or star-patterned base for the back of the head and continued with a border that covered the top and sides of the head (plate 44). Examples show a range of fine knitted-lace designs, some with heavily textured patterns and others gossamer light with frills or beaded in floral patterns (plate 43).

Typical of the Victorian period are small domestic items such as doilies, dolls' clothes and knick-knacks, including pincushions and pence jugs made in crochet and knitting, for which many patterns proliferated (see p.123). An impressive sample book features 12 different fine lace doilies knitted from aloe cactus-seed thread, known as *pita*, which originated from the Azores Islands and is said to be stronger than cotton (V&A: T.389–2001). One of the distinctive techniques of Azores lace used here includes the unusual wrapping of the yarn round small groups of stitches to produce characteristic decorative 'knops'. Featuring such work in 1893, *Harper's Bazaar* described the lace-making women of the Azores as skilled in knitting fine openwork stockings, shawls, fichus and dresses but very poorly paid.[67]

40 Mitten, 1770–1800, Britain
V&A: T.167–1922
This early hand-knitted long mitten with linen fringe has a gusset at the thumb and a mock seamline, twisted due to the yarn being overspun.

41 Mittens, 1840s–50s, Britain
V&A: T.604: 1+2 –1999
Warp-knitted commercially produced silk mittens, made in one main piece with hand-stitched side seam and inserted thumb. A variety of openwork stitch structures can be clearly seen, finishing with double-thickness welts and lacy edgings.

42 Gloves, mid-19th century
V&A: 963&a–1898
This pair of elegant machine-knitted black and green silk gloves combine the techniques of lace eyelets knitted in diamond formation with silk hand embroidery decoration in floral sprays, giving an impression of beadwork.

43 Baby's bonnets,
19th century, Britain
V&A: T.89–1928, T.97–1929,
T. 71–1912, T.31–1922
These four baby's bonnets in
cotton illustrate a range of
knitting techniques used in
sometimes complex
combinations, including lace,
beading and raised stitch
effects. Each has a different
arrangement of the central
circular-knitted star-shaped
patterns at the back of the head.
Similar fine lace caps were worn
by ladies as night caps.

44 Bonnet,
19th century, Britain
V&A: T.31–1922
The back of this intricate
textural bonnet forms an
unusual six-pointed figure
made up of bordered leaves
on an openwork mesh ground.
A separate lace border outlines
the circle, where it joins to a
raised leaf pattern, made by
increasing and decreasing in
succession. The bonnet is
finished with a separately
knitted frill.

45 **Cape**, 19th century, Scotland
V&A: T.137–1966
This very large triangular cape with attached hood was knitted in finest silk lace in Shetland. Measuring a massive 243 cm wide and 126.5 cm deep, this would have been worn as a highly fashionable luxury item, requiring months of labour to make.

A central triangle is composed of bands of small interlocking diamonds each with different pattern fillings, similar to those associated with the Isle of Unst. The large border is knitted in two halves, joined by open grafting, as is typical for Shetland shawls. The outer edge is finished with a separate narrow border, knitted in the perpendicular direction and attached during the knitting.

Beaded knitting

Perhaps the most fanciful and decorative examples of Victorian-era hand-knitting are intricately beaded bags, which show both patience and skill. To create these closely beaded pieces, a chart was followed carefully and all the beads threaded onto the yarn in reverse order to correspond exactly with the design, which was often a floral still-life or otherwise figurative, narrative and whimsical – miniature paintings in beads. Each bead was drawn up close between stitches in such a way that the knitted stitches are not visible from the right side (plate 46). So laborious was this that entrepreneurial suppliers of recipes and materials began to produce kits for purses with the beads already strung, ready for knitting up, in single colours.[68] McDonald writes of mourning bags, featuring tombstones, weeping willows and urns in precious beaded knitting, as valuable items:

By the end of the nineteenth century, a knitter could charge five dollars for knitting one, their high price justified by the laborious process of counting out each row's beads, threading each onto thread often spun from home cocoons…Though one could reasonably duplicate an existing bag by counting its stitches, carefully diagrammed patterns were closely held secrets, and written rules were only divulged to friends.[69]

The bags were lined in fabric, often finished with metal handbag clasps, which were easily available, and

46 Circular beaded bag,
19th century, Britain
V&A: T.1165–1913
Closely beaded, this circular bag is knitted in the same manner as the bonnets, commencing at the centre and working in circular formation with nine gores formed by regular stitch increases in the same position. The beaded patterning moves from the three colours in the central star to multicoloured paisley and floral designs. Complete accuracy of threading beads and knitting was required to achieve this miniature work of art.

47 Beaded purses,
19th century, Britain
V&A: T.1181–1913, T.71–1961
More rigid than the common-place stocking purses, beaded purses were knitted in the round, with a slit in the middle made by knitting to and fro. Note the finishes with either a button or a beaded fringe, and the gored ends of the purse on the left. This one is incomplete without the rings needed for keeping money secure.

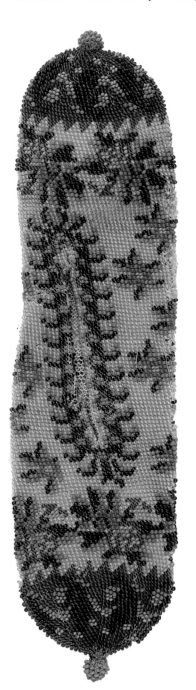

48 Pineapple purse,
1800–30, Britain
V&A: T.1348–1913
Worked in coloured silks, this purse shades from green to yellow and orange, representing the colours of a pineapple. A glass bead is knitted in at every three-dimensional point, and beads also form a pattern at the circular base. The purse is finished with separately knitted leaves.

49 Pineapple purse (detail),
19th century, Britain
V&A: T.22–1910
One of three pineapple purses in the V&A, this is constructed in the round with overlapping leaves, each incorporating an edging of tiny beads. It is worked in salmon pink (now faded) and green silk, with lilac and green glass beads. The garter stitch triangles were knitted first, then knitted into the stocking stitch base.

50 Apron, 19th century
V&A: T.30–1950
This English rose-patterned decorative apron is knitted in brightly coloured wools, possibly the Berlin wools newly available in England in the 1830s, and in its style is reminiscent of folk-craft traditions from central Europe. The rose and grape motifs and their foliage are in several naturalistic colours, each worked individually in the intarsia style, but with stranded colours within each motif area.

It is a decorative version of what is essentially work-wear, and may be an example of commercial hand-knitting for the fashion trade. Although highly accomplished, it is a little unfinished on the back, where the ends of coloured yarn have been left hanging.

decorated with beaded fringes or other ornamentation. They might be circular in shape and knitted with gored construction, as in a bonnet, or of cylindrical construction, similar to an upside-down cap, with drawstring fastening.

Simpler stocking purses and reticules appear to have been made prolifically both as practical small items for personal use, as simple gifts or for charity work. Long stocking purses were used by both men and women in the nineteenth century and thus were items commonly knitted by women as love tokens and given to sweethearts. A typical style is the soft miser's purse, made to fold over a belt, formed in a long tube with an opening in the centre and secured by metal rings. Knitted beaded stocking purses were also made. These are shorter in length than the miser's purses and, being naturally more rigid, are designed not to fold over a belt but to be carried perhaps in a pocket. They were knitted in circular construction and, because of the angle of the beads as they sit next to each other on the thread, the central slit is diagonal (plate 47).

One of the quirkiest purse designs of the times, found in several instruction books, is the 'pineapple' purse – a complex construction of relief patterns and 'leaves' worked in the round, with chevron patterning creating the pointed pineapple surface texture (plates 48 and 49). Patterns for such purses featured prominently in many nineteenth-century manuals and the Pearsalls company produced a wide range of silk yarns in hundreds of 'washing and non-fading' colours, one specifically called 'Purse Silk', 'for Ecclesiastical embroidery and netting purses'.[70]

These and similar items represented the pinnacle of hand-knitting in the mid-nineteenth century, but the rapid development of industrial machine-knitting ensured conclusively that hand-knitting would henceforth be confined to the domestic craft and leisure spheres. Given the continued growth and sophistication of knitting technology, it appears unlikely that the achievements of virtuoso hand-knitting will ever again be matched for their combination of skill, technique and the sheer scale and intensity of the work.

51 Lace shawl (detail),
1830–69, Britain
V&A: T.20–1984
This fine hand-knitted wool lace shawl is knitted in an unusual all-over shell pattern. The chevron-patterned border has been knitted separately and joined onto the central panel, with a seam at one corner, and gathering to turn the corners rather than mitring, as in many Shetland shawls.

Livelihood and Industry:
Hand- and Machine-Knitting from the Seventeenth to the Twenty-First Centuries

From the morning till late at night
My knitting wires seldom are still
I can clip & roo, & card & spin too
And knit whatever you will
Knit, knit, knit
A shawl that the Queen could wear
A stocking, sock, or a sailor's frock
To keep out the Greenland air

But my labour is all in vain
Somebody has stolen my luck
For all that I make to the shop I must take
And hand it over to Truck
For calico, sugar and tea
No money I get for the wares that I knit
Or it would be better for me
J. SANDS, *King James's Wedding and Other Rhymes*

HISTORICAL RECORDS from the end of the fifteenth century provide clear evidence of the spread of hand-knitting as both domestic and commercial activity throughout the British Isles, Europe, Scandinavia and the United States. As seen in Chapter 1, during the fifteenth and sixteenth centuries, caps were the most important item of commercial hand-knitting, but they were superseded by stockings for both personal use and commercial industry. This chapter examines the way in which knitting has evolved from a domestic handcraft to a modern industry, from hand-knitting on needles to the operation of hand-frames and the development of powered knitting machines and advanced technology.

Livelihood and subsistence: knitting for income

For many centuries before the Industrial Revolution, in addition to providing practical items of clothing for the family, knitting afforded people from rural subsistence farming and fishing communities a means of earning essential additional income, especially in the winter months. Because knitting was light work requiring only simple portable tools, both women and men could knit at every opportunity – while shepherding, walking to market, sailing or waiting for boats (plates 1, 2). The use of knitting sheaths made knitting faster, more portable and therefore more productive. A simple device tied around the waist or held in the apron or belt, the sheath comprised a stick with a hole or groove in which one knitting needle was fixed in place, helping to free the hands, steady the work and speed up the knitting action. From simple wooden sticks to ornate carved lengths of ivory, this practical tool could also be an elaborate token of love, carved by a suitor for his sweetheart. One example features wooden balls that run up and down inside a carved cage; others might be inlaid, fashioned into chains or sculpted in high relief (pp.54–5). An improvised pad or bundle of straw (a 'wisp') could also suffice as a sheath, and, in the Shetland Islands, knitters still use a leather pouch with multiple holes, stuffed with horsehair and worn as a belt.

The Costume of Yorkshire, published in 1814 by George Walker, includes a well-known watercolour illustration and a description of the peripatetic knitters of Wensleydale – men, women and children all busy with their needles (plate 2):

The Fair Isle Jumper,
Stanley Cursiter, 1923
Edinburgh City Art Centre
A stylish portrait of a society lady wearing the newly fashionable Fair Isle jumper, following the style's adoption by the Prince of Wales, later Edward VIII.

A woman by the name of Slinger who lived in Cotterdale was accustomed regularly to walk to market at Hawes, a distance of three miles, with the weekly knitting of herself and family packed in a bag upon her head, knitting all the way. She continued her knitting while she stayed in Hawes purchasing the little necessaries for her family, and worsted for the work of the ensuing week. She was so expeditious and expert that the produce of the day's labour was generally a complete pair of men's stockings.[1]

Across the British Isles, the woollen industry was the backbone of the medieval economy. Although there is no extant evidence, it is likely that everyday items for warmth such as stockings and caps for women and children were knitted from locally handspun coarse wools. The development of the spinning wheel in the fourteenth century enabled finer yarns to be produced in greater quantity and, from the late sixteenth century, skilled artisans fleeing religious persecution in Europe helped improve the British textile industry with 'New Draperies'.[2] The spread of finer knitting prompted the replacement of cloth hose with knitted hose. At the same time, Spanish, Italian and French fashions stimulated production of knitted goods to service the needs of fashionable society in many parts of Britain; the demand for silk stockings, for example, in emulation of the Spanish court, reached a height in the Elizabethan era, making stockings the dominant knitting industry. As better-quality worsted-spun yarns became available through the use of Midlands long-haired fleeces, wool was increasingly used to knit the finer stockings desired by all classes, rivalling the quality of silk and broadening access to the stocking market.

Expansion in the seventeenth century transformed stocking knitting from a domestic craft to a commercialized cottage industry that flourished in trading centres throughout the country, including London, Yorkshire and Nottinghamshire. Quality was inevitably variable and needed control, which was enforced by hosiers, who gave out wool – sometimes ready spun – collected in finished work and supplied them to merchants. However,

designs, colours and quality of production still varied widely across regions; coarser stockings for children, soldiers and peasants were, for example, made in northern areas. Daniel Defoe, himself a merchant hosier in London, writing after his tour of the British Isles in the early eighteenth century, commented that Stourbridge in Dorset was 'once famous for making the finest, best and highest prized knit stockings in England', but that in Richmond, Yorkshire, the stockings were 'coarse and ordinary' and consequently cheap.[3] Prices also varied enormously. In the 1670s, silk stockings worn at Charles II's court cost between 10 and 18 shillings, while high-quality worsted stockings from Guernsey cost between 2 shillings and 6 pence and 10 shillings wholesale. In Leicester, however, in 1690 worsted stockings cost as little as 1 shilling and 6 pence to 2 shillings and 6 pence per pair. Indicating the

growth in knitting production, prices had fallen considerably from a century earlier, when imported silk stockings were affordable only to royalty.[4]

Demand was high, and domestic trade grew during the seventeenth century, alongside trade with Spain, Portugal, France and Holland. It was common practice among the gentility to wear two pairs of stockings, not only for warmth but also to protect the more expensive pair, just as woollen boot hose might have protected precious silk stockings from chafing by the boots. At her execution, Mary Queen of Scots wore a pair of fine white jersey stockings underneath her decorative blue worsted stockings.[5]

By the eighteenth century, the stocking knitting industry in Scotland, centred in Aberdeen, was of a size to be regulated by a 1720 act of Parliament, which

The Tools of Hand-Knitting

The beauty of hand-knitting lies partly in the simplicity of its tools. Originally these were nothing more than sticks of wood, bone or quill filed to a point, or wires and rods made of metal. Four or more double-pointed needles were used for circular knitting or two longer single-pointed needles for flat knitting. The V&A collection includes needlework cases, needles and accessories predominantly from the nineteenth and twentieth centuries, although the earliest knitting tool is a wooden knitting sheath dated 1679 (V&A: 774–1907), which was fixed around the waist and held one needle in place to enable knitting on the move (see pages 52 and 104).

Water-powered wire drawing mills, first set up in the mid-sixteenth century, made finer wires and metal knitting needles widely available. The standard numerical gauges utilized for wires were adopted as knitting needle sizes. Relatively coarsely knitted woollen caps and stockings gave way to finer silk, linen and worsted stocking knitting as spinning methods also improved, inspiring the mechanization of the handcraft. Reliable manufacturing of fine steel needles enabled the development of fine stitchcraft and lace which has left a remarkable legacy of intricate hand-knitted pieces from the eighteenth and nineteenth centuries. The skilful mastery of coloured stitchwork, controlled in Europe by medieval guilds, is seen in silk brocade knitting and magnificent carpets, although the tools that created some of these virtuoso earlier works cannot now be reliably determined. From the late nineteenth and early twentieth centuries, the commercial development of plastics such as casein and Bakelite transformed knitting tools, which became lightweight, colourful and inexpensive. Today knitting needles are made from aluminium, bamboo, wood or plastics and are sized in metric measurements, with larger gauges for thicker yarns and speedier results.

Shown here is a selection of tools and accessories from the mid-eighteenth to mid-twentieth centuries.

Green leather needlework case, c.1910, Britain V&A: T.107:1 to 20–1999

'Mitrailleuse' metal needle case manufactured by J. Ahncke, late 19th century, Britain Contains four sets of steel needles, sizes 13 to 16 V&A: T.713:1 to 26–1995

Bell-shaped metal needle gauge, 1847–99 (patented 1847), Britain V&A: T.276–1979

Carved ivory needle case and needles, 19th century, China, V&A: T.129–1915

Pair of carved ivory needles, 1840–1900, Britain V&A: T.73:1&2–2000

Set of four size 18 needles in paper packet, John James & Son, late 19th century, Britain V&A: T.714:1 to 5–1995

Pair of wooden needles, 19th century, Britain, V&A: T.283&A–1979

Turned wood and ivory sheath, 18th century, Spain, V&A: T.7–1930

Wooden sheath, early 19th century, Britain, V&A: T.56–1920;
Curved 'goose wing' wooden sheath, 1842, Britain, inscribed 'AWG Nov 16 1842', V&A: T.192–1960;
Two metal sheaths, 18th century, Italy, V&A: T.60&A–1937

Wool holder, two-part mottled brown Bakelite sphere, mid-20th century, Britain Sandy Black collection

Wool holder, Patons & Baldwins, red Bakelite two-part 'Beehive' shape with needle gauge, mid-20th century, Britain Sandy Black collection

Mauchline ware souvenir wool holder, two-part wooden sphere with transfer applied of West Pier Brighton, 19th century, Britain V&A: T.49–1980

Two Bakelite darning mushrooms, mottled brown; brown with removable yellow top and battery-powered light bulb inside, mid-20th century, Britain Sandy Black collection

Emerald silk knitting on steel needles, about 1825, Britain Unfinished, possibly a purse V&A: T.126: AtoD–1972

Pair of novelty glass needles, 20th century, Britain Marked 'N' on the ends V&A: T.18&A–1986

stipulated that stockings made in Scotland must conform to precise standards: 'Wrought of three threads, and of one sort of wool and worsted and of equal work and fineness, free from left loops, hanging hairs and burnt, cut or mended holes and of such shapes and sizes as the patterns marked by the several deans of guild.'[6] Similarly, in 1765 the Tewkesbury Act – the only piece of eighteenth-century legislation relating to the English hosiery industry – outlawed the use of the inferior single two-ply yarn unless it was marked as such.[7]

The town of Kendal was the centre of the hand-knitting trade in Cumbria, which in 1770 was observed as 'employing near five thousand hands…one-hundred and twenty wool-combers each employing five spinners, and each spinner four or five knitters. They make five hundred and fifty dozen [stockings] a week the year round.' Prices ranged from 22 pence to 4 shillings a pair.[8] By this time, frame-knitting was beginning to spread. A contemporary writer in 1759 stated that the 'poor are chiefly employed in knitting of stockings, caps, waistcoats, etc, mostly of cotton, tho there are of late seven stocking-looms set up'.[9]

Whereas the capping industry, based in towns such as London, Coventry and Monmouth, was regulated by statutes as early as 1488, the dispersion of stocking hand-knitting as a rural domestic industry carried out largely by women and children may have contributed to a lack of guilds and limited regulation by acts of Parliament in England, although stockings were certainly subject to taxation at the end of the sixteenth century.[10] In contrast, as the stocking frame spread, professional frame-knitters in London protected their trade, establishing the Worshipful Company of Framework Knitters in 1657 (see p.37).[11]

The Shetland knitting industry

Isolated in the North Sea, the Shetland Islands are at the centre of major shipping routes between Scandinavia, Iceland, Greenland, Scotland, the Mediterranean and the United States, providing an important staging post for supplies and mutual trade. Knitting here can be traced back to the early seventeenth century.[12]

An important find of knitted clothing from a grave at Gunnister in Shetland is datable to 1680 because of the Dutch and Spanish coins found in the clothes.[13]

Knitting of stockings, underwear, caps, gloves and jerseys supplemented income from fishing and crofting, and the Shetland islanders could not have managed without it, especially if a woman had lost her husband to the sea. Given that knitting was such an essential part of everyday working life, to be 'hand idle' was considered sinful. Knitting was a livelihood, not a handicraft, and was learnt at a very young age. To one woman recalling her early twentieth-century childhood, knitting was associated with hardship: 'I had to put the fingers in gloves before I went to school so I always vowed I'd never knit for anyone.'[14] Women and children knitted because they had to – to keep the family warm and to exchange knitting for goods or money. The enforced barter or 'truck' system, referred to in the song at the beginning of this chapter, was endemic throughout the knitting trade in England and Scotland.

In 1872 the Truck Commission Enquiry, investigating conditions, found that a Shetland knitter might be paid 10 shillings for a lace shawl that took a month to knit but often was forced to take half the sum in goods, whether these were wanted or not.[15] Women therefore had to negotiate with local businesses to exchange, for example, tea for cash, so they could buy what they actually needed, including more wool. Even though the Truck Amendment Act of 1887 legally banned barter payments, the practice carried on until 1897.[16]

Initially trading with visiting ships, hand-knitters later supplied plain goods for both domestic and export markets. By 1901, two-thirds of the Shetland people were involved in the hosiery trade.[17] Both spinners and knitters were highly skilled. Knitters worked without written patterns and regularly devised new designs for the requirements of the market. Hand-knitted lace was introduced to the Shetland Islands in about 1833 in the form of a Christening bonnet – a gift to a Mr Ogilvy, which was duly copied.[18] Inspired by the demand for high-quality lace goods in cosmopolitan London, Shetland knitters were then encouraged to create new

3 **Fine lace shawl**, 1951, Shetland Islands Shetland Museum and Archive An example of the magnificent Shetland lace shawls, knitted from hand-spun wool for the high class London market, worn here by Greta Coutts.

products.[19] Knitted lace was developed and perfected to a high art, particularly on the northernmost island of Unst, combining the Shetland women's skills in spinning extremely fine, even yarn, with the form of their everyday shawl or 'hap' – plain in the centre with a striped wave-patterned border – to create ingenious new patterns. Coarser work could be done while going about daily chores, but the finest lace was knitted in the evenings at home. Shetland wools have a reputation for softness, as a result of the finer hairs produced – paradoxically – by Shetland sheep kept on the poor grazing grounds of the windswept hills. Made from the finest wool hand plucked ('roo'd') from the sheep's neck, legendary 'wedding ring' shawls were created for export, knitted from about 120 grams of wool, and fine enough to pass through a ring. The products of the lace-knitters' labours were sold via merchants, who traded the goods both within Shetland and to the growing fashionable elites in England and the developing tourist trade (plate 3).

The particularly intricate and colourful patterned knitting practised from the late nineteenth century on one tiny island, Fair Isle, has become known the world over, giving its name to a generic style of colour-stranded hand- and machine-knitting. It is recognizable by small, repeating, geometric patterns in several colours, arranged in horizontal bands, traditionally in variations of the OXO formation – alternate lozenges and crosses with numerous filling patterns. The islanders emphasize the inaccuracy of the oft-cited legend that the patterns were brought by sailors wrecked in the Spanish Armada.[20] The similarity with colour-stranded knitting practised since 1800 in the Baltic countries, which increasingly traded with Fair Isle in the nineteenth century, is the most plausible theory of the origin of Fair Isle patterning.

Small items including fishermen's caps, scarves and socks were among the first all-over-patterned items to be made, plain goods having previously been the mainstay of the Shetland knitting trade.[21] A merchant's knitted goods catalogue from the Shetland Archives dated 1910 offers items for everyday use and warmth –

sleeves, a body belt, bedsocks, gloves, mitts and wristlets – in plain knitting, as well as fancy Fair Isle sweaters, berets and socks (plate 4). The patterned sweater is expensive, priced at 25 shillings, whereas a girl's tam-o'-shanter is 1 shilling and 6 pence.

The name Fair Isle is commonly misused in relation to knitwear; it strictly refers to the typical patterns of no more than two colours in a row, on natural or red-coloured grounds, with colours frequently changed and skilfully blended. The islanders have fought legal bat-tles to retain the integrity of the name as 'Fair Isle knit-ted in Fair Isle', just as campaigns have been fought for Champagne and Harris Tweed, and in the 1950s the Shetland Hand-Knitters Association was formed to pro-tect the knitters' interests. Patterned bands in the OXO formation are found in both Fair Isle and Shetland work: Fair Isle work is distinguished by either plain ribs or two-by-two checkerboard-patterned welts, whereas Shetland knitting tyically features two-coloured ribbed welts (plates 5 and 6).

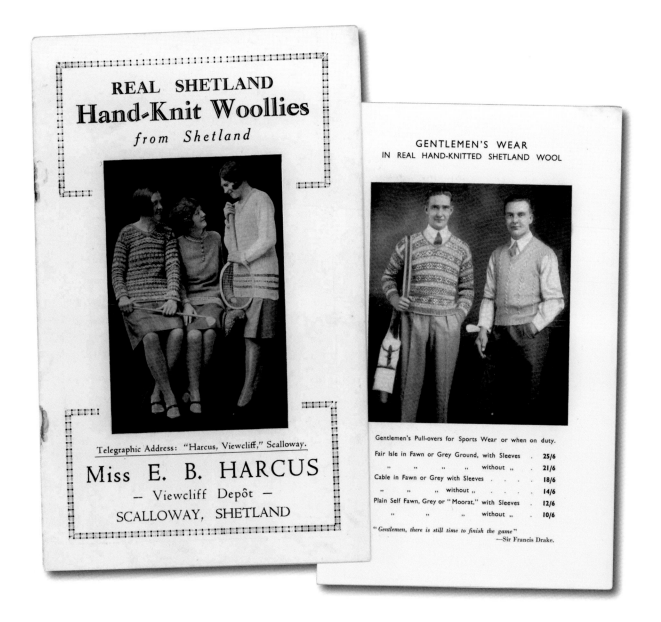

5 Fair Isle sweater,
1996, Shetland
V&A: T.77–1997
Annie Thomson, one of the last surviving commercial hand-knitters of Fair Isle, knitted this genuine Fair Isle sweater, commissioned especially for the V&A *Cutting Edge* exhibition. Knitted in the round using five needles and a knitting belt, it is made in five colours using natural and synthetic dyes.

The distinctive patterns and symbols of Fair Isle knitting have given rise to their own mythology. One wonderful story tells of the 'Robes of Glory' knitted by older women for their grandsons' coming of age. Typically the knitted patterns flow in a sequence resembling first the 'water of life', then the 'seed of life', which is nurtured into the 'flower of life'. This is followed by the 'anchor of hope', accompanied by the 'star of Bethlehem' to guide the boy through life, with the 'crown of glory' rewarding a life well led.

There is a good deal of mathematics embedded in the construction of Fair Isle textiles, as well as in other knitted items such as circular hats and doilies, ganseys, seamless stockings and lace patterns. All require the ability to hold repeat information, divide and multiply pattern units, calculate tension and distribute shap-

ings.[22] The principles of vertical and horizontal symmetry are clearly seen in the classic OXO banded patterns typical of Fair Isle designs. Rather than deriving from religious or other symbols, the patterns can be seen as variations within the geometric constraints of a given format. As Alice Starmore, a knitter from Stornoway, states, 'the dazzling illusion of complexity in this work is achieved by juggling a very small number of variables'.[23]

The knitters have always taken pride in choosing colours, resisting the urgings of London buyers to use more fashionable colours to increase sales, as knitter Jean Hardie emphasized in an interview in 1985: 'To me it's just like painting a picture. If you choose the right colours your picture will be a good picture…if you choose the wrong colours it wouldn't be a success.'[24]

However, the Shetland hand-knitting industry relies on the outside world for survival.[25] Making gifts to royalty has been one of the clever ways that Shetland Islanders have promoted their work, a lace shawl having been presented to the young Queen Victoria in 1837. Edward, Prince of Wales was presented with a long-sleeved sweater that he wore to play golf in the 1920s, setting a fashion trend.

Hand-knitting continued in the Shetlands until World War II but later declined in the face of competition from machine-made items. In order to compete, from the 1960s simpler coloured hand-knitting was combined with domestic machine knitting of plain sections to speed up production – an activity that some men also took up. The resulting cardigans and sweaters with distinctive circular patterned yoke were prevalent throughout Britain and the United States in the mid-twentieth century (plate 7).

In Fair Isle, the population fell severely as a result of difficult economic conditions, and in the 1950s the island was taken under the management of the National Trust for Scotland, who appealed for people to return to live there, despite the lack of electricity and running water. Annie Thomson, one of 70 or so current residents

and one of the last commercial hand-knitters of Fair Isle, returned in 1957 with her family after 13 years away. Born and brought up on the island, she began knitting for income at the age of 14, when she and her sisters finished their formal education, ironically generating income to help pay for their brother's further education. On her return, knitting again became an important source of family income.[26]

Poignantly, until the 1990s, the Fair Isle islanders did not wear their own patterned hand-knitting, as it was too valuable a commodity and had to be sold. Today on Fair Isle, knitting is no longer essential to the economy and, with an ageing population of hand-knitters, its sustainability is under threat, despite a resurgence of fashionable interest in the genre in 2010 (plate 8).

6 **Sweater**, 1920s, Shetland
V&A: T.185–1982
Knitted in the round, this sweater in natural shades of thick brown and cream wool has the signature two-coloured 'corrugated' ribbed edgings, seen in Shetland knitting, which is less elastic. Each band of pattern is different, based on crosses and six-sided lozenges with geometric fillings in the familiar OXO arrangement, but here including an anchor motif separated by bands of small 'peerie' motifs. The sweater has been carefully patched at the front to mend a hole.

7 Sirdar advert, 1947
AAD/8/4–1991
This is a hand-knitted version of the simplified Fair Isle yoke sweater, from a Sirdar pattern leaflet advertised in *Vogue Knitting*. This style continued to be popular in knitting patterns throughout the 1960s and 1970s.

8 Marks and Spencer advertisement, 2010
The trend for cosy and nostalgic 'Fair Isle' patterned knitwear grew to a crescendo in Autumn/Winter 2010 when, following the lead of high fashion designers such as Dolce & Gabbana, many mainstream market stores, including Marks and Spencer, produced their own lines.

The growth of the mechanized hosiery industry

It seems logical that the combination of constant knitting in the home, the popularity of knitted stockings in the second half of the sixteenth century and the economic importance of knitting would have provided the inspiration for 'Renaissance genius' William Lee to develop the first stocking knitting frame in 1589 – some 150 years before the Industrial Revolution proper.[27] One of several legends says it was to win the love of a woman, who later spurned him. However, the impetus must also have derived from an entrepreneurial spirit hoping to capitalize on the contemporary knitting boom.

Initially, the products from Lee's revolutionary stocking frame machines were coarse and could not match the quality of skilful hand-knitting. Other factors also made competition with hand-knitting difficult, as frame-knitting required capital investment and payment of wages, while the labour element of hand-knitting was virtually free. Lee was refused a patent by Elizabeth I when he presented her with the coarse woollen stockings produced on his early machine, perhaps because his invention threatened the livelihood of stocking hand-knitters.[28] Some years later, in about 1598, despite Lee's having doubled the number of needles so that the finest silk yarn could be knitted, as desired by Queen Elizabeth, Lee was again refused a patent and he was forced to seek patronage in France, where the luxury silk trade was developing strongly. In 1612 Lee contracted with Pierre de Caux of Rouen to manufacture stockings and to supply both frames and English workmen who would teach apprentices to knit

and manufacture looms.[29] A number of frames were duly taken to Rouen in northern France, but sudden changes in circumstances, including the assassination of Lee's potential patron Henry IV, appear to have left him with no prospects, and the father of machine-knitting died in France, by all accounts a broken man. Having left a technical legacy from which the French industry clearly developed and benefited, Lee's invention was brought back to England by his brother James and was further improved.

Lee's original apprentices set up workshops in London and Nottinghamshire and framework-knitting slowly spread. By 1655 the hosiery industry was grouped in three main sectors: the highest-quality framework knitting in silk was based in London; worsted-wool framework-knitting became a speciality of the Midlands, which, according to Defoe, had 'no other manufactures';[30] and the northern regions continued to produce coarser, less expensive hand-knitted stockings.[31] By the beginning of the eighteenth century, framework-knitting had begun to have a serious effect on the livelihoods of stocking hand-knitters. The two industries, hand- and frame-knitting, survived side by side for a considerable time but, in the face of changing fashions, technological progress and increased machine productivity and quality, the hand-knitting industry declined and was all but finished by the early nineteenth century, except in remote rural areas.

Fashion inspired many new developments in framework knitting in the second half of the eighteenth century (see p.26). For example, Nottinghamshire knitters began to specialize in knitted cotton lace as an economical alternative to fashionable bobbin lace. Unlike hand-knitting, frame-knitting could produce both lengths of fabric and pieces intricately knitted to shape – and these two types of mechanized production, with their differing labour costs and processes, still characterize the industry today. At the end of the eighteenth century a frame-knitter could produce 12 pairs of stockings in four days when work was plentiful, earning 18–30 shillings a week for fancy work, or 10–12 shillings for plain cotton and worsted goods.[32] This represents four times the productivity of the Kendal hand-knitters (see p.56) and up to two-and-a-half times the wages, but with much greater overheads.

As the industry grew, supply began to exceed demand, and life became harder for the frame-knitters who, particularly in England, were at the mercy of mid-

dlemen or 'bag-hosiers', who controlled the flow of work, payment levels and the supply of orders and raw materials. As cottage weavers had done before them, most framework-knitters rented a frame to work either in their own home as a cottage industry or in one of the new frame shops, managed by master hosiers who owned the frames. Frame-knitters therefore found themselves in an iniquitous situation between self-employment and dependence on an employer for work and materials.

The precursors of the factory system that developed in the mid-nineteenth century, the frame shops were tightly packed with several knitting frames to maximize rents (plate 9).[33] In addition to rent, each frame-knitter had to pay someone to wind the yarn and finish the stockings. Inevitably these tasks were delegated to family members – the wives seaming stockings and children winding yarn from hanks to spools for the machine. Working on 'piece rates' at a fixed price per pair of stockings, set by the master hosiers or via middlemen, frame-knitters were often in dire poverty as foreign competition increased and demand fluctuated and their frame rents still had to be paid. As early as the mid-eighteenth century, the saying 'as poor as a stockinger' became commonplace in the Midlands, where the bulk of the industry had migrated.

As fashions changed and were simplified in the early nineteenth century, the market for stockings suffered a further serious decline. A period of extreme turbulence and technical change in the industry was marked by the Luddite uprising of 1811–12, when knitting frames were smashed in Nottinghamshire, their birthplace. The knitters were protesting against high standing rents for frames and extremely low wages, but the uprising was also a protest at the de-skilling of fully fashioned framework knitting, which was threatened by new technical improvements and increasing competition from cheaper 'cut-ups' – inferior stockings cut and sewn from plain-knitted fabric.[34]

Knitters in the Midlands petitioned for regulation of the framework-knitting industry, first in 1779, then

10 Striped stockings,
1860s, Britain
V&A: T.209&A–1928
Fully fashioned silk stockings in bold stripes of pink, yellow and blue, with narrow yellow-and-blue stripes appearing green, and white soles. Marked W in the welt, they may have been worn by a man or a woman. Probably frame-knitted, utilizing striping attachments, they have neat hand-sewn seams.

11 Green stocking, 1923, Britain
V&A: T.147&A–1975
Emerald silk fully fashioned stockings made by I&R Morley, suppliers to the royal household. They manufactured stockings in silk, lisle cotton, merino (wool and cotton) and artificial silk, dyed in many colours. Fully fashioned stockings were knitted on both hand and rotary power frame machines and marked with the letter M in knotted stitch. Home workers added the 'chevening' embroidery – a narrow line and arrowhead – a legacy of the elaborate embroidered clocks of previous eras.

in 1812, but without success. A parliamentary enquiry into the conditions of framework-knitters in England did take place, however, in 1844, concluding that 'the general condition of the framework knitters is very deplorable. They work generally from daylight until 10 o'clock at night, five days a week in winter and during daylight in summer very frequently. The average is about 14 hours a day.'[35] The situation was complex, however, and the commission also concluded that the knitters' distress was fundamentally due to excess of labour over demand, and little change resulted.[36] Nevertheless the Truck Commission Enquiry of 1872 considered that the charging of substantial frame rents to knitters was still a form of truck.[37] Thus the development of the knitting industry, from such pioneering beginnings, took a much troubled course.

The progress of framework knitting

The spread of frame-knitting throughout the British Isles and Europe took place both legitimately and through industrial espionage, despite protectionist export bans. In France, for example, Jean Hindret made detailed drawings in 1656 for the politician Jean-Baptiste Colbert, and these were later published in Denis Diderot's *Encyclopaedia* and now provide the earliest detailed technical records of the frame.[38] Knitting frames were smuggled to the American colonies and copied and improved by many inventors during the eighteenth century, and so the knowledge was diffused.

The making of stockings on the frame was many times faster than hand-knitting but still a craft activity, based on a sequence of eleven arm and leg movements per cycle, plus hand manipulation of stitches to achieve intricate designs. Stockingers were apprenticed for seven years to learn the many techniques employed in the making of fashionable stockings, from stripes, inlaid colours and ribs to turn-stitch patterns and openwork lace made by transferring stitches between needles using specially made eyelet tools.[39] The welts of many stockings show their maker's mark – perhaps a group of eyelet holes or short lines of contrast colour or initials knitted in with pride (plates 10 and 11). The manufacturers used one, two or three holes to mark sizes, and even their locations were carefully knitted into the welt. Sometimes these were deliberately misleading: following a protectionist ban on imports of desirable French stockings in 1766, Nottinghamshire knitters were instructed to knit 'Paris' into the welts.[40]

Technical improvements in spinning, weaving and knitting continued throughout the eighteenth and nineteenth centuries, but the basic knitting technology remained largely unchanged. A major shift came in 1849 when Matthew Townsend, a Leicester hosier, patented the latch needle as an alternative to Lee's bearded needle, simplifying the knitting process and paving the way for a new generation of machinery, including rotary frames and circular machines. Machines for improved production were developed, such as William Cotton's patented

12 Queen Victoria's stockings (detail), late 19th century, Britain V&A: T.74–1955
12 Queen Victoria's stockings (detail), late 19th century, Britain
V&A: T.74–1955
An elaborate crown and the letters V R are worked into the top of these silk stockings, using eyelet lace technique. The letter S is knitted into the welt, and the number six below the motif may indicate the precise pair within the wardrobe inventory. The legs are black with chevening-embroidered clocks. The pulls stitched to the welts are made of linen cloth. During the knitting, the back of the fabric faces the knitter, and the motif and letters would be upside down and reversed, as the stockings were knitted from the top down.

13 and **14** **I&R Morley trade catalogue**, 1917, London

I&R Morley was one of the UK's largest merchant hosiers supplying underwear, stockings and many other knitted items for men, women and children to the retail trade. Plate 13 shows fleecy-lined merino wool combinations and a bodice for women and a shirt and drawers for men. Plate 14 illustrates women's bodices and knickers. The company also exported hosiery worldwide and plate 14 reinforces the British manufacture with a flag. Morley's extensive catalogues ran to 400 pages and some 40,000 items.

multiple frames, in which many stockings or other items could be knitted at once – first 4, then 12, 18 or even 24.[41] During the 1870s steam power was applied to the machinery and manual frame shops gradually gave way to true factories in which all operations, including knitting, winding and making-up, took place under the employer's roof.

Labour was plentiful, however, and the organization of the industry changed only slowly over a period of a hundred years as the work moved away from small frame shops to become concentrated under the larger merchant hosiers, such as Brettles, I&R Morley, Corah and Wolsey. These companies set up major factory operations in the Midlands from the mid-nineteenth century, for a time using both manual frames and steam-powered rotary frames to supply their own large Midlands or London wholesale warehouses and thence the burgeoning retail trade (plates 13 and 14). Activities in the factories were largely divided along gender lines: the men, having operated the labour-intensive heavy stocking frames, generally continued to run the powered machines[42]; the women workers, meanwhile, handled the making-up and finishing processes – a division that persists in knitwear factories today. Both handframe- and power-frame-knitted stockings had to be made as flat fabric and subsequently hand-seamed, mainly by women and children. Despite industrialization, many home workers continued to be employed through the 'putting-out' system until the late twentieth century, carrying out finishing operations – seaming and embroidery – for factory-knitted pieces.

The French wars in the early nineteenth century created new demand for knitted hose for the troops, who also required undergarments, and gradually the market for machine-made knitted underwear developed. By the mid-nineteenth century, knitting had become a major British industry, with the supply of both goods and machinery overseas. Such well-known hosiery and underwear brands were established as St Margaret's, Wolsey, Vedonis and Meridian.

The frame-knitting industry resisted the application of power to the machines longer than other textile areas, maintaining the craft of patterning and fashioning to shape alongside developments in automation, but today handframe-knitting is rare. One firm, G.H. Hurt of Chilwell, Nottinghamshire, still produces fine lace shawls on both modern-day powered machines and original handframes in order to preserve the historical and industrial heritage of the area. Hand-operated semi-industrial machines are also still used widely in Asia and by designers creating fabric samples and prototypes.

Circular and warp-knitting

A direct competitor to frame-knitting emerged in the late nineteenth century in the form of small-diameter hand-operated circular machines, such as the Griswold, which could produce seamless hosiery knitting. These machines were used both in factories and by home workers to make socks for the army, particularly in World War I in Britain and North America (see p.136). They were later automated to produce seamless fine-gauge hosiery. In the mid-1920s there were 348 seamless machines at one of Morley's factories, producing 500 dozen pairs of stockings per week.[43]

Powered circular knitting developed in the mid-nineteenth century, based on the circular frame developed in England by Marc Brunel in 1816 but later improved in France and the United States. Large-diameter machines created continuous lengths of extremely finely knit tubular fabrics which were cut open for 'cut-and-sewn' manufacturing. Originally termed 'circular web' or stockinette, the fabric later came to be referred to as 'jersey'. It could be produced as plain or striped single jersey (as in T-shirts), or double-weight jersey, plain or intricately patterned and textured.

Another rival to frame-knitting was the warp-knitting process, created by Josiah Crane's adaptation of the knitting frame in 1775 to produce a cross between knitting and weaving that instigated a new branch of the knitting industry, developed most strongly in Germany. This process was not based on replicating hand-knitting techniques but aimed to imitate the structures of netting, lace and other openwork fabrics. As in weaving, the technique uses a warp beam, which holds many warp threads, feeding into hooked needles to form a chain of stitches laterally intermeshed with its neighbours via the knitting operation to produce either open or solid fabrics, with additional yarns inserted for pattern effects.

Unlike weft-knitting, warp-knitting is relatively inelastic and does not unravel, so it is suited to lengths of fabric for cut-and-sewn construction and is now used for furnishing, fashion and industrial fabrics. Where weft-knitting favours horizontal patterning and allows two- and three-dimensional shaping, warp-knitting often features vertical patterning and design. It was popular for vertically striped stockings from the late eighteenth century, exemplified by a pair of fine stockings in cream silk with a blue vertical stripe, dating to the early nineteenth century (plate 15). A shawl dating from around the 1850s, worked in two colours, shows a highly distinctive complex chevron patterning technique that is possible only in warp-knitting (commonly known as Raschel fabric after one of the manufacturers of warp machinery), (plate 16). Warp knitting has found modern fashion applications in, for example, the zigzag patterning in several colours that has been a signature fabric of the Missoni fashion house since the 1950s, made on original machines (see p.201), and the 'A-POC' concept for knitted seamless garments developed by Issey Miyake and Dai Fujiwara in 1997, providing an instant cut-out wardrobe (see p.186).

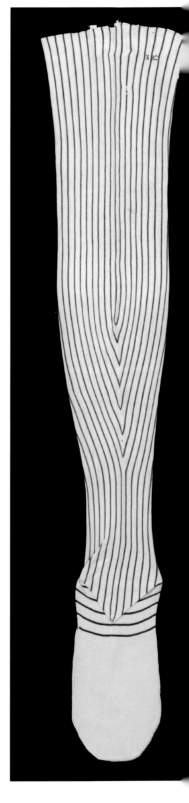

15 **Striped warp-knit silk stockings**, 1800–24, Britain
V&A: T.1723&A–1913
These stockings have been fully fashioned and hand sewn, in the same manner as weft-knitted stockings. The heel is simply shaped to a right angle, forming a point when flat, whereas the instep and sole of the stocking are shaped by fully-fashioned weft knitting. The stripes form attractive chevrons at the back of the calf where the stockings are shaped.

16 **Raschel knit shawl**,
1850s–60s, Britain
V&A: T.64–1989
Silk shawl warp-knitted in four colours: yellow, green, purple and brown. The meandering flame-like effect is a distinctive feature of the warp-knitted fabric. Despite the appearance of horizontal chevrons, this fabric has been knitted in the perpendicular direction. Each of the colours is knitted continuously in the vertical direction, representing one thread on the warp beam, but shogging left and right to create the meandering effect. Its use has continued to the present, revived in the 1950s by the Italian designers Missoni to become one of their signature fabrics.

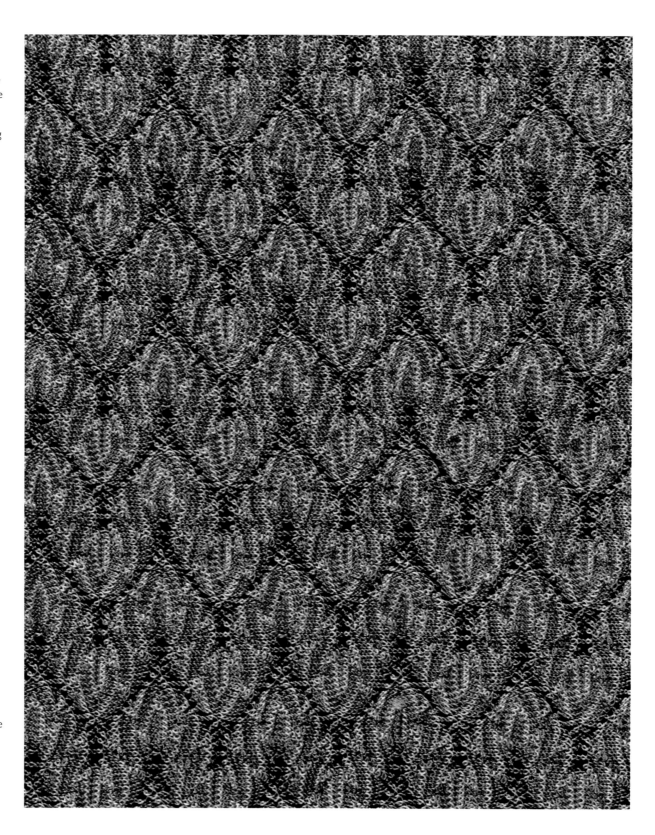

Underwear to outerwear
and the development of sportswear

From medieval times, simple garments in the form of a shift or shirt were worn to protect more elaborate outer layers of clothing from the dirt and odours of the body, and for ease of laundering. For women this garment became known as a smock or chemise; for men the shirt or waistcoat. Linen was worn by the higher social classes, but it is likely that ordinary people wore coarser woollen undergarments. By the sixteenth century, many layers of clothing were worn under fashionable outer garments, including evolving forms of the male shirt worn next to the skin, which in Tudor times was exposed by slashing the outer garment.

In the eighteenth century, men's formal fashions consisted of a skirted coat worn with knee-length breeches and stockings and a waistcoat that may have been made of silk brocade woven fabric or of a plain fabric decorated with embroidery or frogging (see pages 27, 33). Machine-knitted fabric began to replace traditional woven fabric as new techniques and surface effects were developed, and by the late eighteenth-century men's breeches and longer pantaloons, worn as part of suits, were made of machine-knitted cotton or silk jersey in cut-and-sewn construction (plate 17). They were tight fitting and tailored in the same manner as woven fabrics, with woven facings, pockets and fall-front fastenings, but the use of knitting for the main parts would have given an element of flexibility for active movement in, for example, riding. Some show a great deal of wear and tear and mending in the crutch area. From the mid-nineteenth century, breeches gave way to pantaloons and then trousers. One intriguing pair of fully knitted silk pantaloons, complete with feet, was constructed on the frame in such a way that the lower half mimicked jockey boots (plate 18).

The wardrobe of Thomas Coutts (1735–1822), the founder of Coutts bank, was preserved on his death in February 1822 and is interesting here for its hosiery and knitted woollen underwear. Mostly made from undyed wool, this includes two sets of garter-stitch wristlets (with seams), four tubular-knit knee warmers in stock-

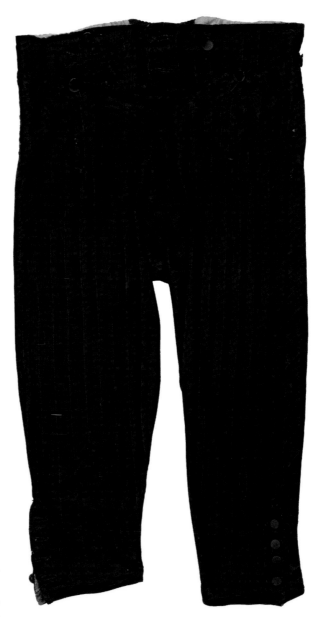

17 Men's breeches,
late 18th century, Britain
V&A: T.745A–1913
There are examples in the V&A collection of breeches made from machine-knitted plain-cotton double-jersey fabric (V&A: T.41–1986), or, as here, from knitted-silk double jersey in black or brown. The textual ribs of the knitted-silk jersey fabric have been cut to create subtle chevron effects.

ing stitch with ribbing and three tubular double-layer wool nightcaps shaped at each end (plate 20).

Two machine-knitted undershirts in heavy, undyed, woollen fleecy jersey have openings at the front bound with woven linen fabric.[44] Traditional men's knitted vests, important for warmth, had been simplified to plain knitting by the time they were produced industrially. Unusually, in these examples, the underarms also have bound openings for ease of movement under

18 All-in-one pantaloons with stockings,
1780–90, Britain
V&A: T.68–1935
This pair of frame-knitted silk pantaloons emulates jockey boots, down to the last detail of the linen loops to pull on the boots. Knitted in yellow, brown and black silk, a subtle detail at the back of the leg is knitted in cream using intarsia technique, possibly imitating stocking tops.

other clothes, with the possible added benefit of enabling longer wear between launderings. The functional detail of the open bound underarm was used as a design feature of heavy rib-knitted dresses and sweaters shown on the catwalk by Yohji Yamamoto in his Autumn/Winter 2010 collection.

Three pairs of Thomas Coutts's hand-knitted ribbed footless stocking gaiters in navy wool are in good condition. Otherwise, most of the knitted underwear items, in contrast to the relative elegance of the outerwear, are well worn, mended and heavily stained. The slightly matted appearance of some pieces indicates they were frequently washed. Mr Coutts's woollen nightcaps and thick fleecy-lined undershirts are carefully repaired, and a shirt and cream stockings show many stains, suggesting long use without replacement which is surprising for a man of his position (plate 19). It is thought that Mr Coutts may have been bedridden for his last years.

Woollen undergarments made of circular-knitted stockinette were developed for men from the late eighteenth century and for women from the early nineteenth century, spurred by the increased concern for health and fitness that came to prominence in late Victorian times. Industrial knitting manufacturers produced ranges of underwear – for example, Pringle's 'Rodono', Peter Scott's 'Pesco' – often made of finely knitted jersey fabrics, produced using circular-knitted single- and later double-weight fabric that could be slit open and cut and sewn as woven cloth. In parallel, upper-body garments were often made by hand-knitting, and knitting patterns became widely available. Men's shirts, later known as undershirts or vests, had a round neck and button-front placket opening. This classic style, with short or long sleeves, became a hybrid of underwear and outerwear as it was adopted for sporting wear, wool jersey being highly absorbent of sweat. Similar styles were registered as football and rugby jerseys by Corah of Leicester and produced from the 1870s (plate 21).[45] A drawing of the Oxford and Cambridge rowing teams from the *Illustrated London News* of 1863 shows the men wearing short-sleeved 'jerseys' with front plackets offset to the left side of the

19 Undershirt, worn by Thomas Coutts, 1800–22, Britain
V&A: 371X–1908
Machine knitted woollen vest made from fleecy-backed stockinette, bound with linen on the front and underarm openings, showing heavy staining from prolonged use. Thick woollen underwear was a necessity for warmth, especially in infirmity.

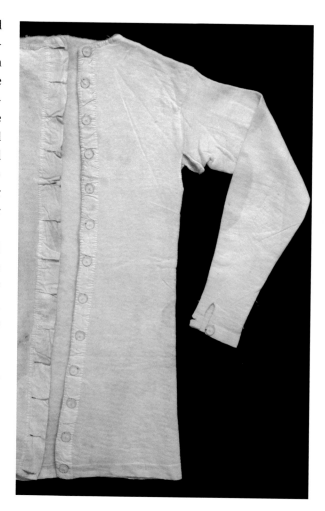

neck, looking like a vest – a forerunner of the modern T-shirt.[46] This basic undershirt or vest style was seen unchanged in underwear throughout most of the twentieth century. Knee warmers continued to be worn until the twentieth century, likewise emphasizing the continuity, practical nature and enduring relevance of much of knitting's history.[47]

Underwear became a mainstay of the knitting industry, accounting for most of the output of many firms until the middle of the nineteenth century. By this time jersey had also become popular for outerwear for men and boys. In the late nineteenth century working men's jackets using jersey fabrics were extensively produced, bringing flexibility in movement to practical working clothes.[48] This was the jersey-knit fabric so radically adopted for women's wear by Chanel in the 1920s.

Sanitary clothing – Dr Gustav Jaeger

Throughout the eighteenth and nineteenth centuries, elite clothing had to meet the increasingly extreme demands of fashion while also protecting against the elements. Intricate layers were often required, restricting movement, especially for women. Towards the end of the nineteenth century, the complexity of such clothing

systems came under attack. Social and medical research centred around bodily hygiene, and 'rational' clothing gave rise to new thinking that eschewed fashion and took a lead from simpler, functional working-class clothes.

Dr Gustav Jaeger, a professor of zoology and physiology at the University of Stuttgart, having long observed animals, wrote his treatise *Health Culture* in 1880, extolling the health-giving virtues of woollen and other animal-hair clothing over clothes made from vegetable fibres. His philosophy of 'sanitary clothing' was based on the need for clothing to absorb and pass away the 'noxious exhalations' of the body, including perspiration. Wool, as a porous fibre, could absorb these vapours when worn next to the body more easily than could linen or cotton, which he referred to as 'chilling materials'.[49] (The scientific basis for the claims is sound, as wool is a hygroscopic fibre that absorbs moisture and in doing so gives off heat so the body does not feel cold.) The book expressed the need for a sanitary clothing system made entirely of wool, from undergarments to outerwear. For the system to function, coats, it was claimed, must be kept buttoned up or taken off altogether, but never worn open.

Health Culture was translated by an aficionado of Jaeger's ideas, English businessman Lewis Tomalin, in 1884. Formerly the head of finance for a grocer's firm in London, Tomalin licensed the Jaeger name and founded with two others the company Dr Jaeger's Sanitary Woollen System to manufacture knitted underwear and outerwear for gentlemen and ladies. The company opened its first London shop in 1887 and was renamed Jaeger and Co. Ltd in 1914. Patrons of this radical new concept included Oscar Wilde, George Bernard Shaw and several Arctic and Antarctic explorers (plate 22).

In the 1930s the health-giving properties of wool were explained in a series of bulletins written by Mr Garrett, the head of the Jaeger technical laboratory:

The foremost elements to give proper protection and comfort in what you wear are – slow conductivity, to enable the body to maintain a normal temperature, absorption to eliminate damp,

20 Thomas Coutts's wardrobe, 1800–22, Britain
V&A: 371O&P–1908; CIRC. 718:12–1912; CIRC.717:9–1912; CIRC. 718:11–1912; 371ff&gg–1908; CIRC. 718:10–1912; CIRC. 718:8–1912; CIRC. 716:11&A–1912
This selection of Mr Coutts's knitted accessories, mostly made in undyed wool, includes a pair of large hand-knitted plain stockings, probably boot liners (foot length 33 cm); two finer hand-knitted stockings with purl-stitch clocks, one with red top edge; two garter-stitch wristlets (with seams) and four tubular-knit knee warmers in stocking stitch with ribbing (not quite matching pairs); a tubular-knitted double layer nightcap; a lacy cotton hand-knitted seamless cap lined with purple silk; one of three pairs of hand-knitted ribbed footless stocking gaiters in navy wool and a pair of angora gloves with much of the long hair worn away.

21 Rugby football team, early 20th century, Powys, Mid Wales, in shirts made of knitted jersey fabric,

22 George Bernard Shaw, 1886, in a Jaeger suit of brown stockinette,

ventilation and moderate weight. Adequate cover of the human frame is essential for the maintenance of health and good wool possesses all the elements named…ideal sportswear is always made from wool for the reasons given.[50]

Garrett also hailed wool's ability to absorb and transmit 'healing rays' from the sun to the body as a superior treatment for rheumatic illnesses.[51] From around the same time, however, the emphasis in Jaeger's promotional materials began to rest less on the health-giving properties of fabrics and more on tailoring and fashion, and sports clothing, including golfing knitwear, became important to the Jaeger brand as it developed a full men's and women's fashion range.

In his original text, Dr Jaeger revived a form of stocking and sock manufacture originally proposed in 1792 by Englishman Walter Vaughan: the five-toed stocking. An earlier version of the five-toed stocking exists in the V&A (V&A: A.P. 421-1).[52] Similar in manufacture to gloves, the digitated woollen stocking (plate 23) was heavily promoted by Dr Jaeger for those with sensitive feet:

> The objectionable condition of the skin between the toes, which no amount of cleanliness and care can wholly avert, and which frequently causes soft corns and even sores, is due to the inability of the perspiration to escape when the surfaces are in contact…[When wearing the toed stockings] the skin between the toes becomes dry and wholesome.[53]

Digitated socks remain a novelty in Britain but split-toe and five-toed knitted socks are popular in Japanese culture, where foot coverings are regularly exposed indoors because shoes are removed. They relate to the white fabric *tabi* socks with split toes worn with wooden *geta* sandals by women wearing the kimono costume in traditional Japanese dress, while Japanese workmen commonly wear *tabi* split-toe boots – cotton ankle boots with light flexible soles – for easy grip on bamboo scaffolding.

23 Jaeger stocking,
1890–1910, Britain
V&A: T.394-2001
Dr Jaeger believed the
separation of the toes
promoted foot hygiene, so the
Jaeger company produced
digitated woollen socks, made
in the same manner as gloves.
Machine knitted in black with
ecru sole, the socks have fully-
fashioned shaping for each toe
and the heel. Matching
darning wool was also
supplied.

24 Pope & Plante stocking,
1851, London
V&A: A.P. 421:2
Shown at the Great Exhibition,
this white elasticated cotton
stocking is inscribed 'Pope &
Plante 1851 Let Us Love As
Brethren' in the welt. The
stocking, with its wording and
textured welt, would have been
painstakingly knitted on the
hand frame, with lettering
worked upside down and in
reverse. The soles and heels of
the lace stocking are in stocking
stitch for strength.

Industry shows its paces:
exhibits from the Great Exhibition of 1851

With machine knitting a significant industry in Britain
and hosiery and underwear its bedrock, the Great
Exhibition of 1851 offered machine builders and manufacturers the opportunity to show up-to-the-minute
innovations. The catalogue lists 58 British hosiery manufacturers, many of whom showed underwear and new
products to demonstrate their expertise and manufacturing capability, with some of the finest work still being
made by handframe. Products for men, women and
children included vests, drawers, underpants, spencers,
combinations, kneecaps and nightcaps in addition to
guernsey and jersey frocks, shawls, socks and stockings,
in wool, cotton and silk. London-based hosiery manufacturers Pope & Plante exhibited finely knitted
commemorative stockings with intricate lace patterning and inscriptions, made with rubber elasticated
yarns to give better fit (plate 24). Capper & Waters of
Regent Street, London, exhibited a man's woollen vest,
'The Sottanello', which featured an innovative sleeve
design, shaped and seamed to allow more fabric at the
point of the elbow, thus avoiding strain and premature
wear (plates 25 and 26). Another significant innovation
was a woman's woollen vest, its manufacturer
unknown, created manually on the handframe and
accurately shaped to the body with three-dimensional
seamless gores at the bust (plate 27). Also shaped to fit
snugly at the waist, this garment was designed to give
women greater comfort and fit, avoiding bunching of
excess fabric when worn over or even under a corset.
Both the Morley and Pringle companies also came up
with the seamless three-dimensional bust shaping concept independently around the mid-nineteenth
century, but neither was able to patent an invention
that was in its time quietly revolutionary.[54] At the Great
Exhibition, no medals were awarded for hosiery as
there was 'not enough originality or inventive
power' but the 'excellent quality, diversity of
useful products and low prices of goods suitable for the mass of consumers' was
remarked upon.[55]

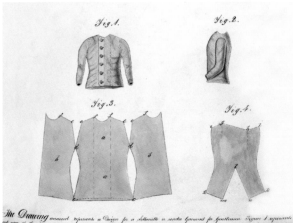

25 'Sottanello' vest with elbow shaping from the Great Exhibition, 1851, Britain
V&A: T.54–1959
Gentleman's machine knitted fully-fashioned cotton vest, shaped to fit the waist and elbow, with off-centre front placket bound in woven cotton, fastened with pearl buttons. The manufacturer Capper and Waters claimed this design was 'an improvement in undergarments (woven in stocking looms) suited to the personal form and especially the action of the elbow' and registered the design by submitting the technical drawing shown.

26 Capper & Waters,
Design for the 'Sottanello' undergarment, 1850, Britain
National Archives
The body and sleeve shapes represent innovation, creating a bent elbow in the manner of tailoring. The accompanying text states: 'By the peculiar form of the sleeves they will approximate nearer to the form of the arm and the peculiar form of the body *a a* and *b b* a better fit will be ensured rendering the whole much more comfortable than undergarments usually are.'

27 Woman's vest with shaping,
1851, Britain
V&A: T.55–1959
This vest is machine knitted in wool and fully fashioned, with cotton placket and pearl buttons. The process of shaping the bust was laborious. The gores were knitted separately and then picked up loop for loop into vertical gaps in the garment. Several manufacturers used cut-and-sewn gores to create three-dimensional bust shaping, necessitating seams, so this seamless gore was an innovation.

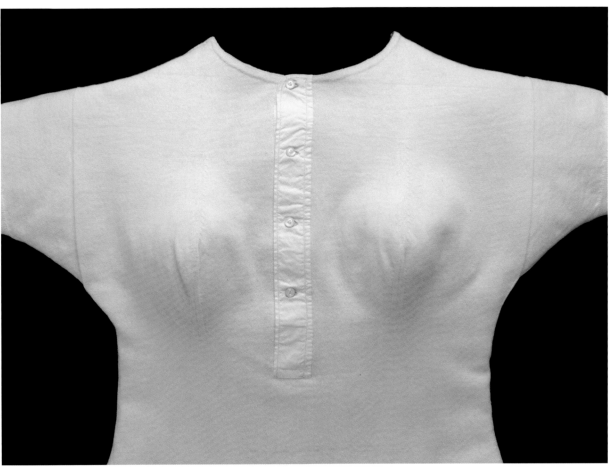

Modern technology

Changes in society, industry and fashion are accelerated during and following major conflicts, and the clothing requirements of the military also prompt changes in production. Knitted sweaters, for example, became standard issue for the British services in the late nineteenth century, providing practical garment forms that remain popular today. Woollen underwear was also taken up by the military, providing large orders for emerging factories, and such underwear continued unchanged for many years (plate 28). In the twentieth century the effect of war on trade in the fashion and textile industry was mixed: those companies who gained government contracts, such as Pasold's and Wolsey, were able to thrive, while others were subsumed, or found difficulty obtaining materials as supplies such as silk and later nylon were diverted to war use. The decades following World War I were a boom time for the hosiery and knitwear industry as production expanded and technology developed in Britain, the United States and Germany. During World War II, the British Civilian Clothing Scheme for essential 'utility' clothing was developed in close collaboration with the industry. Although sweaters and outerwear overtook production, underwear was still one of the key products of the knitting industry and came within the utility regulations, being provided by companies such as Wolsey, Morley, Corah, Smedley and Pringle among others, with Pasold's specializing in children's wear. In the second half of the twentieth century, knitting-machine technology made further great advances, enabling the most complex patterning and structures to be individually programmed and knitted, with infinite design possibilities for knitwear and hosiery. From the mid-1970s, electronic control enabled vast improvements in jacquard patterning compared with the early mechanical systems (consisting of metal plates punched with holes and using pegs to select the pattern) or the numerical machine programming necessary before graphical computer interfaces. In the mid-1990s, complete garment knitting and seamless knitwear was the new technological revolution in the weft-knitting industry, in both flat-bed and circular knitting. In flat-bed work complete seamless garments can be made by knitting and joining three tubes side by side, one each for body and sleeves, thereby eliminating most of the labour-intensive making-up processes of classic fully fashioned knitwear and saving costs on up to 40 manual processes (plate 29). Medium-diameter circular-knitting machines can create body-sized tubes to be made up into body-contouring garments without side seams, such as lingerie and sportswear, using precision-knitted fabric structures and synthetic yarns. These replicate the skills of the earliest hand-knitters, who achieved the same results in stockings, socks, hats

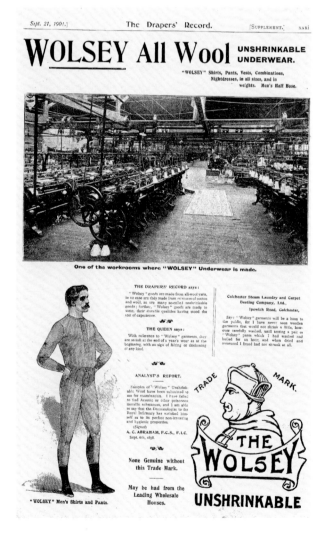

28 Wolsey advert, 1901
Drapers Record,
21 September 1901
One of the major hosiery manufacturers, Wolsey supplied wholesalers with underwear manufactured from wool, cotton and silk. The workroom, shown here, illustrates several Cotton's Patent straight-bar rotary-powered machines for knitting and fashioning to shape several articles at once. Most manufacturers promoted 'unshrinkable' finishes for woollen garments, based on chemical treatment of the wool (see V&A: T.107–1989).

and gloves (albeit more slowly) using nothing more than four or five straight wires.

The economies of mass production combined with cheaper synthetic fibres meant that by the mid-twentieth century the price of hosiery, underwear and knitwear was driven in a downward direction towards the economy end of the market, where price sensitivity was most important. This exacerbated a polarization of the industry that had begun in the nineteenth century with the mass production of knitwear and hosiery centred in the Midlands around Leicester, Nottingham and Derby, supplying many brand names such as Meridian, Vedonis, Bear Brand and Pretty Polly (both stocking brands) to department stores and multiple retailers. In contrast, Hawick in the Scottish Borders developed a niche industry focusing on high-quality woollen products, especially cashmere, that were both exclusive and fashionable. This schism in the industry continued, with Scotland producing luxury knitwear and the Midlands industry generally focused on the commodity end of the business. The contemporary British knitwear industry, vastly reduced by overseas competition in the 1970s and again in the 1990s, is today once more focused on traditional high quality, but with greater innovation in style and design rather than commodity production.

From natural to man-made fibres

In tandem with developments in machinery and technology, the materials used for knitting have evolved. In Britain, local wool was used to make early examples of basic knitting such as caps, stockings and other domestic items, and wool and woollen cloth became extremely important to the British and European economies from medieval times. In the Houses of Parliament in London, the Lord Chancellor still sits on a ceremonial 'Woolsack' – a seat stuffed with wool, first introduced in the fourteenth century by King Edward III as a sign of prosperity and a reminder that England's traditional source of wealth was the wool trade. Of course, linen was also used for knitting and, for the most luxurious items such as the finest knitted stockings produced for royalty and the aristocracy, silk. This much-prized fibre had been

29 Yoshiki Hishinuma seamless jacket, 2005
Powerhouse Museum, Sydney, Australia
This totally seamless tailored jacket was made using flat-bed knitting technology, developed by Yoshiki Hishinuma in collaboration with Shima Seiki, Japanese knitting machine builders. Even the buttons are incorporated in the process.

30 Courtelle advert 'New Generation' jersey, 1966
Vogue April 1966
In the 1960s and early 1970s the new branded synthetics such as Courtelle, Bri-Nylon and Crimplene were widely adopted by the knitting industry for their easy knitting properties. Their 'easy care' consumer branding saw a fast growth in textural knitted double-jersey fabrics, which replaced woven fabrics in dresses and suits in a 'new generation' of fashion.

COURTELLE

imported from China and India since medieval times and was eventually cultivated successfully in Mediterranean countries, although attempts to rear silkworms were made as far north as England.

With the Industrial Revolution, carding and spinning machinery improved quality in worsted-spun wool yarns, using longer staple fleeces, particularly imported merino from Spanish Merino sheep bred in Australia, which was of finer quality than any of the British wools.[56] Merino and botany wools spun in England and cashmere spun in Scotland became the hallmark of high-quality knitwear. However, the Industrial Revolution also saw wool lose its dominance as imported cotton became the principal fibre.

As industry progressed, the quest to produce cheaper materials to cater for an increasing population gathered pace, aiming to create artificial fibres in mimicry of natural ones but, importantly, easier to maintain than wool, cotton or silk. The first man-made fibre, rayon, produced at the end of the nineteenth century, was a regenerated cellulose fibre derived from natural wood by artificial processes, commercialized by Courtaulds in Britain in 1905 and known as artificial silk because of its lustrous sheen. Nylon was the first fibre synthesized entirely in the laboratory, produced in 1938 by Dupont in the United States and launched to the American public in 1940 in the form of 'indestructible' stockings, although the new 'nylons' did not become widely available until after World War II. Other synthetics such as acrylic and polyester fibres were produced in Britain by Courtaulds and ICI and in the United States by Dupont and Dow Chemicals. These were marketed under modern brand names such as Orlon, Bri-Nylon, Dacron and Courtelle, and featured in the optimistic advertising of the 1950s and 1960s, heralding new freedoms and prosperity (plate 30).

For the knitting industry these yarns were revolutionary, creating a new age of easy-care, machine-washable knitwear, baby clothes and underwear, longer-lasting stockings and tights and new lightweight but rugged sportswear and outerwear. What is more, the advent of synthetic fibres stimulated a growth in the circular-knitting branch of the industry that focused on textured and

Modern Stockings and Tights

The rise in the use of powered machines in the hosiery industry from the mid-nineteenth to the mid-twentieth century saw the transition from decorated hand-knitted stockings and hand-embroidered silk stockings to the commonplace mass-produced nylon hosiery of today. Stockings knitted on the handframe survived in tandem until the 1920s, both inside and outside the factories. For example, extremely fine pink silk stockings (V&A: T.96–1960) made in France about 1920 still have clocks worked in eyelet lace, but clock decoration disappeared soon after.

From the late 1940s, following World War II restrictions, synthetic nylon yarns began to change the hosiery industry forever and, with the adoption of circular technology, seamless modern 'nylons' soon became the affordable norm. The next shift for the industry was inspired by the 1960s designer fashion for short skirts, creating a major demand for tights in many colours and weights, and Mary Quant developed a mainstream hosiery brand to capture the market she helped create. Eventually, stockings created their own niche market. In the latter part of the twentieth century, the British company Funn Stockings, using rare nineteenth-century machinery found in manufacturers in the south of England and the Midlands, re-created the heavier lisle and wool stockings of previous eras, catering for costume dramas and keying into a nostalgic fashion mood. Today, tights and stockings continue to be made in plain and fancy textures, stripes, lace, colour patterns and prints, in seemingly unending variety.

1. **Advertisement** for Bear Brand stockings from *The Tatler*, November 1937
Sandy Black collection

2. **The Hardwear Ladderless Hose**, cream seamless stockings in artificial silk with cotton heel, toe and welt, British, 1920s
V&A: T.108&A–1981

3. **Klingsil fully fashioned silk stockings**, British, 1940s (non-utility)
V&A: T.214 to D–1982

4. **Mary Quant white nylon tights** with butterfly appliqué, British, 1960s
V&A: T.101C–1983

5. **Libelle Dentelle brown lace nylon stockings**, German, 1960s
V&A: T.164&A–1980

6. **Twiggy lilac nylon tights**, British, 1960s
V&A: T.99–1983

7. **Fully fashioned nylon stockings** with black inlaid heels and feet, British, *c.*1945,
V&A: T.86:1&2–1992

8. **Cards of nylon mending threads**, British, 1940s
V&A: T.58–1986

9. **Nevertity 'American style' nylon stockings**, British, 1960s
Packaging states 'this lovely pair of sheer stockings is made of nylon the amazing new material developed through Du Pont chemistry U.S.A.'
V&A: T.100C&D–1983

patterned double-jersey fabric, especially popular for cut-and-sewn suits and separates in the 1970s. Soon the domestic knitwear industry was rife with mergers and acquisitions. In the 1960s and 1970s the major fibre companies diversified into knitwear, supplying large multiple stores such as Marks and Spencer with bulk merchandise. Yet this was the time when the seeds of the British designer knitwear boom were sewn – a reaction to mass-produced products with little perceived design value. A similar duality has characterized the beginning of the twenty-first century: the fibre giants themselves have become the subject of takeovers and mergers while 'couture' knitwear has blossomed.[57]

The rise of nylon, like the varied fortunes of both the hand-knitters and framework-knitters, vividly illustrates how changes in fashion and technology can create or ruin industries. The invention of nylon, launched just before the United States entered World War II, then immediately commandeered for parachutes, ropes and other wartime supplies, created unprecedented demand for the new sheer nylon stockings after the war. Compared with the heavier rayon and lisle stockings previously available, nylons were a symbol of modernity, but they had been excluded from the list of rationed clothing, creating the conditions for a lively black market. Fully fashioned nylon stockings were exactly that – knitted to shape on the machines and seamed to give the distinctive and seductive line up the back of the leg, just as in the original frame-knitted stockings but infinitely finer. Famously, during the war women even mimicked the seamlines of fully fashioned nylon stockings by drawing lines with make-up on their bare legs. By the 1960s the latest nylon stockings were knitted seamlessly and heat-set to the shape of the leg, thus decimating the fully fashioned stocking industry, which retracted and remains a niche segment of the market. The emergence of the miniskirt in the 1960s stimulated the demise of stockings and the emergence of tights, previously a specialist product for dancers and children. Similarly, footless tights, hitherto confined to the dance and exercise market, unexpectedly became high fashion in 2007.

31 Combination skirt and top swimwear, *c*.1910, Britain
V&A: T.336/a–1987
This bathing costume is typical of the late Victorian and Edwardian era. Nautical blue with white ribbon trim, it is a short-sleeved loose-fitting all-in-one, modestly worn with a wrapped skirt, which is easily removed, still displaying considerable propriety but allowing significant exposure of skin.

32 Bathing party, September 1911, Houlgate, France
Edwardian photograph of women in the sea, wearing typical bathing outfits: dresses and drawers (two with braiding), bathing caps, stockings and bathing shoes.

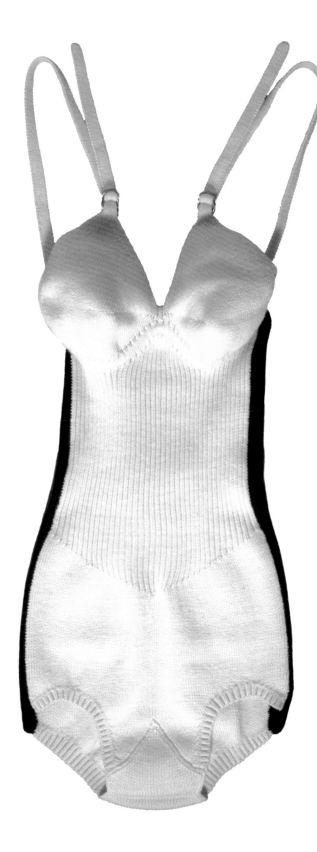

33 Neyret swimming costume,
1937, France
V&A: T.293–1971
Made in Paris and machine knitted in cream wool using a combination of flat double rib and stretchy 2x2 rib fabrication, the costume has been meticulously fashioned to shape. Three-dimensional shaping of the bra cups has been achieved by *flèchage* technique (partial knitting), also used to achieve the curved rib central panel. The back is scooped low and the leg edging is plated with elastic yarn. Despite this complex construction, the wool would have sagged when wet. A streamlined slimming effect is created by the blue stripe down each side.

Swimwear

The changing mores of society, as well as developments in fibres, can be read from the evolution of underwear, sportswear and especially bathing costumes. As the nineteenth century progressed, attempts to simplify clothing saw knitted combinations – all-in-one vest and drawers – proving popular with women as well as men, and corsets being discarded as the greater freedom of movement enjoyed in sporting activities pervaded everyday life. Swimwear followed a similar path (plates 31 and 32). Both mass-produced and home-made bathing costumes of the early and mid-twentieth century were famously made of wool. Wool's stretchiness for fit was excellent until the costume came in contact with the sea, whereupon it would absorb several times

34 Samantha de Terain swimming costume,
1992, Britain
V&A: T.183–1993
This one-piece costume is cut and sewn from 92% nylon and 8% Lycra jersey fabric, featuring a ladder construction for bold effect at the back, with a plain V-neck front. The high Lycra content was heavily promoted as imparting enhanced fit.

its weight in water and gravity would take over when the hapless bather emerged. Perhaps as an ironic echo of this tradition, the risqué topless bathing costume or 'monokini' designed by Rudi Gernreich in 1964 was still made predominantly of wool double jersey in a dogstooth check pattern, although blended with 13 per cent cotton and 4 per cent rubber (V&A: T.257–1974).

A striking 1920s patchwork bathing costume in cotton jersey makes a statement (V&A: T.307–1992). An elegant 1930s hand-knitted feminine style from Paris is more complex in construction, utilizing ribbed sections and bi-colour design to make the figure look slim (plate 33). Many knitting patterns for swimwear ensembles were produced in the 1930s and 1940s, often including wraps or coats for modesty, and all promoting stylish and healthy pursuits. A swimsuit pattern for men proudly proclaims 'For You to Knit – For Him to Wear'. Everyday bathing costumes continued to be manufactured from double-jersey wool by companies such as the American-owned Jantzen (plate 35) and British Meridian (V&A: T.299–1982). As synthetic fibres took over, swimwear was one of the areas to benefit from improvements in fabric performance, with finely structured jersey fabrics becoming the norm. The final step was the introduction of Lycra and elastomeric content into jersey fabrics for body-contouring swimwear, often with inbuilt support structures for women. One of the earliest elasticated stretch fabrics was the ruched Maxxam, patented by British designer Rosemary Moore in 1985. This nylon single jersey with Lycra was quickly taken up for Liza Bruce swimwear in the USA. With the new fabrics, swimwear designs became ever more revealing and inventive, as shown by cut-away panels in Samantha de Terain costumes from the early 1990s (plate 34), in a blend of 92 per cent nylon and a relatively high 8 per cent Lycra to ensure cling fit.

However, bikinis had meanwhile become the prime vehicle for minimum coverage of the body, developing from the relatively modest two-piece bathing suit to the extremes of small triangles of fabric. Controversially launched in 1946 in Paris by Louis Réard, bikinis were not an immediate success, owing to moral objections, but they overtook one-piece costumes in the 1960s.

Crocheted and hand-knitted bikinis were surprisingly fashionable again in the late 1960s, and new patterns have emerged for modern knitters to create with humour and irony.

Outdoor sports

Developments in swimwear were part of a wider expansion of outdoor sports and leisure activities at the end of the nineteenth century. Special clothes were designed for particular sports, in addition to the versions of the popular jersey for rugby and football. Corah produced a jersey cycling suit in 1883 (the Fred Wood Champion Suit), alongside children's dresses and ladies' bodices.[58] A man's cycling suit dated to the 1890s, made by Marshall E. Smith & Bro. of Philadelphia, demonstrates the use of jersey for 'Streamlined close fitting garments which allowed free movement…when pitching body and bicycle against the elements'.[59] Worn for cycling on the new lightweight bicycles of the period, the suit would have cut a dash (V&A: T.7–2000).[60] The breeches are of fleecy wool fabric, smooth on the outside but textured on the inside for warmth, and are designed with fabric reinforcements at the seat. Today a similar reinforced design can be found in contemporary nylon-jersey cycling shorts, which have a high elastomeric yarn content and are designed to fit tightly like a second skin for ultimate streamlining.

Much research has been carried out to design optimum-performance fabrics for sportswear. In swimming, for example, Speedo Fastskin is a textured warp-knitted fabric, designed to mimic the rippling texture of shark-skin, which channels the water at microscopic level (plate 36).

Now synonymous with the American concept of simple and relaxed casual clothing, sportswear developed as a strong element of the twentieth-century knitwear trade. The simple sweater became emblematic of certain sports: the cricket sweater is cream wool or cotton, V-necked with contrasting navy and red striped edgings and a cable pattern (plate 37); the golf sweater is typically round-necked wool or cashmere, with the traditional argyle diamond pattern over the body; the plain wool or cashmere sweater in heathery

35 **Left: John Smedley**, 1930s; **Right: Jantzen**, 1950–59; **Below: Pattern booklet**, 1930s, Britain
V&A: T.252–1990; T.113–1999; V&A: Furniture, Textiles and Fashion Archive
The turquoise costume is knitted in fine woollen textured jersey with transfer stitch patterns. It is constructed in a double layer and has knickers beneath a small skirt. The navy costume is pique cotton jersey with red grosgrain ribbon trim. The front panel is double layered with vertically wired bra. Note the signature Jantzen diver appliqué logo. The pattern booklet shows hand-knitted woollen bathing costumes for men and women.

colours has become a classic for hunting or shooting trips to Scotland; the ski sweater is, in contrast, thicker and knitted in bold geometric or figurative patterns and bright colours with white. Knitting patterns have naturally been designed for all of these to be made at home, with subtle changes in detail and fit appearing with each passing decade.

Unrivalled for stretch properties and flexibility of movement, fine knitted jersey fabrics with elastomeric yarns provided the basis for the women's exercise-wear boom that emerged in the body-conscious era of the 1980s. Stretch-knitted fabrics, however, had long before

made an impact in other areas of clothing, including footwear. One of the innovative exhibits at the 1851 Great Exhibition comprised two pairs of ankle boots, made either in Britain or in Germany from a combination of elasticated knitted (rubberized) fabric with leather toe caps and soles (plate 38). Since the beginning of the nineteenth century, boots had been fastened with laces or many buttons, but these new stretchy ankle boots eliminated the need for either and were said to allow the foot to move more freely. Their lightness of construction and uncluttered design looks remarkably modern, and contemporary designers continue to utilize stretch knit for footwear. Both the famous Chelsea boots of the 1960s and humble plimsolls or tennis shoes (made from canvas and rubber) featured inserted elasticated panels to ease putting on and taking off. At the beginning of the twenty-first century, knitted footwear has become fashionable for boots and an updated version of plimsolls (plate 39).

Sportswear has also evolved in casual wear, with synthetics blended with natural materials such as polyester and cotton becoming popular due to a combination of easy care and comfort. Knitted cotton jersey has continued to be a staple of casual wear in T-shirts and sweatshirts (made from cotton jersey fleecy fabric, brushed on the inside), and at the end of the twentieth century knitted polyester fleece fabrics became widespread, usurping the position previously held by the knitted sweater to provide warmth without weight. Generically termed a 'fleece', this type of polyester garment is of a different construction to the earlier sweatshirt or underwear fleece fabrics, being knitted in an integral pile structure that allows the outer fabric surface to trap air.

38 Stockinette ankle boots,
19th century, Britain or Germany
V&A: T. 269&A–1963
This elasticated pull-on style
replaced multiple button
fastenings.

39 Ugg boots, 2011, Australia
Ugg boots, made of sheepskin,
became cult fashion footwear
for both winter and summer in
the first decade of the new
millennium. A popular knitted
fabric range called Ugg 'Cardy'
boots utilized heavy ribbed
wool, complete with button
fastenings and fringing. More
recent versions have Aran-style
cabled textures or knitted
patchwork.

Knitwear manufacturers and production

Despite tremendous upheavals in the British knitwear industry, there are still a number of knitwear manufacturers in England and Scotland whose heritage can be traced in an unbroken line, some for more than two centuries. Most of these companies have survived by establishing a high-quality niche product and heritage brand. Two of the most well-known are Pringle of Hawick in the Borders area of Scotland and John Smedley in Derbyshire in the Midlands. Others include Johnstons of Elgin, Lyle & Scott, Peter Scott and Ballantyne.

Pringle of Scotland

The story of Pringle, established in the early nineteenth century in Hawick, reflects the tumultuous transitions of the knitting industry.[61] The Borders area was important in the wool trades, having long been involved in spinning yarns using wool from plentiful local sheep.

Hand-knitting of bonnets and stockings was well established in Scotland by the sixteenth century, and the first stocking frame-knitting machines and knitters came to Hawick from England in the 1680s. After a faltering start, many hosiery firms were established in Edinburgh and Hawick, and, with the Union of Scotland and England in 1707, the Borders wool trade received financial encouragement in the form of grants. However, growth of the Scottish industry was slow in comparison to England: by 1812 there were over 28,000 frames in England compared with 1,450 in Scotland. In 1851 there were 80 'stocking shops' in the Hawick area making woollen hose, but wars and industrial unrest took their toll and stocking knitting gradually declined in favour of underwear, then outerwear. By 1870 stocking shops using handframes were becoming obsolete, replaced by power machines in factories.

40 Pringle sweater,
1950s, Britain
Photographed by Peter Clark
Pringle was one of the first
brands to introduce knitwear
as outerwear for sportswear,
catering for fashionable
socialites from the 1920s. The
intarsia 'argyle' diamond became
a signature design, popular
amongst golfers, and appealing
to a new audience in the late
20th century.

The Pringle company, however, kept handframes for several years longer. The partnership of Waldie, Pringle and Wilson had begun in 1815, and developed into Robert Pringle and Son in 1842. Typical of the Borders wool trade, they produced stockings and underwear in many different qualities and yarns – cheaper in plain lambs' wool or 'fancy' in merino (wool and cotton) – but Pringle developed silk knitting in particular and by 1892 had added silk underwear to their lines sold in London. In 1899, the Pringle list for men included vests, long underpants and golf and cycling hose, and the list for women combinations, cycle drawers and bodices. Fashionable handmade lace was copied in knitting for 'Princess' tops with the aid of special new machinery. Innovative vertically striped gents underwear was introduced, and in 1910 a special department was set up for ladies knitted coats, making 17 styles in wool, art silk (rayon) and spun silk. As fashions and society changed, the market for underwear such as combinations evaporated, and from 1959 Pringle focused on outerwear, particularly outdoor jackets, cashmere sweaters as fashion items and the now-famous golf sweaters (plate 40).

With the hosiery industries in England and Scotland vying for superiority, innovation was increasingly important. As the twentieth century progressed, design became a key focus for Pringle. In 1930 their first designer, Otto Weisz, later managing director, began a series of 'dress-maker style' fashion-conscious knitted tops for ladies, perfecting the classic 'twinset' – a matching short-sleeved sweater and cardigan. The American market was vitally important in the 1950s – the 'era of knitwear' – and Hollywood stars were photographed in figure-hugging Pringle sweaters (plate 41). Colour knitting and coordination with woven fabrics was a key point of differentiation for Pringle, and from the 1930s they developed intarsia knitwear as a speciality, creating intricate graphic and pictorial designs course by course and colour by colour like tapestry – a return to the slow, highly skilled manual operations typical of the old stocking frames. Other Scottish knitwear companies including Ballantyne also adopted this at the turn of the twenty-first century Pringle was bought by Hong Kong company Fang Brothers. The new management team reinvented Pringle, giving it a luxury fashion status and appointing designers Stuart Stockdale and then Claire Waight Keller to revive the brand while capitalizing on its 200-year heritage and history. Fashion shows and a flagship store in London cemented this transition, although Pringle's core product remained the sweater and its contemporary variations. However, in a sad coda to nearly two centuries of manufacturing, stiff competition and changing markets led to the decision to close the production site in Hawick in June 2008, transferring it to China and leaving just sales and marketing activities in Scotland. As a response to the brand's enviable heritage, students and staff at Central St Martins College, University of the Arts London, have worked with the company to document its archive material and develop new designs for new markets.

John Smedley of Derbyshire

The progress of the Midlands knitting heritage is represented by the John Smedley company. This vertically integrated knitwear business has been operating from the same factory premises in Derbyshire since 1784 (plate 43) and is still family owned, having maintained continuous production through eight generations since the beginning of the Industrial Revolution. It is now one of the oldest manufacturing businesses in the world. Smedley produces around half a million items per year from its main Lea Mills site and two others nearby, and over 70 per cent of these are exported.

The company started by spinning cotton for local cottagers to weave into muslin but expanded into woollen hosiery in 1795. At first handframes were used, then the River Lea provided water power for the machines before the introduction of electricity. Underwear was the original product, especially one-piece combinations for men and women in wool, cotton and silk, or sometimes with silk legs and tops and wool drawers in the same garment. The company invented many techniques, such as women's combinations

41 Dorothy Lamour, 1948
Dorothy Lamour wears a beaded bouclé evening sweater with scoop neck – an example of the 'dress-maker style' knitted evening tops made popular by Otto Weisz at Pringle.

technique, however, and in time it was largely replaced by electronic machinery.

The 1970s saw a decline in demand from both home and American markets in the face of increasing overseas competition, and Pringle's market position faltered. Following a series of takeovers in the industry,

42 John Smedley underwear, 2009
A range of men's and women's plain and lacy underwear is still produced by the company, including 'long johns' for men.

43 John Smedley factory, Lea Mills, Derbyshire, 1927
The image shows female workers attaching separately knitted welts to the underwear.

shaped with gores for the bust and a special S-wrap flap opening for the men's version. In the early twentieth century, Smedley added hosiery, nightwear and swimwear to its range, sold through wholesalers such as Brettles (plate 35). Outerwear was developed in the mid-twentieth century with the rise of American sportswear, and the now classic fully fashioned Smedley sweaters first appeared in the late 1950s.

The company has maintained tight control of production throughout its history. In 1819 the second generation John Smedley pioneered the spinning of worsted wools using high-quality Merino fleece imported from Australia (now sourced from five dedicated ethically run sheep stations in New Zealand) together with the long-staple high-quality cotton known as Sea Island cotton (originating from islands off the south-west coast of the United States, but now grown in several countries). The fourth generation, John D. Marsden Smedley, was responsible for updating the machinery in 1893. The many processes required to get from fibre to garment, including spinning, dyeing, knitting, scouring, pressing and finishing, were all originally conducted on the main site, and the water of the River Lea is said to be important to the softness of the wool and cotton. Since 2003, the majority of spinning and wool dyeing has taken place in Germany and Italy, although all yarns are prepared and conditioned for knitting in Lea Mills, where an 'unshrinkable' chemical finishing process is applied.

Smedley sweaters are 'fully fashioned' – knitted to shape – using both old and new technologies: the oldest is William Cotton's patent multiple frame – which can knit up to 24 identical garment pieces at once – developed from William Lee's frame using the original bearded needles. In this type of production, the ribbed welts of the garments are knitted separately on different machines and 'run on' or transferred to the multiple frame. Fully fashioned garment pieces, collars and trims are assembled by skilled women workers and finished stitch for stitch using the manual 'linking' machine technique. The entire manufacturing process entails some 35 different steps. In contrast, the latest electronic complete-garment machines, which make seamless fashioned knitwear automatically, garment by individual garment, requiring virtually no making-up processes, are now used for a small proportion of the Smedley production.

Smedley has a reputation for strong use of colour and now creates its own fashion ranges, as well as producing knitwear for designer labels, including Margaret Howell, Paul Smith, Vivienne Westwood, Comme des Garçons and Agent Provocateur. At the same time, underwear – including 'long johns', named after the first John Smedley – in Sea Island cotton and merino/silk blend are still made, although the market is in slow decline (plate 42).

The hidden makers of fashion: cottage industry and couture hand-knitting in the twentieth century

Much of the high-quality knitting carried out in the nineteenth and early twentieth centuries, such as that of the Shetland Islanders, is produced anonymously, the exquisite products reaching royalty and the high-class fashion trade through intermediaries. In contrast, individual designers and makers such as Maria Luck-Szanto, Eve Sandford (see p.131) and specialist knitwear company Ritva (see pp.176–7) represent the development of knitting from the viewpoint of the designer and producer of knitted fashion.

Knitting craft skills, passed on through generations by word of mouth, have been significant in twentieth century fashion. Elsa Schiaparelli, for example, admiring a sweater worn by a friend, discovered that it had been hand-knitted by an 'Armenian peasant'. Schiaparelli's fertile imagination invented the image of a scarf tied in a bow, which she sketched for the woman to copy in knitting. It took two unsuccessful attempts until the third was exactly what Schiaparelli wanted. Wearing the sweater herself, Schiaparelli was besieged with requests, and her iconic *trompe l'oeil* sweaters, which became so fashionable in the 1920s, were born (plate 44). The 'little woman' soon gathered and trained a group of hand-knitters, and the sweaters were made to order in Paris.[62]

Behind all high-fashion knitwear are companies and individual makers who create the designer's vision through skilful interpretation and technical know-how in a symbiotic relationship. Two significant contributors to this area, Szanto Models and the Women's Home Industries (WHI), both operated at the highest couture end of the market.

Szanto Models

Before World War II, in addition to the comfortable pullovers, hats, scarves, children's wear and socks that were a staple of everyday home-made knitwear, knitting began to be applied to sophisticated and stylish day- and eveningwear, inspired by tailoring techniques. The 1940s and 1950s were to become a zenith of fashionable knitting, as the quantity of knitting patterns and fashion records show. Hand-knitting designers Jane Koster and Margaret Murray produced many volumes of home-knitting patterns throughout the war rationing period, emulating woven tailored styles for the home-knitter (see pp.138–9).

In a lecture to the Wool Education Society in 1957, Jane Koster referred to the work of Maria Luck-Szanto as one of three 'high style' fashion knitwear designers operating in London at that time: 'Unlike many people in the fashion world, Madame Szanto does not use knitting as a fabric to cut up and turn into an ordinary dressmaker's or tailored garment. She believes in using it to fashion shape and design.'[63]

Hungarian by birth, Maria Luck-Szanto came to England in 1935. She had trained in tailoring, design and handcrafts – including crochet, embroidery and knitting – in Vienna, where she conceived the idea of hand-knitted tweeds, designed to have the strength and durability of woven tweeds, but with the elasticity and softness of knitting. She decided to come to Britain to establish her ideas, partly because of the availability there of excellent yarns and skilled labour. She had to wait until after World War II to start her business, Szanto Models Ltd, based in Harrington Street, South Kensington, London. She held her first fashion show, 'Hand-Knitted Tweeds', in February 1946 at the head-

44 Elsa Schiaparelli, *trompe l'oeil* sweater, 1928, France
V&A: T.388–1974
This example of the bow sweater was donated by Elsa Schiaparelli herself, following the 1971 Cecil Beaton *Fashion: An Anthology* exhibition at the V&A. The use of a weaving-in technique created a double-layered effect with the colour of the woven-in strands discreetly 'grinning through'. It was hand-knitted in Paris by an Armenian home worker.

quarters of the prestigious International Wool Secretariat, and continued to hold twice-yearly presentations of her designs or 'models' in London and also overseas in Toronto, Canada. Wools were favoured, in inventive combinations of the fine worsted tweed yarns used for weaving, together with two- and three-ply knitting wools, but mohair, angora and cashmere were also used. Many designs were made in a special blend of wool and rayon gimp called Spintex, which had both good body and sufficient drape.

Luck-Szanto was a supreme technician of both patterns and knitting, utilizing the special qualities of the knitted construction to create dress designs that could not be made in woven fabric and were 'shaped on the needles'. The marriage of carefully chosen yarns and stitch structures with three-dimensional sculpted shaping for the body resulted in flattering and easy-to-wear pieces that were in fact quite complex in construction.

Luck-Szanto found ready export markets in Canadian and American high society for her elegant designs, which soon caught the attention of the fashion press in London. Clients included royalty and the actresses Vivienne Leigh and Ava Gardner among many others.

An article featuring the 'Barbara' dress in *Harper's Bazaar* of November 1951 states: 'Handknitted clothes, long loved by elegant women in America and

France... combine fashion with warmth, are wonderful for travelling, completely uncrushable and the pleated skirts stay pleated.'[64] The 'Barbara' dress epitomizes the elegance and smooth lines for which Luck-Szanto came to be known (plates 45 and 46). The first example, made in 1947, was knitted by Mrs Dorothy Elvin in Spintex, made in two main sections – bodice and pleated panelled skirt, grafted together – and worn with a knitted and lined belt. The cowl-fronted bodice with plunging crossover back is worked all in one piece in a highly unusual curved shape designed with integral back sections, armholes and side gussets. The short sleeves are knitted separately and grafted to the armholes, then the underarm seam sewn. The overall construction, with almost invisible joins, is extremely sophisticated and well finished, to the point that the dress was often described as seamless, which indeed other designs are.[65]

By advertising in *The Lady*, Luck-Szanto built up a circle of 'gifted and intelligent knitters'. Writing in 1975 for the company portfolio prepared by her husband, she recalled:

> Looking back on the 40 years of my professional occupation with knitting, it seems to me, the then prevailing social conditions were specially conducive to allow me to develop knitting to the kind of sophisticated craft-industry which it became by the end of the period. There was an abundance of material: wool in a fantastic variety of tempting colours and textures; easy availability of labour, a nearly untapped pool of skilled and intelligent women whose social position was such that they needed a supplementary income but were not able to take a job away from the home either because they had to look after their household and family or because there were not enough jobs about anyhow. There was also a large and eager demand for hand-knitting.[66]

Luck-Szanto ran the business with the aid of her husband, Frederick H. Luck, and her right-hand woman, Mrs Lil Fleming – the first person to answer one of her

BARBARA HORIZONTAL RIB

1st row: knit
2nd row: purl
3rd row: knit
4th row: purl
5th row: purl
6th row: knit all increases and decreases on this row.

Barbara Dress

adverts – plus a dedicated team of girls in the workshop. There were 500 to 600 knitters all over Britain, working part time as outworkers, including many seaside landladies who were glad to earn extra income during the winter months. Routinely, one garment would be made by several knitters working on different pieces at the same time in order to achieve a reasonable delivery time of four to six weeks – a risky strategy needing careful management. For example, according to the

cial hand-grafting technique virtually eliminated obvious seams. Each model was given a name, and no two were identical, although popular designs such as the 'Barbara' dress were continually made with slight modifications and inspired a number of variations (plate 46). In the early years, they could be sold either finished or, for a lower price, in parts ready to make up. For firms overseas Szanto Models would provide a model garment and the instructions for making it, replicating the practice of Parisian couture houses, which sold calico toiles to department stores and manufacturers.

While Frederick Luck concentrated on the organizational side of the business, setting up a detailed card-index system to track production and record the work and knitting style of each outworker, Luck-Szanto was the creator and would retire to a hotel to design her models and write the master patterns (all in size 14) – a complex affair. The creation of her pleated skirt was a major landmark, and Luck-Szanto went on to use many variations of knife or kilt pleats in designs for suits and dresses. She also introduced many complex new stitches and specialities such as beaded knitting (plate 48, 50), all-over two-colour patterns, 'tapestry knitting' in several colours and lace designs.

Luck-Szanto's 'Jane' dress (plate 47), made by Mrs Peggy Cope, dates from the 1950s and is a tour de force of lace knitting, being made in one piece in the knitting, with no sewn seams at all and just an opening for the zip at the back. The dress is fitted to the waist with a flared skirt and scalloped edge and is made from a fine cobweb of wool, weighing only 6 ounces. Unusually, the knitting started at the neck and worked down the garment to the hem, with all the shaping ingeniously worked into the lace pattern. By the time the knitter reached the hem of the skirt there would have been hundreds of stitches to manage across several needles. Casting off the lace pattern would have naturally created the scalloped edge after careful blocking, which is finished in crochet to neaten (plate 49). The sleeves were knitted downwards, picking up stitches from the bodice, then tapering to the wrist and finishing with a ribbed cuff. At the time, the dress would probably have

records, one 1966 order for a navy-and-white racing suit was divided between five knitters. They were paid by the weight of yarn despatched to be knitted, at a rate of 7 shillings per ounce, plus one shilling: a coat back using 7 ounces of yarn was paid at £2 and 10 shillings, two skirt panels at 8 ounces was therefore paid at £2 and 17 shillings. The knitted pieces were received from the outworkers, then washed and blocked to size before making up. There was strictly no cutting, and the spe-

47 Szanto Models,
Jane dress, 1956, Britain
V&A: T.314–1984
Knitted in worsted wool, the circular construction of this dress may have made it easier to keep track of the patterning and shaping, as the right side of the work was always facing the knitter. A circular yoke was knitted for the shoulder area, backwards and forwards to create the back opening while the bodice was knitted in a decreasing tube to the waistline, after which point increasings begin for the skirt shaping.

48 Szanto Models,
beaded sleeveless dress,
c.1960, Britain
V&A: T.121–1986
Szanto's beaded dresses revived the technique used in the 19th century. With one bead knitted between each stitch, floral sprays decorate the border of this all-over beaded design. It is knitted in rayon yarn in two pieces, front and back, with integral edgings.

been worn with an underslip that may have been specially made to match.

A cardigan-jacket from the 1950s in beige bouclé wool, in a subtle self-coloured textured stripe, is at first sight rather ordinary in comparison. Importantly, however, the jacket is seamless and knitted sideways, including sleeves, which have a raglan-shoulder shaping. This piece may have contributed to the experimental development of 'integral garment knitting' with which Luck-Szanto became increasingly involved in the mid-1950s (V&A: T.120–1986).

Through a serendipitous connection with a former engineer, Luck-Szanto forged a notable connection between hand-knitting and the technological progression of twentieth-century machine knitting, becoming, in her words, the 'mother of the invention of a tailor knitting machine'.[67] The development of integral garment knitting – completely shaped on the knitting machine and requiring little or no making-up – had been a vision for the commercial knitting industry since the advent of machines that could knit one-piece socks. The idea of eliminating many of the labour-intensive and highly skilled (and therefore costly) making-up processes was obviously appealing. In the 1950s, there was one product on the market, the Basque beret, that achieved such an approach, being knitted sideways in a circular formation of wedge shapes and requiring only one seam to complete. In 1955, Luck-Szanto was asked to design a Rembrandt-style beret by Kenneth Macqueen, at that time public relations manager for Kangol, a firm that manufactured berets in Cumbria. She visited the factory to see for herself how the flat knitting machines used horizontal shaping by knitting short rows to create the wedge shapes – *flèchage* or partial knitting – rather than vertical increasings and decreasings, and was inspired to try to use this concept for garments. She immediately hand-knitted a coat using the sideways principle, starting at the right front edge and finishing at the left front edge, and suggested to Macqueen that he adapt the beret machine to make complete garments. This began a series of developments that led to Macqueen Tailor-Knitting.

The project proved ambitious and required significant investment in electronics as well as mechanics. A patent was eventually filed in August 1957 and granted in Macqueen's name in May 1960.[68] In the same year, the *Hosiery Trade Journal* introduced the concept of Macqueen Tailor-Knitting to the industry, showing the knitting sequence of a jacket alongside illustrations of Maria Luck-Szanto's hand-knitted designs and the strapline 'Fully automatic electronic unit can revolutionize jersey dress trade'.[69] The article claimed that Macqueen Tailor-Knitting could create 'complete garments – sleeves, collars, cuffs, pleats, bows etc in a single operating cycle, without the need for skilled knitting operatives'. It went on to say: 'The potential application of this machine to the jersey dress-goods field is virtually limitless, and it may well contribute to a change in the entire structure of the dress trade.' Three years later, the concept was publicized in *New Scientist*, under the heading 'Cybernetics and Haute Couture'.[70]

Macqueen proposed a process whereby six machines were to be electronically controlled at the same time from a central processing unit. He envisaged that a design would be scanned into a computer (at that time still in development), which would print out magnetic punch tapes to control the machine and the needle selection row by row. The intention was for the designer to be free to use different instructions within each row, selecting any needle and making non-repeating patterns in up to eight colours. This revolutionary ambition for a technology enabling total design freedom was at least 20 years ahead of its time, both in terms of computing power and the microelectronics required to drive the system.

Unfortunately Macqueen died suddenly in 1964 and the project was abandoned. The patent expired in 1972 but was a foundation for other inventors and knitting-technology developers around the world – an echo of the fate of William Lee's invention and vision. Research based on the Basque beret construction was taken up by Courtaulds in Britain. Emma Pfauti in Switzerland took out her own patent in 1960 to produce garments with a circular segmented yoke, inspired by classic Fair Isle hand-knit designs.[71] The important breakthroughs in flat knitting, however, would rest on combining control of the knitted fabric with electronic individual needle selection. Research continued throughout the 1970s and 1980s, and the problem of fabric control was solved by the presser foot attachment, developed by Courtaulds and then with Dubied in Switzerland. This simple device pressed down on the knitted stitches –

unlike previous systems, which pulled down from below – enabling knitting to be built up in some areas of the flat needlebed and not others to create integral shapings such as pockets and collars, or relief-texture stitches such as cables and blackberry stitch in imitation of hand-knitting. The issue of controlling individual needles was solved in 1975, when Stoll of Germany introduced a completely electronically controlled flat knitting machine, eventually enabling individual needle selection through a computer interface. The stage was set for 20 years of competitive development of integral knitting on flat-bed machines, culminating with Shima Seiki launching their 'Whole Garment' technology in 1995, followed two years later by Stoll's 'Knit and Wear' concept, both finally achieving, in different ways, what Luck-Szanto, Macqueen and others had envisaged forty years previously. Maria Luck-Szanto's involvement and technical expertise had provided a catalyst for this technological development from the perspective of the designer at a crucial early stage.

Women's Home Industries

Despite technical developments in machine knitting, hand-knitting was responsible for some distinctive trends in the second half of the twentieth century. During World War II a countrywide knitting drive in Britain to make comforts for the troops was organized by the Women's Voluntary Services (WVS). They created an impressive network, which, after the war, was converted into a production unit – the Women's Home Industries (WHI) – that subsequently played a significant role in fashion.[72]

The WHI was set up in 1947 by the Dowager Marchioness of Reading, chair of the WVS, initially as a non-profit business, with the support of Stafford Cripps, then president of the Board of Trade. The aim was to contribute to the post-war export drive to earn dollars for the economy by calling on the innate skills of British women. The inaugural press release said, 'Housewives and home workers will aid in the export drive…Women will make modern art treasures to be sold abroad. We intend to organize the making of carpets, tapestries,

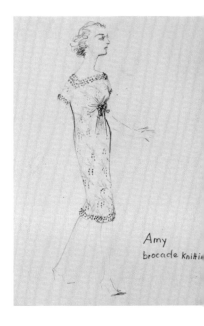

50 Szanto models, design for Amy dress, 1950s, ink on paper
Maria Luck-Szanto archive, V&A: vol.6
The Amy dress features the stitch pattern shown in plate 51 worked in repeat across the short-sleeved design, similar in style to plate 48, with a decoration applied under the bust.

cushions, chair seats, church kneelers, quilting and the best quality knitwear.'[73] They were supported in their efforts by Queen Mary, who donated to the organization six needlepoint chair seats she had stitched herself. Lady Reading was inundated with offers and rigorously selected 1500 women (and one man) whose quality met the WHI's criteria from over 30,000 who sent in samples of their work: 'The demand is only for work of really exceptional quality and execution,' she said in one report.[74] The women were supplied with free export-quality yarns not otherwise available to knitters at home, with which, for an agreed price, they produced knitwear of the highest standards, made to order on couture principles.

Clients included many high-fashion houses abroad. Designers found the services of WHI Couture Hand-knits invaluable. Elsa Schiaparelli ordered a large black ski sweater and tiny cardigans called 'shrugs', and for Christian Dior they made a cardigan patterned with geometric shapes knitted in Fair Isle technique, crochet evening shawls and later a sporty striped wrapover top. British couturiers Norman Hartnell and Hardy Amies, and Digby Morton from Ireland, also used the services of the WHI in this early post-war period, when fashion was again in the ascendant. The WHI supplied fashion stores in the United States and Canada – including

Neiman Marcus in Dallas and Sakowitz in Houston. Private clients, mainly from high society in London and the States, including Princess Margaret and actress Lauren Bacall – could place personal orders through the London shop or during sales trips to New York, Washington, D.C., Philadelphia, Boston and Montreal undertaken by Constance Gold, sales manager in the 1950s. Salon presentations were held in hotel suites, where local models were hired to show off the garments to best advantage.

One example of WHI knitting is a stylish fitted dolman sweater named after the couturier Edward Molyneux, who had ordered it. The WHI company records of October 1949 report 'a sale of a model to Molyneux who had asked for exclusivity for six months'. It was further hoped that 'Molyneux would let us have a toile of his own design for us to copy for him'.[75] Beautifully designed and knitted in fine purple wool with a small shawl collar, it is made in two main pieces, having dolman sleeves, all in one with the body, and diagonal front darts (plate 53). This sweater was clearly a popular design for many years, one version costing 7½ guineas in 1965, when it was featured in the pages of *Vogue* (plate 52). Perhaps helped by the society connections of WHI's founders, many items, including lacy stockings and dresses, featured in the fashion magazines *Harper's Bazaar*, *Queen* and others at the organization's peak in the 1960s and early 1970s (plates 52 and 54).

From its headquarters in London, the WHI continued to develop commercially under the design leadership of Beatrice Bellini, who was appointed general manager in 1949. The work was originally organized in regions nationwide. At its height the business was dealing with 5000 knitters; the postage bill alone for 1947 amounted to £1000. The average pay for a woman working for WHI for five to six hours per day was about 10 shillings a week in the 1950s. Knitting or embroidery provided valuable income for many who were bedridden. Pricing was highly market sensitive, and company minutes show the tensions between quality, reasonable pay for the knitters and the need to

51 Szanto models, swatch of beaded 'brocade' knitting, 1950s, Britain
Maria Luck-Szanto archive, V&A: vol.6
A further example of Luck-Szanto's couture knitting techniques, worked in Spintex wool and rayon, combining a purl-stitch design of foliage with steel beads knitted in and flower sprays formed by knitted raised knops. The design was inspired by the 17th-century knitted jackets in the V&A.

52 Women's Home Industries,
Molyneux sweater
Photographed by Brian Duffy for
Vogue, 15 April 1965
The back and front are knitted in a
very subtle chevron construction
on the cross. To tailor the fit
further, two diagonal darts are
knitted into the front, while the
side waist is also simultaneously
shaped. A high level of skill was
required to follow the complex
pattern, which is carefully
explained inch by inch, in page
after page of detailed instructions.

53 Women's Home Industries,
Molyneux sweater, *c*.1950, Britain
V&A: T.207–1985
The original design for this hand-
knitted sweater in purple wool was
made for the London-born, Paris-
based couturier Molyneux. The
two-piece sweater with shawl
collar has graceful lines, achieved
through subtle but intricate
shaping of the panels with knitted
front darts and central chevron
decreasing creating angled lines of
stitches. There were no armhole
seams to interrupt the line, just
one overarm seam and side seams.

gain sales. The total bill for outworkers in 1951 was
almost £20,000 – a substantial figure representing thousands of small transactions.

Two women, Mrs O'Rourke and Mrs Leggert, wrote
the patterns in several sizes, and these were typed and
copied and sent out with a sample swatch of knitting.
Constant vigilance was maintained over quality and
patterns contained instructions for a tension swatch to
be sent back for approval. Any rejects were sold in special sales. In common with the early traditions of the
knitting industry, knitting of the garment pieces was
separated from the making-up processes. Orders were
returned to London for couture finishing, from inspec-
tion, pressing and blocking to size to making-up, lining
and adding buttons and buttonholes.

In 1966 Bellini and her husband bought the business, forming Beatrice Bellini Handknitting and
retaining the WHI name for the tapestry business, both
run from a shop in Pimlico, London. Bellini was not
herself a knitter or a dressmaker, but she had a keen eye
for fashion and devised styles based on current ideas
in conjunction with her team. Knitwear designs were
made to order and for stock available in the shop and
ran from stockings and hats to jackets and occasionally
full-length wedding dresses. Knitted suits were a speciality, with one designed especially for Norman
Hartnell. At the workshop, individual clients would be
measured and adaptations of patterns especially
drafted. The design approach of the workshop was one
of flat pattern cutting, as in dressmaking, with complex flat shapes knitted and sewn up into
dresses as woven fabrics would be, with
darted shapings – a combination of
traditional knitting and fashion. This
tailored approach was made possible
by fabrics and stitch patterns that were
often dense and firm. The knitwear became lighter as
time went on, however – in common with knitwear
generally and the rise of centrally heated homes. A
handwritten sample notebook, or stitch 'bible', was
kept as a master reference, containing the instructions
for many intricate lace and textured patterns and key

54 **Women's Home Industries**,
Tattershall check
dress and stockings
Photographed by David Bailey
for *Vogue*, August 1965
The 'total look' in fashion was at
its height in the mid-1960s, as
shorter skirts emphasized legs,
and stockings became a key
coordinating statement within
an outfit. Prints and lacy or
patterned knits were especially
popular. The WHI had great
success with its hand-knitted
stockings, here with a tailored
slim dress creating a top-to-toe
look dubbed 'Totalisation' by
Vogue.

information for the knitters. Small samples might show the same stitch in alternative colours and yarns, or perhaps a lace pattern plain and decorated with knitted-in beads – a wealth of possibilities for the couture service.

Bellini Handknitting continued to knit for designers, and the bespoke service for individual clients continued throughout the 1980s and 1990s, although business slowed with changing fashions and greater competition and choice. The number of knitters could be counted in hundreds rather than thousands in the later years. Beatrice Bellini died suddenly in 1998, signalling the end of an era.

From their former ubiquitous position in every locality, needlework and knitting shops have become a rarity in the contemporary British high street. The WHI shop, first opened in 1959, finally closed in December 2005 along with the knitting business, but the tapestry business, managed for the last forty years by Frankie Salter, survives as a mail-order service still under the venerable name of the WHI Tapestry Shop.

The influence of designer knitwear on commercial industry

The 1970s and 1980s saw an explosion of designer knitwear in Britain, reinventing the traditional art of knitting. Many designers emerged, some trained in textiles or fashion and others self-taught, but all with the desire to create something original, expressive and highly covetable. Respected fashion journalist Suzy Menkes aligned this revolution with the changing status of women:

> From subservient wife knitting balaclavas for the troops (and later knitting for victory), we now have a creative flowering of hand-knitting that has become high fashion and a serious commercial business…the designers who have transformed knitwear form the dull necessities of winter woollies to imaginative, elegant and even amusing garments, are almost entirely female.[76]

The functioning of these designers was often based on special relationships with husbands, partners and other

55 **Women's Home Industries**, Cashmere twinset, Photographed by Norman Parkinson for *Vogue*, February 1951
Norman Parkinson was commissioned by *Vogue* to photograph quintessentially British fashions in various iconic locations. This classic hand-knitted cashmere twinset was featured in the setting of the Hobnails Inn at Washbourne and is modelled by Wenda Parkinson.

family members intimately involved in creating and running small design-led businesses, often following the format of cottage industries. Labels included Mary Farrin, Ritva, Patricia Roberts, Sasha Kagan, Sandy Black, Edina Ronay and many others. At the same time, many British fashion designer companies introduced significant knitwear elements to their collections, including Betty Jackson, Body Map, Clements Ribeiro and John Galliano.

Much of the designer knitwear of this time was focused on a basic sweater form, with simple rectangular shapes often the norm. Design features included intricate relief textured patterning, floral imagery and abstract geometric or narrative elements that did not repeat over the garment or were asymmetric. These manually achieved techniques were often used in combination, rendering the garments impossible to knit on any commercial machinery of the time. Emerging knitwear companies consequently produced their designs either by hand-knitting or domestic machine knitting, and occasionally both, using outworkers knitting at home – exactly as the early stocking knitting trade had used the 'putting-out' system. Cottage-industry knitting was thus reinvented, using the abilities of some of the six million hand-knitters across the country, with direct relationships between designer and makers.

In the 1970s the British knitwear industry was focused on large orders of basic, plain styles for mass-market efficiency, and was incapable of supporting small designers' production runs, even if the design concept was simple. The economic necessity in the commercial industry of keeping expensive investments as productive as possible, coupled with lack of design flexibility and a disinclination for sampling prototypes in the British factories left a gap in the market that enabled the small design-led knitwear companies to flourish, providing unique ideas for an increasingly affluent high-fashion market, especially attracting export sales. Through small boutique shops and prestigious international department stores such as Harrods and Harvey Nichols in London, Saks Fifth Avenue and Bloomingdales in New York, or Takashimaya and Isetan in Tokyo, designer knitwear became an established part of fashion.

The success of this colourful knitwear in turn opened up a new fashionable market and created demand in the mainstream industry. The machinery builders therefore concentrated their efforts to develop the patterning capabilities of flat-knitting machines, which have since proved to be the most versatile technology available. Today almost any pattern and texture that a designer can imagine can be knitted on an industrial power-knitting machine – a far cry from the limited production capabilities available when designer-knitwear cottage industries were at their most prolific, but not so different from the 'fancy hosiery' of the skilled frame-knitters. The entire phenomenon was therefore an important influence on the commercial knitwear sector, from both design and technological

perspectives, gradually raising standards for knitwear on the high street. As knitting technology has advanced to new levels and economic factors such as the minimum wage have come into force in Britain, the viability of European cottage industries for knitwear has declined sharply, leaving room for just a handful of specialist small companies who can sell their knitwear based on handmade production and the heritage of traditional forms (see p.172–6).

In contrast to this British scenario, the Italian knitwear industry has been modelled on an entirely different system, in which small, family-based production units using industrial knitting technology have grown up in geographical areas that provide complementary skills, in an evolution of the artisan guilds of the Renaissance period. Investment following World War II provided the means for this development, which led to the high reputation of Italian-made knitwear. The industry is characterized by a responsiveness to design challenges, due in large part to direct links between designer and producer, who, in the case of pioneering knitwear company Missoni and many others, were often within a single family. This combination of flexibility, quality and diversity within the Italian knitwear industry has kept it buoyant for longer than the knitwear industry in Britain and other countries.

The new millennium has seen greatly increased competition to European and American production from emerging economies. The world's production base has shifted towards South Asia, especially China, and takeovers and closures have rapidly occurred in a drastic rationalization of the industry. Innovation is seen to have the competitive advantage, but the industry now, as in the 1960s, has been resistant to complete garment technology. Since the 1990s, however, seamless knitting technology has slowly begun to have an impact first on the lingerie and bodywear sectors, then on the fashion-knitwear market. In the process, some of the most sophisticated technologies for design and automatic production of knitwear of all kinds have been created, and the industry has arrived at the revolution that Kenneth Macqueen predicted.[77]

WELDON'S SIXPENNY SERIES No 212

SPORTS WEAR

*In Knitting
and Crochet*

Knitting in the Home:
from the Eighteenth Century to the Present Day

Madame Defarge with her work in her hand was accustomed to pass from place to place and from group to group: a Missionary – there were many like her – such as the world will do well never to breed again. All the women knitted. They knitted worthless things; but, the mechanical work was a mechanical substitute for eating and drinking…So much was closing in about the women who sat knitting, knitting, that they their very selves were closing in around a structure yet unbuilt, where they were to sit knitting, knitting, counting dropping heads.

CHARLES DICKENS, *A Tale of Two Cities*

*The aunt looked up. She sat on the round bed, knitting a cloud of angora as fast as a machine. Warren slumped at her feet, only the scarlet-rimmed eyes moving. Bunny tear-stained in a chair with a torn cushion…
'Nephew, we've got to do something. These children need a place to go.'
The aunt drove her needles furiously. Wool twitched through her fingers…
Her sentences speeded up, tripping out as if to catch time with her clicking needles.*

E. ANNIE PROULX, *The Shipping News*

Weldon's Sportswear pattern booklet (detail), 1920s
Sandy Black collection
Full of the optimism of the post-WWI jazz era, this booklet features a knitted golf cardigan, sports gloves, flared skirt and jumper knitted in a simple 'jazz pattern' of chevrons in stripes, as shown on the front cover: 'just the thing for sports – a jumper that can be worn tucked in or outside the skirt'.

A S A FAMILIAR EVERYDAY experience, knitting has often been used as a metaphor in literature to express a wide range of emotions – from the detachment of Dickens's *tricoteuses* at the guillotine in *A Tale of Two Cities* to the high dudgeon of the aunt in E. Annie Proulx's *The Shipping News*. The knitting industry may be relatively young but knitting as a domestic activity is embedded in social history and the collective consciousness. In rural communities, many remember hand-knitting as a communal activity, with 'knitting bees' or 'sittings' to while away the long evenings. Wartime memories of 'make do and mend', knitting for economy and women's work still evoke an emotional response. Across Britain and the United States patriotic 'knitting for victory' became part of every war effort, providing socks, balaclavas, sweaters and other 'comforts' for the troops of the Crimean War, American Civil War and World Wars I and II. More recently, knitting has been the butt of jokes in film, television and popular advertising as an easy stereotype for the ridiculous, incongruous or old-fashioned.

As has been seen, since the rise of the hand-knitting industry in the sixteenth and seventeenth centuries knitting at home has been an accepted means of earning extra money for many groups of people, whether for additional comforts and small luxuries, for a small independent income or as a crucial means of earning a livelihood. This latter necessity in turn related to the development of the mechanized knitting industry: from the mid-nineteenth century, smaller knitting machines targeted specifically at the woman in the home came into use. Whatever the motivation, domestic knitting has always been a way to provide for the needs of family and community – from children's clothing, underwear and coarse, warm clothes for outdoor labour to items such as bedspreads, playthings for children and gifts. And sometimes it has been a sociable leisure activity in itself.

The evolution of domestic knitting reflects the changing role of women from providers to consumers and their evolving status in relation to men – from financial dependence to greater autonomy and emancipation. This is in turn charted in the gradual evolution of a women's press, printed needlework and knitting instructions and the growth of specialist publishing and advertising.

Social knitting

Historians can chart the path of domestic hand-knitting from knitting manuals published from the mid-nineteenth century, but information from before this time often comes incidentally from documentary and literary sources, including wills, inventories and other transactional records. The writings of travellers of the seventeenth, eighteenth and nineteenth centuries give clear accounts of the areas in which hand-knitting, and later frame-knitting, flourished.[1] What emerges from such accounts is that early rural knitters were often peripatetic, knitting to be doubly employed while walking to or from market, shepherding or collecting peat (see pp.51–3), using a range of devices, from sheaths to 'a broach, a wooden stick on which the wool was wound, tucked in at the side of the shoe or clog … latterly the "clue of garn" [ball of wool] was pinned to the apron with a safety pin, or suspended from the waist on a length of wool.'[2]

Being such a portable activity, hand-knitting contributed to community discourse, especially in rural areas, where it was purposefully carried out in groups or 'knitting circles' to while away long winter evenings and socialize when the outdoor work of the day was done. Thomas Pennant, travelling through Wales in 1773, observed at Bala:

During the winter the females, through love of society, often assemble at one another's houses to knit, sit round a fire and listen to some old tale or some ancient song or the sound of a harp, and this

is called *cymmorth gweu* or the knitting assembly… Close to the southeast end of the town is a great artificial mound called Tommen y Bala, in the summer time usually covered in a picturesque manner with knitters of both sexes and all ages.[3]

William Howitt, writing in 1844 of Dentdale, Yorkshire, in *The Rural Life of England*, noted:

As soon as it becomes dark, and the usual business of the day is over, and the young children are put to bed, they rake or put out the fire, take their cloaks and lanterns, and set forth with their knitting to the house of the neighbour where the sitting falls in rotation, for it is a regularly circulating assembly from house to house throughout the particular neighbourhood. The whole troop of neighbours being collected, they sit and knit, sing knitting songs and tell knitting stories. Here they often get so excited that they say 'Neighbours, we'll not part tonight', that is until after 12 o'clock.[4]

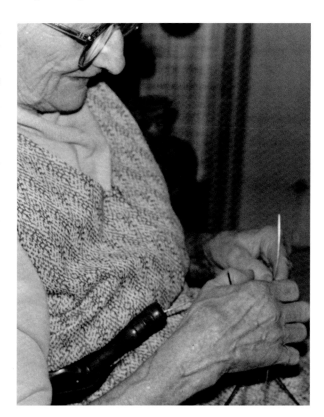

1 Wooden knitting sheath, 1980s, Settle, Yorkshire
V&A Archive, RP/1989/54, acquisition of gansey jumper, gift of Mrs Kathleen Kinder

Clara Sedgwick, formerly a knitter of Dent, Yorkshire, shows the use of a wooden knitting sheath, tucked into a belt round the waist. It is of the curved 'gull wing' type commonly used in Yorkshire at the height of the hand-knitting industry. A set of four double-pointed needles is being used, for circular knitting, with one needle positioned in the hole in the end of the sheath to give stability (see pp.54–5).

In the United States, a similar knitting culture emerged. Having been colonized initially by settlers predominantly from Britain, the U.S. has a history of hand-knitting that runs parallel to British developments. Imports from Britain provided stockings for the more well-to-do society of New England, as well as spinning wheels for those who had to make their own yarn and cloth. Self-sufficiency in all respects was the norm for the frontier pioneers and those living in rural areas, where 'industrious knitting was a prescribed accomplishment of a "good dame"'.[5] The coming of independence in the late eighteenth century meant that 'homespun' traditions in spinning wool, knitting stockings, dyeing and weaving cloth came to be seen as virtuous pursuits that would help break colonial ties, and home-made clothes could be worn in society as a badge of pride. The clandestine importation of stocking knitting machines from England at this time gradually developed into a major American knitting industry in both jersey fabric and knitwear. However,

despite burgeoning industrialization, ready-made goods were expensive, and, in a society where idleness was perceived as 'the unforgivable sin', it was not uncommon for the whole family, including young children, to be busy knitting at every opportunity.[6] For example, the journal of a young girl, Abigail Foote, written in Colchester, Connecticut, in 1775, recounts daily chores, including 'carding, spinning, weaving, dyeing, knitting, making bonnets, washing, ironing, and cooking' – a typical workload of daughters in colonial times.[7]

Folk knitting

The folk traditions of peasant communities around the world indicate how the social aspect of knitting can result in localized knitting cultures, and how hand-knitting has become embedded in everyday life, particularly in the colder parts of the northern hemisphere across northern and eastern Europe and the Baltic states, where wool is the common fibre used. Many of these communities, often remaining in some isolation because of their remote location, developed strong local customs and rituals celebrating the rhythms of the agricultural cycle and important family occasions with special versions of daily clothing. Knitted items, including stockings, hats, socks, mittens, gloves, jackets and leggings, were important elements of these folk and festival costumes (plate 2, see also pp.12–13).

The defining characteristic of such folk knitting was that it was made for private use not for the market, ignoring fashion and remaining essentially unchanged. The fisher ganseys of the British Isles and Nordic countries might be viewed as examples (pp.106–110). While there is little evidence of such costumes before the seventeenth century, many seem to have started to die out at the beginning of the nineteenth century.[8] Twentieth-century fashion and knitwear designers have often turned to these traditions, and many knitting pattern books use folk knitting as inspiration.[9]

Period photographs and postcards from the nineteenth and twentieth centuries show domestic knitting activities across the British Isles and many countries in Europe and the Americas.[10] Although these would have

2 Postcard,
20th century, Europe
Sandy Black collection
Postcards often provide a snapshot of cultural clichés, based on folk traditions, familiarity and humour. Here, two male admirers flank a young woman knitting a stocking in an amusing scene. All are dressed in folk costume, with both men wearing knitted stockings and breeches. Knitted stockings or leggings were integral to folk costumes in many countries and could take on the role of currency, or be used as tokens of affection. Who will be favoured here?

been staged for the photographer and the tourist trade as idiosyncratic or nostalgic, the regular occurrence of knitting in the postcards indicates that they reflect a commonplace activity, much as the 'knitting Madonna' paintings from the fourteenth and fifteenth centuries showed a familiarity with the everyday process of knitting (see p.15). Dutch and Welsh knitters seem to have been especially popular, as they appear most frequently in postcard collections, their national costume contributing to the folk history the postcard manufacturers sought to portray. The Dutch knitters are shown in a traditional costume of clogs, aprons and bonnets, and the Welsh knitters in tall hats, shawls and aprons. Many knitters are shown working outside their cottages – a common practice to make use of the daylight and no doubt also to be sociable.[11]

Other customs are evident in postcards and objects deriving from South America, especially Peru and Bolivia, where Spanish and Portuguese colonists introduced knitting into a culture with a strong textile-weaving practice. The nineteenth- and twentieth-century tradition of knitting finely patterned conical caps and bags continues there today in its coarser popular form for the tourist trade. Unusually in folk knitting, these fine caps with earflaps (*ch'ullu* in Quechua) were often knitted by men for themselves and their children in a wide range of distinctive figurative and geometric designs as a mark of identity and regional area.[12] Wool and alpaca sweaters and hats are also still knitted for the western fashion markets, and a new popular fashion has arisen based on the traditional Peruvian/Bolivian hat (plate 3).

Fisher ganseys

From the mid-nineteenth century to the mid-twentieth century, the hand-knitted seamless gansey was an important item of everyday functional clothing for fishermen of the British Isles, even though machine-made knitwear was available (plate 6). Featuring distinctive textural patterning and diamond-shaped gussets knitted under the arms to give ease of movement and reduce strain on the garment, the body of the gansey

3 Bolivian hat with earflaps
(*ch'ullu*), 20th century,
Potosi district
Sandy Black collection
This type of hat was traditionally knitted by men and worn by men and children in the *altiplano* (high plains) of the Andes. Synthetic yarns in strong colours have largely replaced the natural alpaca and wool used originally. This example is notable for its spiral patterning, which gradually converges to the point of the conical shape as the stitches (and motifs) are decreased.

was knitted in tubular fashion, with seam stitches as markers. Armholes were made by dividing the stitches for front and back and knitting to and fro. Shoulders were grafted or cast off together to make a visible ridge, then the neckband picked up and knitted in the round. Finally sleeves were picked up and knitted onto the body from the top down, narrowing the tubular shape towards the cuff, thus enabling easy re-knitting. Some style variations have a shoulder strap merging into the neckband. The yarn traditionally used was a hard-wearing oiled four- or five-ply worsted wool in dark blue, closely knitted using inventive combinations of purl stitch and cable patterning for a thicker, warmer and more windproof fabric, the oil helping to repel water. Ganseys were relatively short in the body and sleeves to prevent cuffs becoming wet or getting caught up in lines, and the garment was measured during knitting so that it would fit the wearer snugly for warmth. Jackets or, in bad weather, oilskins (originally made from sealskin) were worn on top for greater protection. Coarsely hand-knitted sea-boot stockings were a less celebrated part of the fishermen's everyday clothing and can also be seen in many photographs.

The knitted gansey became integral to the fishermen's identity, as shown by the many surviving photographs of ganseys worn with pride. Every year the fisher wives would knit a new one that was kept for Sunday best, as Mrs Lily Crooks, a gansey knitter from Staithes in Yorkshire, wrote: 'The fishermen always had three jerseys or ganseys, one for Sunday best, one for evenings and one for working in. As the working one wore out they got a new one for Sunday, took the best one for evening and the evening one for work' (see plate 6).[13]

A gansey might have all-over textural patterning, but the decoration was often on the top half of the body and sleeves only. The stories of fishermen whose home town could be identified by the patterns of their ganseys are testament to the skills and individuality of the knitting but are part of the unverified folklore and mythology that surrounds traditional knitting. It is logical that in small village communities ganseys included localized motifs, handed down by word of mouth through generations of families or perhaps made by particular women knitting for others. A pragmatic view would be that there are obvious ways of arranging plain and purl stitches in simple but pleasing geometric configurations that are easily remembered. Variations of these patterns can be found wherever knitting is practised. Several authors have researched and collected patterns for knitted ganseys from the islands and east coast of Scotland and Northumbria through Yorkshire to East Anglia and then to Cornwall and the Channel Islands, identifying many patterns that include local and recurring motifs with names such as 'marriage lines' (a vertical double zigzag pattern).[14]

But while the recurrence of motifs may, to some extent, be inevitable, patterns were also passed on through the fishing trade. Alice Starmore, a knitter and writer from Stornoway on the Isle of Lewis in the Outer Hebrides, recalls stories from her aunts, who were 'herring girls' in the 1920s and 1930s (plate 4) following the herring fishermen up and down the Scottish coast and east of England as far south as Yarmouth and Lowestoft during the many months of the seasonal migration:

Many communities and indeed individuals, created their own unique patterns, so that a fisherman's home port could often be identified by his gansey. Balanced against this insular, individual creativity, however, was an exceptionally strong interaction that diffused many of the patterns, particularly those of the Scottish east coast, around the coastline. This interaction…can be explained in one word: herring…This mixture of women from all the major fishing communities would sit or stand around the [curing] yard chatting, knitting and examining each other's work and, of course, patterns were exchanged and ideas copied. Never in written form but by memory or chanting the rows.[15]

Mrs Noble, an elderly woman from Whitby on the Yorkshire coast, remembers:

> The moss and the diamond [pattern] came from the Scottish when they came for the herring … they used to knit on eight short needles. They taught me the anchor and the chevron and they did a plait instead of a cable. There was another one from Scotland – the half flag – me mother used to do that one without any ropes [cables].[16]

The Cornish traditions of ganseys or 'knit frocks' were of much plainer design, often using 'fisherman's rib' (a thick warm rib). This may be because ganseys, not stockings, were the main product of the Cornish commercial hand-knitting industry, so productivity rather than decoration was the key factor. Fishermen on the south coast of Britain in Brighton and Hastings, who also travelled to Yarmouth and Scarborough for the herring fishing, wore simple ganseys – often machine-made naval jerseys – under smocks (plate 5).

The etymology of the word 'gansey' relates to the thriving knitting industry on the Channel Islands of Guernsey and Jersey, that possibly pre-dated other areas, which were known in Elizabethan times for high-quality goods, supplying large numbers of stockings to

5 **Fishermen**, 1860s, Brighton
The Royal Pavilion and Museums, Brighton and Hove
Fishermen on the south coast of Britain in Brighton and Hastings wore simple ganseys under their smocks until the mid-twentieth century.

6 **Fisherman's gansey**,
knitted by Lily Crooks, 1977, Staithes, Yorkshire
V&A: T.47–1989
This gansey knitted in the round in four-ply wool shows an all-over design of vertical alternating panels of cables and double moss stitch, with plain gussets (typical of all ganseys) and cabled shoulder straps from the sleeve to the neckline. See the pattern in Thompson (1955).

England, including the royal court, with hosiery named 'jersey stocks'. Trade to Britain, France and the United States continued throughout the eighteenth century, using (duty-free) imported wool from Britain to meet growing demand, particularly from the Navy. In his book *The Coinage of the Channel Islands* (1949), Lieutenant Colonel W. Marshall-Fraser gave the following explanation:

> It was Sir Walter Raleigh, Governor of Jersey from 1600 to 1603 who caused the establishment of an extensive trade between that island and Newfoundland, a trade which endured for some 300 years and gave rise to local shipbuilding and the supply of woollen garments for the mariners... Almost invariably guernseys are in thick dark-blue wool, while jerseys are thinner and of various colours. Jerseys became better known owing to the very large number of Jerseymen who entered the Newfoundland enterprises.[17]

The Channel Islands thus gave their names to key items of knitwear, but even more importantly to the basic knitted fabric – fine stockinette or plain knitting, now universally known as jersey fabric. The traditional Guernsey sweater – also called a 'Guernsey frock' – is, however, of much simpler design than the typical fisherman's patterned gansey, having a plain-knit body, a distinctive divided welt and shoulders in garter stitch – a design easily reproduced by machine. Similar styles can be seen in the French coastal ports of Brittany.

The gansey's popularity spread to Scandinavia and other countries around the North Sea and soon developed into a generic style of sweater, although not always seamless. After a brief moment of poularity in late Victorian fashion, hand-knitted fisher ganseys gradually died out in all but the most remote communities owing to the widespread availability of cheaper machine-made versions. However, interest was revived for both historical and fashion purposes during the hand-knitting boom of the 1970s and 1980s, when several books tracing the last vestiges of the original craft were published. The fashion knitwear company Artwork produced their own version of a gansey knitted in indigo-dyed blue-cotton yarn, complete with monogram and fashionably 'distressed' by washing to look worn (a trend that gained wide popularity throughout the following decade) (plate 7). Another postscript to fisher gansey knitting survives in charity work: replacing the knitting of ganseys for the former Seamen's Aid Missions, the Sailor's Society now appeals for knitters to make woolly hats to be sent 'to

7 Artwork sweater, 1991, Britain
V&A: T.384–2001
This sweater is hand-knitted in 'denim' rope-dyed indigo cotton yarn, giving a faded effect after several washings, like jeans. The initials 'GT' have been knitted in for Artwork's George Trowark second label. Note parts of the hem, cuffs and shoulder unraveling, through constant wear and tear over a period of five years, which have been left unmended, similar to many 19th-century fisherman's ganseys seen in photographs. Artwork gave the owner a replacement sweater and donated this one to the V&A.

enrich seafarer's lives worldwide', distributing 15,000 hats each year.

There is a strong similarity between the fisher gansey and early Fair Isle and Shetland multicoloured sweaters, both seamlessly constructed by knitting in the round, with underarm gussets and sleeves knitted down from the body. Both were originally made within their respective communities as part of the local economy, and each has had its moment in the fashion limelight and become an iconic classic, albeit in machine-made and simplified form (plate 8).

Everyday knitted clothing

Sweaters such as the gansey were one of the key products made by hand at home for the family, along with gloves, stockings, socks, hats and underwear. Such items were (and still are) a basic part of the everyday wardrobe, making use of the inherent flexibility of knitted fabric to mould to the shape of the body for comfort and practicality – ideal for underwear, work activities or sports. Many such items have remained essentially unchanged for centuries (plate 10).

While ecclesiastical gloves are among the earliest surviving knitted artefacts, preserved because of the elevated social status of their wearers (see pp.16–17), everyday gloves, important as practical items, were subjected to much wear and tear and so do not figure in many collections. Gloves and mittens for outdoor work or activities need to be as dense and protective as possible while allowing the fingers to move and are generally thicker than gloves worn solely for warmth (which trap air in the openwork of the stitches). A fine example of heavy work mittens is a pair in cream-and-red wool from nineteenth-century Rättvik in Sweden (plate 9). They demonstrate a technique typical of the region since the mid-seventeenth century, known as two-strand or 'twined' knitting, which uses two threads of the same colour yarn knitted alternately to create a thick, warm, protective fabric, closely stranded on the back. It is also called two-end knitting, as the yarn is usually taken from both the outside and the inside of the ball simultaneously, the strands being twisted over

8 Hand-knitted Fair Isle tunic jumper, 1920s
Shetland Museum and Archives
Although this is a black-and-white image, the subtlety of the colour variations is evident within the distinctive OXO patterning. This jumper has the two-colour ribbed edgings typical of Shetland knitting and a V-neck – newly fashionable at the time.

9 Heavy mittens in twined knitting,
19th century, Rättvik, Sweden
V&A: T.396–1920
Each mitten is knitted in the round with deep gauntlet cuffs bordered in red. The knitted fabric has a dual appearance: smooth plain knit on the outside but horizontally ridged on the inside, consisting of strands of yarn. It shows the remains of a nap raised by brushing, now mostly worn away. The narrow wristband and top of the mitten are knitted in 'chain stitch' texture pattern, made by alternately bringing one of the strands to the front and knitting with the other. The red cuffs have subtle diamond patterning, made with much finer white yarn or thread, creating surface depth in the pattern.

10 Byssus (sea silk) gloves,
19th century?, Italy
V&A: T.15–1926
Hand-knitted in Taranto, these gloves are made from byssus, the silky threads extruded by molluscs of the genus *Pinna* to enable them to attach to surfaces. The longest threads were from the very large *Pinna nobilis* especially common on the shores of Sicily. In colours varying from gold to cinnamon brown, byssus was highly prized and denoted high status. These gloves are unworn, still tied together as they were finished by the knitter. Identical-looking gloves would today be industrially knitted on automatic knitting machines as commonplace items.

each other between each stitch with two fingers of the right hand.[18]

Many traditionally patterned woollen glove and mitten styles are associated with vernacular knitting from particular European or Baltic regions, such as Latvia, Estonia and Norway, and continue to be made today. Both the cold climate and cultural traditions of these regions have made mittens an important part of the domestic economy. For example, in nineteenth-century Estonia the gifting of mittens to male guests formed an essential part of the wedding ceremony. In Finland, the Helsinki-based Vanhain Tyo organization has, since 1953, provided an outlet for traditional hand-knitted mittens, gloves, socks and hats, all made by retired people over 55.[19]

In the British Isles, certain areas such as Sanquhar in Dumfriesshire, Dent in the Yorkshire Dales (home of the 'terrible [great] knitters'[20]) and Ringwood in Hampshire became famous for particular glove patterns. Sanquhar patterns are distinctively complex, making intricate use of two-colour pattern combinations. Until the 1920s, Dentdale and Swaledale knitters produced gloves in two contrasting colours, usually black and white, often commissioned for grouse shooting, with the owner's initials and names knitted into them (plate 11). Ringwood gloves were more workaday, in a now classic self-coloured textured pattern of purl stitches that was hand-manufactured as a cottage industry well into the twentieth century and is still familiar today.[21] Similarly, Shetland gloves in strong bright colours display the classic patterns associated with the islands and the countries of northern Europe (V&A: T80/a–1916).

In the centuries before homes were well insulated and heated, nightcaps were an essential item of night attire, sometimes worn even during the day in addition to the warm underclothing required inside and outside the home. Men's nightcaps were a simple adaptation of the many types of hand-knitted cap worn since the Middle Ages and were manufactured in quantity when frame-knitting and mechanized machine-knitting took over. Such nightcaps were essentially tubes that could be made in one piece or cut and seamed from lengths of fabric. The top might be shaped or just gathered and finished with a knot or tassel (plate 12). Some caps of double thickness comprised a tube shaped at both ends, then one half turned inside the other – a style familiar in fishing communities. In the mid-nineteenth century, ladies' nightcaps were intricately knitted in lacy designs, in a similar manner to children's caps (see pp.42–3). Nightcaps have not survived in use to modern times except for babies, though simple knitted close-fitting hats continue to be popular outdoor wear.

Hand-knitting and commercial knitwear has cycled in and out of fashion for women's and men's clothing since the 1960s, but the knitting of infant and children's clothes has remained a constant, little touched by fashion. Knitting for newborn children is an expression of love that still has potency and that has sustained the last bastions of the British wool shop, which had almost terminally declined by the end of the twentieth century

11 Dent gloves, mid- to late 19th century, Britain
Rachel Kay-Shuttleworth Collection
This pair of gloves knitted for Rachel B. Kay-Shuttleworth, with the initials RBKS around the wrist, is typical of similar gloves made since the mid-19th century. Seamlessly hand-knitted in the Yorkshire Dales from black-and-white coarse strong wool, the gloves have zig-zag patterning on the backs of the hands, whereas the palms and fingers are worked in 'midge and fly' pattern. The cuffs are worked in two-colour vertical stripes.

12 Night cap, 1820s, Britain
V&A: T.214–1966
A typical nightcap for this period, this example is finely machine knitted in maroon-and-cream silk with a delicate hand-embroidered pattern on the double welt and pointelle openwork bands. It has one hand-stitched seam and is gathered at the top by pleating and finished with a tassel. Similar machine-knitted nightcaps with hand-stitched seams are in the Museum of London, including an exceptionally long white silk nightcap belonging to George IV.

(although these have fully revived in the United States). Designed for wear and not often preserved in museums (an exception is the collection in the V&A Museum of Childhood in Bethnal Green, London), home-made children's knitted items can be traced from early pattern books and journals to contemporary magazines and leaflets.

Classic children's designs have changed remarkably little over time: cotton knitted jackets from three centuries ago (see p.31) could be worn in today's society. Examples of infants' knitwear from seventeenth-century British damask-patterned cotton jackets to a series of finely knitted lace cotton jackets from Austria dated to the mid-nineteenth century (plate 13) all exhibit the same fundamental T-shaped construction, knitted in one piece up to the armholes, then divided, with sleeves knitted down from stitches picked up around the armholes.

With the advent of printed patterns, there was a transition towards working separate flat pieces instead of working in the round, but the finished shape of children's clothes remained much the same as earlier designs (plate 14). *Woolcraft*, which was published in 22 editions from 1912 until 1988, featured complete layettes of jackets, leggings, dresses, pilches, bonnets and shoes, and these were unchanged for decades, even if the magazine covers were gradually modernized. The discernible change is in materials, which evolved significantly through the development of synthetic fibres with easy-care properties. Contemporary children's knitwear designs continue to be built on simple rectangular principles, even though the age group considered to be 'children' by the pattern publishers has steadily reduced.

This consistency in production has not always ensured popularity with those who had to wear the clothes. An association of knitting with subsistence living and poverty, workhouses and

13 Infant's lace jacket,
mid-19th century, Austria
V&A: T.4–1946
This is one of a group of five
jackets hand-knitted in fine
cotton, each with different lace
designs but showing the same
simple tubular construction with
straight tubular sleeves. The
body has been knitted in the
round up to the armholes, with a
plain border pattern marking
where it would be cut at the
centre front. Above the
armholes there is a garter stitch
edge. To simplify the knitting,
none of the jackets has neck
shaping; the neckline is threaded
with silk ribbon to close.

poor schools persisted in popular perception to the latter part of the twentieth century, and, despite the ingenuity inspired by World War II rationing, by the 1960s there was a stigma attached to wearing a home-made rather than shop-bought school jumper; some mothers carefully sewed shop labels cut from other clothes into home-made sweaters.

Alongside clothes for infants and children, toys and other comforting items form a little-noted but universal part of the repertoire of family knitting. Some patterns reflect society's domestic concerns: during World War II, in tandem with patterns for comforts for the troops, Bestway published patterns for service dolls dressed authentically in WAAF (Women's Auxiliary Air Force), ATS (Auxiliary Territorial Service) and WRNS (Women's

Royal Naval Service) uniforms. A wide range of patterns for creatures and storybook characters has been continually produced for gifts or for sale at charity bazaars. In the United States in 1915, one George Nelson patented heavy cotton work socks in grey-and-white marl with reinforced red heels, and these were widely appropriated to become 'sock monkey' toys for children. A pattern for knitting red-heeled sock monkeys was published in 1953, and they have since become cult objects.[22]

In times of both hardship and of plenty, all sorts of household items have been fashioned from knitting. These range from simple cushion covers to elaborate doilies and bedcovers, from slippers to rugs and stair carpets. Following the old tradition of pieced and quilted bedspreads, the fashion for white knitting in the

14 Children's knitwear designs
from *Woolcraft* magazine,
published by Patons & Baldwins,
*c.*1937
Sandy Black collection
Typical designs for young
children featured in *Woolcraft*
over many decades and are still
relevant today. These designs
come from an edition that
featured a red skein of wool on
the cover and was priced at 6d.

15 Bedspread with hymn verses, 1855, Britain
V&A: T.196–1984
Measuring 274 x 236 cm, this cotton bedspread is knitted in one large rectangular piece, with added borders in two different patterns depicting smaller and larger floral motifs and scrolls. Knitted at a tension of 30 sts and 52 rows to 10cm, the words and design motifs are delineated in purl stitches on a plain ground. A shield at the top of the bedspread has the words 'Holy Bible, Book Divine' surrounded by 'Precious treasure thou art mine'. Four hymn verses are arranged in a circle around the figure of Truth, separated by images of a tiger, an elephant and a lion. The lower part of the central panel is filled with urns of flowers on either side of a wreath containing the year 1855. The bedspread is finished with an attached cabled and fringed edging.

eighteenth century produced imaginative designs for bedspreads, typically made from individually knitted squares, which could be easily transported to knit anywhere. These often featured relief patterns for an embossed final effect. An unusual heavy-cotton bedspread from Britain, dated 1855, delivers a religious message (plate 15), the central section containing verses from the hymn 'From Greenland's Icy Mountains' surrounding a female figure representing Truth. Two of the four verses read as follows:

> What though the spicy breezes
> Blow soft o'er Ceylon's Isle
> Though every prospect pleases
> And only man is vile
> In vain with lavish kindness
> The gifts of God are strewn
> The heathen in his blindness
> Bows down to wood and stone
>
> Shall we whose souls are lighted
> With wisdom from on high
> Shall we to men benighted
> The lamb of life deny
> Salvation on salvation
> The joyful sound proclaim
> Till each remotest nation
> Has learnt Messiah's name.

Clearly this piece was made to serve a greater purpose than merely decoration. Perhaps it was a homely comfort to a lonely missionary, reflecting the religious colonialism and missionary zeal of the nineteenth century but it is an exception rather than the rule in general household knitting. Patterns for knitted bedcovers abound, from such early serial publications as *Weldon's* and *Godey's Lady's Book* to late twentieth-century designs. Because of the high status accorded to quilts, especially in the United States, and the labour involved in making such bedcovers, many hand-knitted examples from the nineteenth century have survived as heirlooms and several are now in American and British museums.

Knitting schools and knitting at school

As a domestic activity, hand-knitting was learnt by passing skills down through the generations via demonstration in the home. However, when hand-knitting became a major industry in Elizabethan times, it offered an effective way to alleviate poverty and keep children, orphans and paupers occupied, thereby absolving the local parish from any obligation to provide relief. Knitting was therefore taught in schools, the first recorded knitting schools having been set up in the late sixteenth century in Lincoln, Leicester and York.[23] By the eighteenth and nineteenth centuries knitting was taught as one of the practical skills required in the workhouses, along with spinning and sewing. Those in the workhouses were especially subject to the poverty and sickness that claimed the lives of a high proportion of adults and children at an early age, especially in cities such as London. Philanthropic concerns prompted the emerging professional middle class to establish institutions such as the Foundling Hospital, set up by Thomas Coram in London in 1745, and religious and charitable model schools for the education of the poor, both male and female. Here too knitting and needlework figured strongly as part of the regime. Like sewing with its 'thimble drills', knitting was taught by rote, using counting songs and knitting rhymes.[24]

Instruction manuals for school teaching show the exacting work expected of each child. One of the earliest of these, dated 1832, is entitled *Instructions on Needlework and Knitting, as derived from the practices of the Central School of the National Society for the Promotion of the Education of the Poor in the Principles of the Established Church* (plate 16). Published 'in order to provide suitable work for the lower classes', the manual demonstrates methods for hemming (stitches to be evenly spaced and of uniform size), sewing and felling, stitching (taking two threads only), gathering, making buttonholes, darning, marking and knitting stockings. It features nine tiny samples, including a complete knitted stocking, a frilled bonnet and a sewn chemise in 'nineteen necessary parts', as well as worked samples of marking stitches

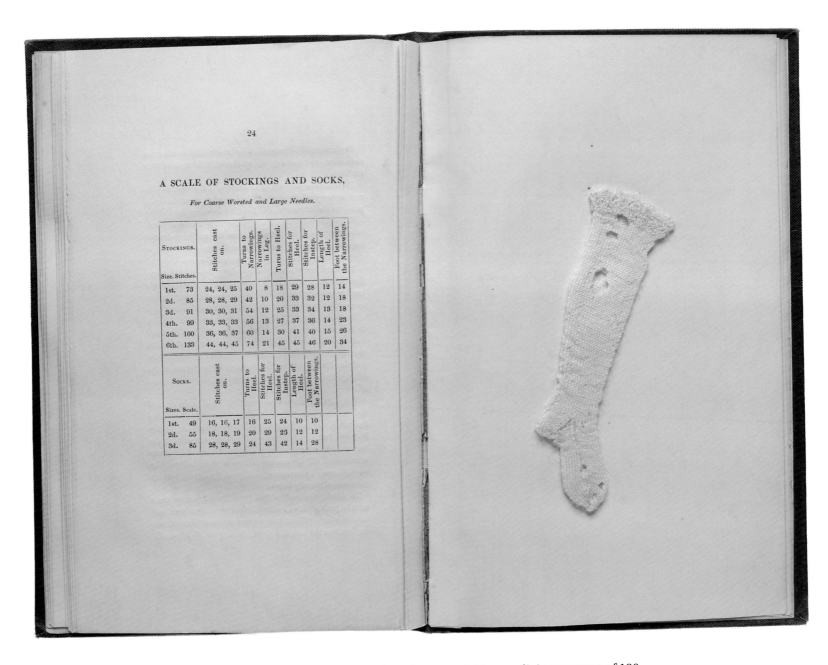

(lettering for identification of clothes) and darning. Further teaching manuals flourished, such as *The Knitting Teachers Assistant* (1838) and *Directions for Plain Knitting for the Working Classes and Schools* (1846).[25]

Ackworth Quaker School, set up in 1779 in Yorkshire for girls and boys who were 'not in affluence' (and still existing as a school today), provides an example of one of the philanthropic institutions where such manuals might have been used. The prodigious output of 120 girls in 1821 included mostly sewn goods – shirts (230), aprons (81), shifts (177), handkerchiefs (277) and counterpanes (46) – but the school was in an area known for its knitting, and 393 pairs of knitted stockings were also produced. Despite mechanization, hand-knitting for income continued in Yorkshire until well into the nineteenth century:

16 Instruction manual,
1838, Britain
V&A: T.307–1979
Once the basic principles of
knitting a stocking to shape
in the round were learnt, the
knitter could vary the size of
the stocking to fit requirements.
Instructions here are given for
six sizes of stocking and three
of socks in coarse worsted wool,
but do not specify needle size.
The chart stipulates for each size
the numbers of stitches and
rounds ('turns') to be cast on
then worked in each section,
such as narrowing in the leg
or length of the foot. This sock
sample measures just 12 cm
long. A first edition of this
manual, dated 1832, is held in
the National Art Library.

**17 *Plain Needlework, Knitting
and Mending, for all, at home
and in schools***, 1879, Boston,
USA
NAL: 43.D.37
This American publication is
based on the earlier English
school manuals *Plain Needlework*
and *Plain Knitting and Mending*,
both set out 'in six standards'
according to the children's ages,
going up to 12 years old. This is
one of a series of diagrams
showing how to darn the worn
heel of a stocking. Other
techniques covered include
Swiss darning, and grafting
together knitted pieces, in
addition to the knitting of
stockings, dishcloths and
'washing gloves'.

Articles requiring complex shaping continued to be made by hand. They were worked at
home, often as cottage industry, but also in
workhouses and workhouse schools. Knitting
tended to be regarded as the work of servants
and labourers…many [Ackworth pupils]
would be able to use that skill when they
moved into employment.[26]

In the United States too, although ready-made
socks, stockings and other knitted items were easily
available by the mid-nineteenth century, knitting was
still felt to be an essential skill: 'Boston public schools
set aside two hours a week for fourth, fifth and sixth
graders…they remonstrated "This time shall not be
shortened… without the consent of the Committee on
Sewing, especially obtained".'[27]

Once the Elementary Education Act of 1870 came
into force in England and Wales, the long tradition of
teaching needlework and knitting in village and charity

42   PLAIN NEEDLEWORK FOR SCHOOLS.

Nine times out of ten all the stitches are there, but have
lost their connecting thread, and fall apart on all sides.
The plan is to take a needle, and carefully search out the
stitches, gradually drawing them together, and then, with
a fine sewing-cotton, fasten them together with care, so as
not to cause a puckered appearance.   This must be done

NO. 3. PLAIN DARNING.

on the right of the stocking, as engraved, because the loops
of the stitches in ravelling fall out on that side. Then
turn the stocking inside out, and darn over the place, and
at least half an inch beyond on all sides.[1]
    A darn should never be in shape either a square or a
parallelogram, because the strain of the thickened part

schools developed into an established curriculum.
Typical drill was laid out in six standards in *Plain Needlework* and *Plain Knitting and Mending*, first published in
1874 (plate 17). The author remarked: 'In times gone by
in the "Society of Industry" in Rutland children of three
years of age were required to learn knitting and in some
parts of England, children of six were expected to knit
socks.' Catering for younger children, *Knitting for Infants
and Juniors* was written by Ethel M. Dudley, a teacher
from Liverpool, who took pride that items of 'practical
use can be accomplished by tiny fingers'.[28] By the time
the book *Knitting without Specimens: the Modern Book
of School Knitting and Crochet* was published in 1914,
schooling in knitting and needlework had become more
gendered – compulsory for girls but not boys. The
authors, E.P. and C.A. Claydon, were at pains to create
more interesting work by 'uniting educational value with
social utility'. Quoting a report on the teaching of needlework that found 'the effect of specimen work on
needlework teaching has been disastrous', the authors –
a school headmistress and a sewing mistress – eschewed
samples in favour of practical items such as dolls' clothes
and stockings and gloves for the child's own use.[29]

The teaching of knitting in schools gradually
declined as social priorities changed. Nevertheless, in
the 1970s, teaching of hand-knitting was re-introduced
to the Shetland junior school curriculum in order to
maintain within the island community a traditional
and potentially lucrative skill that was no longer being
passed on as in previous generations. In 2010, this last
bastion of school knitting fell victim to cost-saving cuts,
and the passing on of knitting skills reverted to the
family and community.[30]

Genteel pursuits and drawing-room manuals
During the eighteenth century, knitting gradually
moved away from its long association with schools,
orphanages, subsistence and poverty and also became
the domain of well-to-do ladies of leisure, becoming
one of the needlework skills that were an essential part
of every female's repertoire, irrespective of social class.
The purpose and products varied, however: the poor

knitted clothes for the family or for income out of necessity; gentlewomen knitted decorative items as a hobby. As the middle classes grew, so did the amount of needlework expected of married women and girls in domestic service. In addition to providing clothing and household needs, needlework of all kinds – including knitting, embroidery, tatting (decorative knotting made using a shuttle) and netting – was seen as morally virtuous and a useful occupation for girls and women. Work was not a socially acceptable option for upper-middle-class ladies – a frustration to many spirited women who were compelled to while away their hours in drawing rooms with the ever-present workbox – and knitting was seen to provide a creative outlet in the production of gifts. Knitting was also an acceptable means of raising money for gentlewomen in personal need, such as widows, or for charitable purposes, many items being sold to raise funds for good causes.

By the mid-nineteenth century, 'fancy' knitting was flourishing, employing the most intricate (and time-consuming) beadwork, stitchery and lace knitting to create trousseau items or simply 'what-nots' such as pence jugs, purses, pincushions, doilies, egg cosies and even frills for Stilton cheese, all catered for in contemporary instruction manuals. Many of these small items were sold in charity bazaars. As a princess, the future Queen Victoria became an accomplished knitter, and continued to knit after she was crowned in 1837: one account tells of the elderly queen knitting six scarves just before she died.[31]

The forerunners of the instruction manuals used for fancy knitting and needlework were the folios of pattern charts published in Germany in the eighteenth century. Comprising charts on squared paper, suitable for various types of embroidery, they could also successfully be used for crochet or knitting; indeed, those published by Albrecht Schmid in 1748, *Allerhand Model zum Stricken und Nahren* ('Assorted designs for knitting and needlework'), were clearly intended for both knitting and stitching (NAL: 43.G Box X). The similarities between motifs in fancy knitted work and embroidered samplers is evident in eighteenth-century knitted pincushions and pinballs, skilfully made in silk and silver-gilt yarn and showing carnations, birds, foliage and inscriptions (plate 18). These were often made as love tokens or gifts for personal use, though some were also made for sale. One Ackworth schoolgirl wrote to her mother in 1823, 'I have been obliged to borrow a little [money] of Hannah Waller which I hope a few pincushions I have to sell will repay.'[32]

To satisfy the growing Victorian vogue for 'fancy work', several women published books of 'receipts' or 'recipes'. One of the first was Mrs Jane Gaugain, whose family was in business in Edinburgh selling the mate-rials for such fancy work. From 1840 she published, with the help of over 500 high-society sponsors, three volumes under the general title of *The Lady's Assistant*, offering knitting, netting and crochet instructions. Volume II (1842) also included receipts for worsted work, raised cut work (a type of embroidery) and tatting. At first, pattern manuals in general were not well illustrated, but gradually more and more detailed illustrations were included. Jane Gaugain published a later accompaniment to her second volume comprising prints 'illustrating all open stitches described in volume II', with a number of 'New and Beautiful specimens of Knitting' (plate 21). Her volume III (1846)

19 Pattern chart by Susana Rieglin, from *Neues und zum Stricken dienliches Modelbuch Hauben, Handschuh und Strimpfe* ('New and useful design book for knitting bonnets, gloves and stockings'), vol.4, 1760, Nuremberg, Germany
NAL: Box 8 95.0.51
Whereas Albrecht Schmid's 1748 volume of 20 charts features lettering, small floral motifs and many designs for stocking clocks, Susana Rieglin's charts include all-over patterns and figurative designs of stags and peacocks, Neptune, and a knight and dragon, clearly allowing adaptation to colour knitting and embroidery. The peacock design can be compared with the embroidered stocking clocks in Chapter 1 (see p.25).

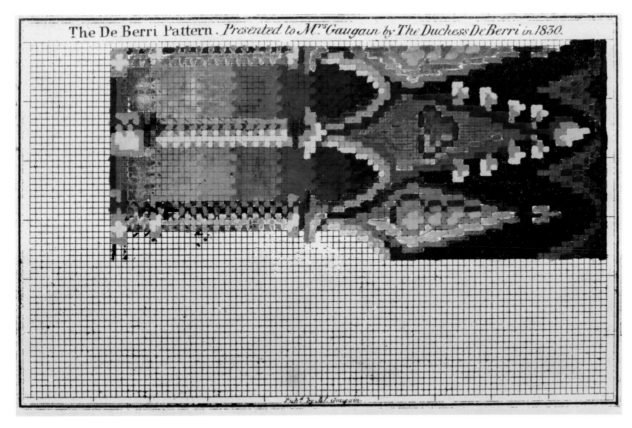

The De Berri Pattern. *Presented to M*^{rs} *Gaugain by The Duchess De Berri in 1830.*

Pub^d by M. Gaugain.

20 Duchess De Berri, pattern from Jane Gaugain, *The Lady's Assistant in Knitting, Netting and Crochet Work*, vol.III, 1846, Edinburgh
V&A: T.69–1975
The design is hand-painted over a chart, similar to the German publications of Schmid and Rieglin. The pattern is intended for worsted-work embroidery, probably using imported coloured wools from Germany.

21 Four lace patterns, from Jane Gaugain, *Accompaniment to Volume II of The Lady's Assistant*, 1844, Edinburgh
NAL: 43.N.6
As well as new recipes, this book contained illustrations of many recipes for fancy lace stitches featured in Gaugain's volume II, which was without visual information. This must have been a boon to knitters, who needed to create samplers to test out the patterns.

incorporates illustrations in the text, including a hand-coloured chart of an intricate design given by the Duchess De Berri in 1830 (plate 20). Mrs Gaugain also invented a range of abbreviations, of which she was justly proud, based on capital letters such as P for plain, B for backstitch (purl), T for take in (decrease), S for slip, and unique inverted letters to denote particular increasings, decreasings or movements. 'F' designates 'bring the thread forward by passing it under the right wire to the front', and an inverted F 'pass the thread to the back by passing it under the right hand wire'.[34] Mrs Gaugain prefaced volume III of her *Lady's Assistant* thus: 'The method of explaining the receipts, though novel…has been found to answer the purpose completely viz, that of giving a simple and clear explanation of them by means of Letters and Figures, which are easily reduced to practice.'[35]

Being privately sponsored, these manuals were relatively costly: volume I of *The Lady's Assistant* cost

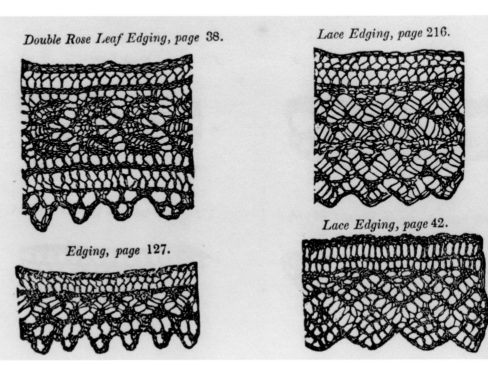

Double Rose Leaf Edging, page 38.

Lace Edging, page 216.

Edging, page 127.

Lace Edging, page 42.

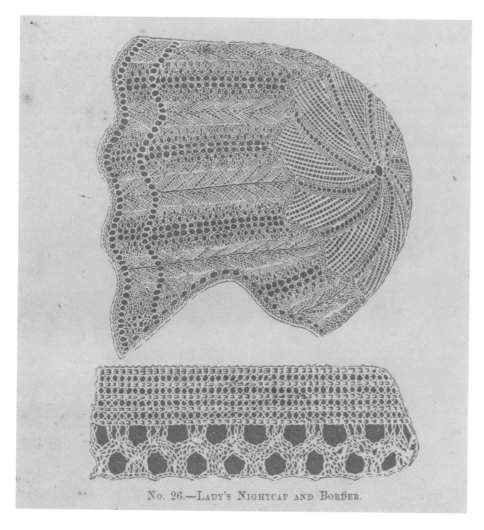

No. 26.—LADY'S NIGHTCAP AND BORDER.

22 **Lady's cap**, from *The Lady's Album of Fancy Work*, 1849, London
NAL: 147.C.5
The *Album*, bound in card covers, stated that its 'usefulness will remain undiminished far beyond the brief season generally assigned to those elegantly bound adornments of the boudoir and the drawing-room'. It contains a comprehensive collection of designs in crochet, knitting, netting and embroidery for ladies, gentlemen and children, together with household items such as doilies.

5 shillings and 6 pence; volumes II and III cost 10 shillings and 6 pence. Conscious of their price and wishing to reach a wider audience, Jane Gaugain deliberately set out to produce more economical volumes, such as the *Miniature Knitting, Netting and Crochet Book* of 1843, priced at 1 shilling. *The Knitter's Friend: A Selection of Receipts for the Most Useful and Saleable Articles in Knitting* (1846) was specifically directed at an audience beyond the drawing room and 'that numerous and useful class of females whose pecuniary means are limited but whose minds and pursuits are well regulated and directed' – in other words, women in need of funds. By 1854 the prolific Mrs Gaugain had published 16 books that included knitting patterns.

Mrs Gaugain's books were part of a veritable explosion of nineteenth-century publications on needlework.[36] As printing processes and paper became more widely available from the mid-nineteenth century, a wealth of manuals and books on the subject were published in English (plate 22). Examples include the earliest English manual, by the Misses Watts, *The Ladies Knitting and Netting Book* (1837). Their *Selections of Knitting, Netting and Crochet Work* followed in 1843. Other notable authors of the period include Miss Lambert, Eleanore Riego de la Brancharderie, who knitted for the English royal family, and Térèse de Dillmont, whose highly successful *Encyclopaedia of Needlework* (1886) was fully illustrated and continued in print until at least the 1930s, by which time it had sold over 800,000 copies in German, French, English and Italian.

Many of the earlier knitting recipes appear frustratingly vague and general to a modern eye, assuming the knitter already possessed a high level of skill. The lack of illustrations and variable quality of different instruction manuals meant that samplers were important for testing the recipes and creating an aide-memoire for the knitter (V&A: T.84–1978).

These earliest pattern publications were primarily for small or decorative items for the household or children. They might give instructions for many stitch patterns to be used as desired, and for specific items including stocking purses, beaded bags and muffatees, as well as methods for renewing the feet of stockings. In the 1840s a fashion arose for knitting 'Polkas' – hip-length jackets shaped tightly into the waist, either tailored in woven fabric or interpreted in knitting – named after the popular dance that swept high society.[37] This was one of the first examples of fashionable upper-body clothing being made by knitting, and it stimulated many patterns by the upper-class writers, including one by Mrs Gaugain in her third volume, followed by her *Knit Polka Book*, published in 1847. The crossover of knitting into fashion had begun (plate 23).

Silk-yarn manufacturers Pearsalls published a small manual, 'Knitting in Silks', in its seventh edition in 1906, which included patterns for ties, as well as for stockings and socks, opera wraps and egg cosies. Knitting in silk was a mark of the gentlewoman's work. At the start of the twentieth century, a vogue for knitting silk ties was evident, as recounted in Ford Madox Ford's 1910 novel, *A Call*:

> The expression upon her face was one of serenity and resigned contentment. She was looking at the farmhouse; she was knitting a silk necktie, a strip of vivid green that fell across her light grey skirt…And suddenly she leaned forward; the long fingers holding the knitting needles ceased all motion. She had heard a footstep…He was leaning over the back of her chair…she whispered: 'Oh take me! Take me! Now! For good.'[38]

The evolution of the knitting pattern

With the development of printing and the rise of literacy, the popular market for needlework and knitting had grown considerably by the end of the nineteenth century. To reach this audience at more accessible prices than the drawing-room manuals, there emerged several series of low-priced monthly journals. Significant among these were the *Family Friend* (1849–66 and 1870–1921) and *Weldon's Practical Needlework* series (1886–1929), including *Practical Crochet* and *Practical Knitter*. Each issue of *Weldon's* cost just 2 pence until 1916, when it became 3 pence. Knitting instructions also evolved. Gradually, more attention was paid to teaching the basic knitting skills in printed form, and reference began to be made to the notion of knitting tension and needle gauge. Instead of continuous prose, instructions were separated into lines. Despite Mrs Gaugain's pioneering efforts, the standard knitting abbreviations now in common use were first established by Weldon's in 1906.[39]

The popularity of these books spread to feed a growing audience in the United States, where the cachet of European designs held much sway in society. Some books were enterprisingly re-published, but much plagiarizing of patterns took place from English, French and German sources, since no foreign copyright laws were in place, as Mrs Gaugain lamented:

Since the year 1837, when I first published a small work on Fancy Knitting – then quite a novelty, though now so popular – I have noticed with much pain, that a number of empirical publications have, from time to time, made their appearance, some of them under spurious pretensions; and a great portion of the Receipts being garbled spoliations [sic] from my various works. I take this opportunity of cautioning the public against those piratical productions, and also of giving this note of warning to Publishers and others, that such pilfering from the works that have cost me so much close study and application, will no longer be passed over with impunity.[40]

23 **Knit polka**, from Mrs Warren and Mrs Pullan, *Treasures in Needlework*, 1855, London NAL 43.N 44
Polkas were knitted in a pliable and springy 'brioche' stitch (similar to fisherman's rib, where alternate stitches are worked into the stitch below), with bodice and sleeves shaped all in one piece, so the sleeves were knitted sideways. Polkas were often trimmed with a fur-like looped edging.

24 Beehive Wools advertisement, from Flora Klickmann, *The Modern Knitting Book*, 1915, London Sandy Black collection J. & J. Baldwin of Halifax were pioneers of the individual pattern booklet. Illustrated are patterns for a lady's cap and raglan jacket, sports sweaters and children's garments. In the second year of World War I, there are also 'Comforts for Men on Land and Sea' and 'Field and Hospital Comforts'.

American publications grew and, although there was no exact equivalent to *Weldon's*, the monthly *Godey's Lady's Book* advised on fashion and health and printed needlework and knitting instructions.

At the beginning of the twentieth century, the individual pattern leaflet became a prime marketing tool for promoting branded yarns that continues to the present day. With sports such as golf and cycling increasingly popular, the first individual patterns were for outdoor 'sports coats' – hip-length jackets with pockets, now termed cardigans, modelled on the tailored male Norfolk Jacket.

The pattern designers of the vast majority of individual knitting leaflets and knitting journals are anonymous, but some influential designers are known and respected for their work. Marjory Tillotson spent 50 years designing knitwear and patterns for many yarn companies, most significantly, from 1908 to 1920, the major British wool manufacturer J. & J. Baldwin, makers of Beehive branded hand-knitting wools (plate 24). At a time when the movement for women's suffrage was developing and women's clothing was becoming less restrictive, Tillotson designed a series of Beehive pattern booklets for garments that crystallized the changing social mores.

Tillotson's philosophy was to make knitting creative, even for schoolchildren, eschewing slavish following of patterns and aligning knitting with fashion. She wrote about the principles of knitting and designing garments and was the first to use stitch-symbol charts and garment-measurement diagrams in order to empower knitters to 'make jumpers, cardigans, babies' woollies etc to their *own* measurements, and to their *own* designs', as she wrote in the preface to the first edition of *The Complete Knitting Book* in 1934. She continued 'The true joy of knitting is only obtained when it becomes a *creative craft*…The decrees of the century and of fashion demand much more than mere utility.' Tillotson also wrote the first edition of the long-lived magazine *Woolcraft*, a comprehensive manual of recipes that included basic knitting and crochet method instructions and proved consistently popular (see p.115), and *The School Knitting Book* (1931). Underwear instructions included combinations, directoire knickers and a child's liberty bodice. The fourth and fifth editions of *Complete Knitting* contained a 'Fashion Supplement' with patterns for a button-through dress, a redingote (long cardigan jacket) (plate 25), and a 'classic style twinset' so that 'even the most inexperienced knitter…can soon evolve entirely new and chic garments to her own size and so keep ahead of fashion'.[41]

Leaflets featuring individual knitting patterns particularly flourished after World War I. British companies such as J. Paton of Alloa, Scotland, who joined forces with J. & J. Baldwin of Halifax in 1920 to become Patons & Baldwins, produced a vast number of patterns for home knitting, reflecting both the everyday needs and fashions of the times.[42] Others included the Scotch Wool Company (in 1960 amalgamated with Patons & Baldwins), Bestway, Bairnswear, Copley, Listers and many more. Listers built sales of high-quality merino wools, later branded 'Lavenda', to meet the needs of, among others, 'thousands of war widows who had turned to knitting to eke out their pensions'.[43] Baldwin's magazine *Woolcraft* became a standard work and paved the way for many future knitting publications such as the influential *Stitchcraft*, launched by Patons & Baldwins in 1932 and running monthly for 50 years – another of a growing number of in-house journals from the knitting-yarn spinners. As well as individual seasonal leaflets, the spinners also produced regular books of knitting collections focused on specific yarns or themes.

As time went on, knitting patterns increasingly featured fashionable outer garments for women, illustrated with new photography, of which John French was an early exponent, bringing fashion flair and glamour to the workaday home knitting pattern (plate 26). Reflecting the trickle-down of high fashion for everyday use, there were many references to fashions from Paris and London, and *Stitchcraft* featured reports from Ann Talbot, the Paris fashion correspondent from 1932 to 1937, with illustrations and tips on the latest styles: 'De War is showing a large collection of knitted costumes that range from sports wear to elaborate evening models. Her amusing

25 Redingote design, from Marjory Tillotson, *The Complete Knitting Book*, 5th ed. 1948, London
Sandy Black collection
Marjory Tillotson was one of the first to bring fashion and knitting together, encouraging her readers to expand their horizons.

bloomer costumes for bicycling are very new, for the cycling craze is now sweeping the Paris *haut-monde*.'[44]

Mary Thomas, a leading writer on embroidery and knitting, noted in the preface to her 1938 *Knitting Book*: 'All ages have contributed their quota to the progress of knitting, and that contributed by the modern knitter is style. A modern knitted garment is not a thing to be dragged on for extra warmth, but has, in its own right, a place in the world of fashion.' Thomas also included some of the history of the craft in her books, which became essential reference works.[45] She made compre-

26 **John French**, photographs for *Stitchcraft*, 1948–51
AAD 1979/9 PL7
John French brought style and *joie de vivre* to the previously formal portrait poses of the knitting-pattern format. His early work for *Stitchcraft* helped establish his reputation as a leading fashion photographer.

PLANNING YOUR WINTER CAMPAIGN

Vest and Pantie Set

IN TWO-PLY WOOL

MATERIALS

5 oz. 2-ply wool for the set, or
3 oz. 2-ply wool for the vest, and
2 oz. 2-ply wool for the panties.
2 No. 8 and 2 No. 12 knitting needles.
¾ yd. elastic for the panties.

MEASUREMENTS

Vest: Length, 28 ins.
Bust size, 34 ins.
Panties: Waist to crutch, 14 ins.
To stretch to fit a 38-in. hip.

TENSION

Using No. 8 needles, 5½ sts. to 1 in.,
measured over the stretched rib.

THE VEST

The Back and Front Alike.—Using No.
8 needles cast on 105 sts. loosely with
double wool. Break off 1 strand of wool
and continue in single wool in moss st. for
1 in. With the right side of the work facing
continue in the following rib:—
  1st row.—K. 2, * p. 1, k. 4; rep. from
* to last 3 sts., p. 1, k. 2.
  2nd row.—P. 2, * k. 1, p. 4; rep. from
* to last 3 sts., k. 1, p. 2.
  Rep. these 2 rows until the work measures 14 ins. from the beginning.
  Change to No. 12 needles and continue
in rib until work measures 18½ ins. from
the beginning. Change back to No. 8
needles and continue in rib until work
measures 23 ins. from the beginning of
the work. Change to moss st. and work
1 in.
  Shape Top and Make Shoulders thus:—
  Next row.—Cast off 7, moss st. to end.

Next row.—Cast off 7, moss st. 45,
including st. already on needle when
casting off has been done, turn.
  Continue working on these 45 sts., dec.
1 st. at both ends of every row until there
are 11 sts. on the needle. Continue working on these 11 sts. for the shoulder straps
until they measure 5 ins. Cast off in moss
st.
  Rejoin wool at needle point and dec.
1 st. at the beginning of the next row,
work in moss st. to the end. Now continue
to shape this side to correspond with the
one already completed, dec. 1 st. at both
ends of the next row and every following
row until there are 11 sts. on the needle.
Complete this side to correspond with the
right side.
  Make Up.—Press the work lightly on
the wrong side, using a warm iron over a
damp cloth. Join the side and shoulder
seams and work a picot edge round the
neck and armhole edges as follows:—
  1 s.c. into the first st., * 3 ch., 1 d.c. into
the first of these ch., miss 1 st., 1 s.c. into
the next; rep. from * to end.

THE PANTIES

The Left Leg.—Using No. 8 needles and
double wool cast on 114 sts. Break off 1
strand of wool and change to No. 12
needles and work in a rib of k. 1, p. 1 for
¾ in., inc. 1 st. at the end of the last row
of ribbing. There are now 115 sts. on
the needle.
  Change to No. 8 needles and continue
in rib as follows:—
  1st row.—K. 2, * p. 1, k. 4; rep. from
* to last 3 sts., p. 1, k. 2.

Expressing warm sentiments: The letter? Undoubtedly, but we were thinking of the vest and pantie set. They're right—and they're so cosy. Come wind, come weather, you'll be warm and with that lovely "well-dressed all through" feeling.

27 Underwear pattern, from J. Koster and M. Murray, *Complete Home Knitting*, 1942, London NAL: NB.95.1172 Jane Koster and Margaret Murray, who were sisters-in-law, continued to design patterns together until the late 1950s for many publications and yarn spinners such as Sirdar, George Lee, Lister, Templeton and Wendy.

hensive use of charts and symbols to explain the principles of knitting and precisely detailed methods of shaping, and promoted variations to express individual tastes and creative expression.

In a similar vein, during and after World War II, Jane Koster and Margaret Murray wrote a series of stylish utility knitting books, published by Odhams, to help housewives create their own clothes for the family while under the constraints of rationing. Patterns covered underwear to outerwear, beachwear to nightwear. The later books included colour photographs and illustrations (plate 27 and 36).

James Norbury, appointed chief knitwear designer for Patons & Baldwins yarns in 1946, went on to become a key knitting authority for home knitting in the 1950s and 1960s. He published a number of popu-

lar books, gave lectures and appeared regularly on the emerging medium of television as the BBC's knitting expert, making his profile and influence greater than that of his female predecessors. In a lecture 'Design in Knitting' given in London in 1952, he criticized the artificial division between art and industry, believing that 'design is implanted within the object: firstly, the purpose for which you are creating it, and secondly, giving a meaning to that purpose'. He admired the craftsmanship of the knitters of Fair Isle sweaters as 'not something conscious, [but] something that emerges out of the individual, in keeping with the particular period in which he is designing'.[46]

The evolution of nineteenth-century knitting-stitch and pattern manuals into serial journals, books and single leaflets provides – along with their later incarnations – a continuous history of home knitting throughout the nineteenth and twentieth centuries, revealing much about the social and fashion contexts of their times. The knitting pattern producers were at pains to appear fashionable, but their simple aesthetic sensibility, combining the everyday with necessary documentary detail – and on low budgets – renders them quaint in retrospect and easily lampooned.

Women's magazines and fashionable knitting

Alongside individual leaflets, knitting journals and books, knitting patterns have long featured in women's fashion magazines. From early beginnings in the late seventeenth century, the publishing of magazines aimed at women has continued to grow. *The Lady's Magazine (or entertaining companion for the fair sex, appropriated solely for their use and amusement)*, published from 1770 to 1847, was the first in Britain to include fashion features and fashion plates in colour.[47] From the mid-nineteenth century, the abolition of duty on paper and improved distribution channels further facilitated magazine publishing. Weekly and monthly society journals such as *The Queen* and *The Lady*, launched in 1860 and 1885 respectively, increasingly featured fashions. From its earliest years, *The Queen* featured 'The Work-Table' – a regular section on home crafts including knitting patterns and answers to readers' craft and knitting queries – as well as occasional knitting supplements with a range of patterns: adult ribbed, spun-silk stockings in 1872; patterns for baby clothes in 1880; sports socks in 1900 (plate 28). *The Queen* also carried advertisements for sewing and embroidery materials, knitting yarns and domestic knitting machines, until, by the turn of the twentieth century, the fashions featured were those for purchase rather than those to be made from patterns.

By this time the market had diversified to meet demand from the more worldly and emancipated women who were entering the workforce rather than domestic service, particularly after World War I. In 1916, in the depths of the war, the high fashion magazine *Vogue* was launched in the United States, soon followed by a British edition. Flora Klickmann's *Popular Knitting Book* of 1921 suggested, 'The revival of knitting seems to be the one and only benefit derived from the war!… Girls and women will now tackle large garments, shaped garments, intricate patterns, introducing ingenious colour combinations, and producing the most up-to-date-styles.'[48]

As the middle classes grew and servants declined it was the housewife who became a key target for many early-twentieth-century magazines, reflected in the change of epithet in their titles, from 'lady' to 'woman'. This new style of weekly women's magazine, utilizing improvements in photographic reproduction, merged domestic concerns and fashion and featured hints and tips on homemaking alongside recipes and romantic stories. From the outset, knitting patterns became a regular feature in magazines such as *My Weekly*, launched in 1910 – the first magazine aimed at working-class women – and *Woman's Weekly*, launched 1911, with patterns for 'the ordinary garments worn by average women'.[49] In the wake of the stock-market crash in 1929, there were further new titles, beginning with *Woman's Own*, launched 1932, which gave away three skeins of wool with the first issue, reinforcing the economic benefits of home knitting and the recognition by publishers of its importance. *Woman*, launched in 1937, competed with *Woman's Own* but soon overtook it in sales, being quick to embrace the new colour lithography. In the 1930s, *Woman's Weekly* sold 500,000 copies per week; in the 1950s, circulation of *Woman's Own* reached 3 million.[50] All of these titles are still in print, including *The Lady*, but only *My Weekly* still features knitting patterns.

Starting in the early 1930s, the publishers of fashion 'bible' *Vogue* produced an offshoot called *The Vogue Knitting Book* (later *Vogue Knitting*), which specialized in a particularly stylish and fashion-conscious genre of pattern aimed at women with responsibilities but also with leisure time. Later in the twentieth century, specialist needlework magazines such as *Pins and Needles* (1949–89) and *Golden Hands* (*c*.1972) were at pains to bring accessible fashion to their readers, but their image was more practical than fashionable. It was not until the glossy fashion magazines embraced knitting in the early 1980s that hand-knitting re-entered the high fashion arena (plate 29).

As with the yarn spinners' individual patterns, the women's magazines knitting features were provided by designers who often remained anonymous. One such is Eve Sandford, who designed for *Woman*, the women's pages of newspapers and the spinners Emu,

Wendy, Sirdar, Marriner and Patons. Sandford trained in fashion and design at Belfast School and turned to knitting while recovering from an illness in hospital. Her first published knitting design was submitted speculatively to the *Daily Telegraph* in 1961 'for those who bemoan the popularity of chunky double knitting and prefer casual elegance to "sloppy Jo's"'.[51] The pattern – a bouclé jacket with scarf and large buttons,

29 Martin Kidman design,
Elle, March 1987
Photographed by Patrick
Jackson
Elle magazine featured monthly
designer knitting patterns from
its UK launch in November 1985
to July 1993. The 16th design was
one of the influential oversized
hand-knitted wool sweaters
designed by Martin Kidman for
Joseph Tricot. It is a simplified
version for home knitters of two
cherub sweaters in the V&A
collection (T.210&A–1990).
Between the border and the
cherub-patterned yoke, one of
the V&A sweaters has a blue-
filled diamond pattern, and the
other has a trellis in gold
metallic yarn. Here there is no
background patterning at all.

30 Eve Sandford designs, 1960s
AAD 6/1–1988 & 6/3–1988
Eve Sandford's first design in
1961 (in pink bouclé yarn) was
made for herself and featured in
the *Daily Telegraph*. Her designs
became classics of the knitting
pattern genre, well designed
with good proportions and
detail, and easy to knit and wear.

lined with chiffon to improve the shape – sold a record-
breaking 7000 copies in a few months. Success
continued, and Sandford's output was prolific: 50
designs for Emu in one year. By 1962 she employed an
assistant and had 12 knitters working for her in order
to produce the made-up designs and written patterns
(plate 30). Another best-seller for the *Daily Telegraph*
was a 'Chanel Style Twinset' in tweedy yarns, but Sandford records it was 'quite a job' to produce the
commission in six weeks – a typically fast turnaround
for the requirements of fashion. A cutting from the
London *Evening Standard*, 16 December 1963, reports,
'Whereas a sweater used to be something you find
round your shoulders on a chilly day, it is now very
high fashion indeed.'

**Domestic machine-knitting
in the nineteenth and twentieth centuries**

Following the success of the domestic sewing machine
in both the United States and Great Britain in the mid-
nineteenth century (an invention that quickly became
a means of manufacturing clothes both in the factory
and in the home), a new market for small domestic circular and straight knitting machines developed. These
appealed particularly to middle-class women wishing
to knit for their family or to 'distressed' gentlewomen
with no means of support, who earned extra money as
outworkers knitting stockings and small items at home.

In the United States, Aiken's Family Knitting
Machine (a small circular machine) was advertised in
1861. Small-diameter circular machines such as this,

31 Hinkley knitting machine advertisement, *The Queen*, 30 July 1870
This early single-needle straight-frame domestic knitting machine originated in the USA in 1866, manufactured in the UK by J. Keighley in Bradford, Yorkshire. Operated either by hand or by foot, the curved needle moved across the needlebed to form each stitch individually.

known as 'ladies' machines' and 'family knitters', were attached to a table-top and hand cranked. They revived a new form of cottage industry, and much of the sock knitting for the troops of World War I was produced by women using such machines, either at home or in small manufactories. Their ease of use was a far cry from the heavy and cumbersome knitting frames that (male) cottage workers had used in the earlier centuries of mechanical knitting or the subsequent machines powered by steam and then electricity in the large industrial factories.

Aiken's early machine was soon superseded by others such as the small straight-frame V-bed made in Britain by Lamb, which could also automatically knit true ribbing. An advert in *The Queen* in July 1870 promoted the Hinkley single-needle straight machine, claiming that it can produce 'any fabric from an "Afghan" to a pair of gloves', and knit 'a stocking complete with a "hand heel"' (plate 31). With the later small machines, such as the popular circular machine made by Griswold (the leading manufacturer in Britain, whose name was applied generically to similar machines), it was possible also to fashion the heels and toes of socks using the 'reciprocal movement' facility to change direction, just like turning the work in hand-knitting. The toes were then finished by hand grafting. Later adaptations to the machine included a second cylinder of needles for ribbing. The typical output of a female worker using such a machine in a workshop was two dozen pairs of worsted socks per day.[52] Because the machines were hand-operated, their products were described as handmade (plate 32).

An advertising leaflet from the 1930s for the Cymbal Home Knitter states:

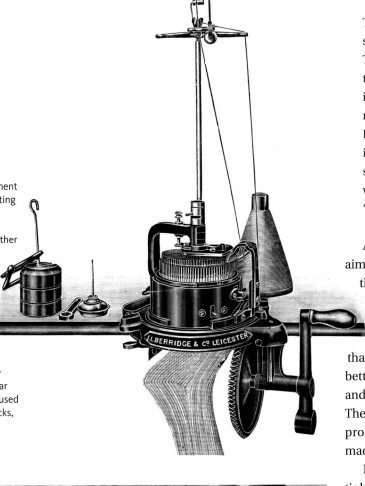

32 Images from Griswold knitting machine brochure,
*c.*1892, Britain
Ruddington Framework Knitters Museum
Following the earlier development of small domestic circular knitting machines in both the USA and Britain, Griswold patented his improved machine in 1872. Further improvements were made by others, and Griswold sold the rights to the machine manufacturers I.L. Berridge of Leicester between 1890 and 1892. At the end of the Victorian era, the brochure emphasizes the contrast between the old way (by hand) and the new way (by machine) to make socks. Similar hand-cranked machines were used to supply WWI troops with socks, made both at home and in factories, as pictured here in Douglas, Isle of Man.

The owner of a Cymbal Home Knitter has one supreme advantage over all other similar industries. There is no slack period at any time of the year… there is a constant demand for ladies' silk stockings…Both artificial and real silk stockings can be made flawlessly and beautifully on the Cymbal Home Knitter, and this could easily be developed into big business. Children's knitted wear, men's socks and sports stockings, etc, and 'pull-overs' are wanted all the year round – and the magic word 'hand made' is a recommendation in itself.[53]

Although the early small machine builders were aiming at both the middle-class domestic market and the factory, the machine's domestic success was not as easily secured as that of the sewing machine. The larger bench-style straight machines were more flexible for narrowing and widening fabric than a fixed-diameter circular machine, but they were better suited to cottage industry than the home parlour and were often used as the basis of a shared workshop. The circular family knitters fell out of favour when mass production of stockings and socks from power machines took hold.

Many new lightweight British and European domestic knitting machines (all straight-bed) were developed in the post-war period, however, and heavily promoted in the women's press and specialist publications such as *Vogue Knitting* to an increasingly affluent but cost-conscious reader. Knitting at home on the new machines was presented as an efficient way both to clothe the family with basics and to earn extra income, and was increasingly aligned to fashion (plate 33). Catering to the growing number of knitters using hand-operated domestic knitting machines, manufacturers such as Knitmaster, Jones, Passap and others produced their own pattern booklets for home-knitted fashions, especially in the 1970s and early 1980s. Capitalizing on the boom in fashionable designer knitwear at this time, domestic machine knitters were able to use their skills to knit as outworkers for new designer businesses (including the author's). Local machine-knitting clubs were formed to cater for

World War II Knitting Patterns

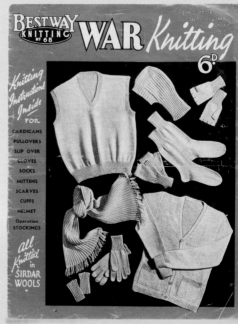

Wartime knitting patterns represent a legacy of complex emotions in the face of extreme adversity. With almost propagandist zeal and a charming visual language exemplifying British stoicism, women (it was largely women who knitted in the home) were exhorted to knit their contribution to the war effort. Every medium of communication was mobilized, including simple but effective graphic design, slogans such as 'England Expects – knit your bit', and direct advertising in the press by the knitting trade and volunteer organizations.

As wartime shortages and restrictions on the size of printed books and pamphlets came into force, knitting patterns and women's magazines were reduced in size. They were passed around between people as precious resources, becoming dog-eared from use and often held together with tape – a tangible symbol of both austerity and sharing. The major spinners such as Patons and Baldwins, Weldon's, Listers and Sirdar produced special pattern booklets under their own names and also for organizations supporting the home front, such as the Seamen's Mission and the Personal Service League, which coordinated service knitting and knitting for distressed children of the unemployed. In addition to warm sweaters, patterns were provided for the ubiquitous socks, balaclavas, body belts, kneecaps, mittens with openings to enable work and seaboot stockings. Those recovering from injury were not forgotten, with simple items handmade at home, during work breaks or in the air-raid shelters and sent to hospitals. The fact that these were universally known as 'comforts' speaks of the place that knitting held within the community, reaching out to those in need far away.

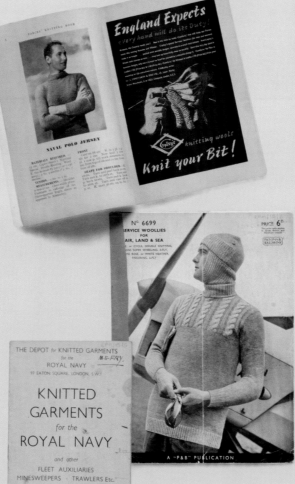

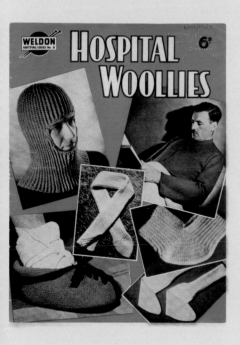

LEFT, TOP TO BOTTOM:
'Woman's Service Cardigan', Patons and Baldwins pattern No. 2760, late 1930s–mid 1940s, Sandy Black collection
'England Expects – Knit your Bit' Copley wools advertisement, *Good Housekeeping's Forces Knitting Book*; late 1930s–mid 1940s, AAD: EPH/24/370
'Service Woollies for Air, Land and Sea', Patons & Baldwins No. 6699, late 1930s–mid 1940s, AAD: EPH/15/6
'Knitted Garments for the Royal Navy', late 1930s–mid 1940s, AAD: EPH/15/5

CENTRE:
War Knitting, Bestway, late 1930s–mid 1940s, AAD: EPH/ 15/4
Home Front Woollies, Weldon Knitting Series No. 26, 1 December 1939, Sandy Black collection
Essentials for the Forces, Jaeger Hand Knit, late 1930s–mid 1940s, AAD: EPH/15/8
Hospital Woollies, Weldon Knitting Series No. 8, late 1930s–mid 1940s, AAD: EPH /15/9

RIGHT, TOP TO BOTTOM:
'Chic for wartime evenings', *Vogue's 19th Knitting Book*, late 1930s–mid 1940s, Sandy Black collection
Coupon-Saving Blouses & Boleros, *Vogue* Knitting Series No. 14, late 1930s–mid 1940s, AAD:EPH/14/5
Patons & Baldwins *Woolcraft* 13th edition, 1942–9, AAD: EPH/24/348
Knitting Book No.1: Garments for Children, The Personal Service League, late 1930s–mid 1940s, AAD: EPH/15/10
'Lady's Moccasin type Slippers', Homecraft Economy Series, late 1930s–mid 1940s, Sandy Black collection
'Economy Jumper', Homecraft Economy Series, late 1930s–mid 1940s, AAD: EPH/16/5

the particular needs of domestic machine-knitters, and many are still thriving in Britain, in a parallel stream to twenty-first-century hand-knitting groups, often affiliated to the Knitting and Crochet Guild.

The twentieth century saw the rise of the Japanese domestic knitting machine industry, due to both a dissemination of machines from Britain and Europe into Japan and the indigenous development of a 'hand-knitting machine for the home' by a Japanese woman, Masako Hagiwara, purportedly in the 1920s. This culminated in the 1980s with the Japanese gradually dominating the market for home-knitting machines.[54] Japanese companies took over the major British manufacturers – Knitmaster became Silver Reed, Jones became Brother – but even these Japanese brands have now almost disappeared from the marketplace in Britain.

Knitting for victory

During each major conflict since the Crimean War there has been a call for knitters to make comforts for the troops. This has provided a much-needed way for wives and sweethearts, mothers and sisters left at home to demonstrate their practical involvement and express their patriotic and personal emotions (plate 34). Their efforts have been coordinated by charity organizations such as the Personal Service League in Britain and Associated Field Comforts in Canada, together with the Red Cross in the United States and in the war zones. In World War I, women knitted helmets, gloves, scarves and especially socks to help counter the 'trench foot' caused by wet and cold conditions, but a lack of skill and quality control was often lampooned in contemporary cartoons. The hit-or-miss quality of the knitting might have been a result of rather vague instructions, which often suggested using 'any knitting wool' on a specific size of needles, with no reference to gauge or tension, as in the *Khaki Knitting Book*, published in 1917 by the Allies Special Aid group in New York. In Hamilton, Ontario, Canada, small circular knitting machines were supplied to increase production, and in November 1915 this region sent 27,892 pairs of socks to the front line.[55] One knitter wrote personal messages to the soldiers, some of whom replied:

33 **Knitmaster domestic knitting machine advertisement**, *Vogue Knitting Book* no. 50, 1957
Sandy Black collection
In the mid-1950s, *Vogue Knitting Book* carried adverts for a range of knitting machines and developed patterns especially for machine knitting. Here, women are exhorted to 'turn spare time into spare cash' by knitting a jumper in 45 minutes or men's socks in 35 minutes, at the rate of 30 rows and 5000 stitches per minute. A chart compares hand and machine knitting timings.

Dear Soldier Boy,

I hope you will find the accompanying socks comfortable. It is a great pleasure to us to send them, and a line from you on this paper telling of their safe arrival would be most welcome. A word from the front is a great encouragement for the workers back home.

Marion Simpson,

Nov 1916

Dear Marion Simpson,

This little note is a very poor medium of expressing my gratitude and conveying my thanks to you for the very very comfy pair of socks which contained your letter. I was 'plumb tickled' (excuse slang) to receive them and sad to confess I needed them badly.

Q.M. Sgt H. Vaughan,

Somewhere in France,

18 Nov 1916[56]

34 *Her Excellency's Knitting Book*, 1915, Wellington, New Zealand
Sandy Black collection
A book of patterns for the Army and Navy includes socks, gloves, balaclavas, cholera belts, sea-boot stockings and a 'coat sweater or cardigan'. Published in Wellington, New Zealand, it has a message from the Countess of Liverpool, wife of the governor: 'To the women of New Zealand who are so nobly responding to the call to provide comforts for the troops in the field, and for our own men which have been wounded in the service of their King and Country.'

In Britain, World War II was fought on home soil as well as overseas, and bombing raids became a frighteningly regular occurrence in the major cities. Far more civilians lost their lives than in World War I. As a form of camaraderie in the face of adversity and as a necessary therapy to keep busy, clothe the family in the freezing winters and try to keep up morale, women knitted together in groups and in the air-raid shelters (plate 41), and parcels were regularly sent off to the front line via the Army and Air Force Comforts offices. A popular slogan was 'If you can knit, you can do your bit'.

The knitting pattern publishers and yarn companies quickly rallied to support the cause by providing detailed instruction leaflets for comforts including balaclavas, socks and gloves (plate 35), hoping to avoid the embarrassment of some World War I efforts. 'These comforts are in great demand and are very much appreciated by the men at the front,' was the response to one parcel from the London Co-Operative Society workers in December 1939.[57] Figureheads such as the American president's wife, Eleanor Roosevelt, and, in Britain, King George VI's consort, Queen Elizabeth, were photographed knitting to inspire home knitters by example. The women's magazines stayed in print throughout World War II, publishing patterns and giving hints on knitting to size, playing a large role in encouraging their readers to take up the needles for the war effort (see pp.134–5).

As textile and clothing factories were commandeered or 'concentrated' to produce clothing for the services and as certain raw materials became scarcer, new clothes for civilians were in short supply. Wool was rationed in Britain from 1940 to 1949, but cotton and silk yarns were not. The strictures of clothes rationing, first introduced in June 1941, and the development of the British Civilian Clothing or 'Utility Scheme' in the same year, somewhat paradoxically produced a wealth of ingenious knitting-pattern ideas. The aim was for normal life to continue as much as possible, and the fashion trade mounted many patriotic campaigns while also continuing to sell non-utility goods. Home knitting for the family became crucial in eking out the ration of clothing coupons. These went much further in buying wool yarns than they did in buying clothes or even fabric, and tailored knitting in firm, close stitches became the affordable substitute for woven fabric clothing. Skilful designs were developed for 'tailor-made' knitwear modelled on the military-inspired and utility woven clothing of the era. The sweater with a skirt or slacks became a wearable, practical and universal style for comfort and essential warmth when fuel was in short supply.

Margaret Murray and Jane Koster's series of comprehensive knitting books – including *Practical Knitting Illustrated* (1940), *Complete Home Knitting* (1942), *Knitted Garments for All* (1944) and *Complete Family Knitting* (1949) (plate 36) – helped women to save precious coupons and still look smart and were reprinted many times. They contained patterns, including basic underwear and pretty lingerie; sweaters for men, women and children; and thrifty jumper fronts, to be worn under a jacket when materials or skill were in very short supply, together with items for the home including rugs, cushions and tea cosies. *Practical Knitting Illustrated* advised:

> You must have at least one hard-wearing cabled
> pullover in your wardrobe. Warm tailored undies are
> a necessity too. Always make sure that your knitteds
> have the careful finish and tailoring that is so impor-
> tant to simple styles. Pad and tape the shoulders to
> give them a bold line. And when you wear these
> jumpers and cardigans…wear them with an air.[58]

By 1941, 'remaking and making do' was embedded as a concept. Pictures of new garments made from worn-out sweaters show a high level of resourcefulness and ingenuity: 'Wool is scarce and precious now. There's a general feeling that, even apart from reasons of economy, one cannot lightly turn last year's jumper into this year's floor-cloth – not without exploring every possibility of giving it a new lease of life.'[59] In the foreword to *Complete Home Knitting*, the authors' tone is intensely practical:

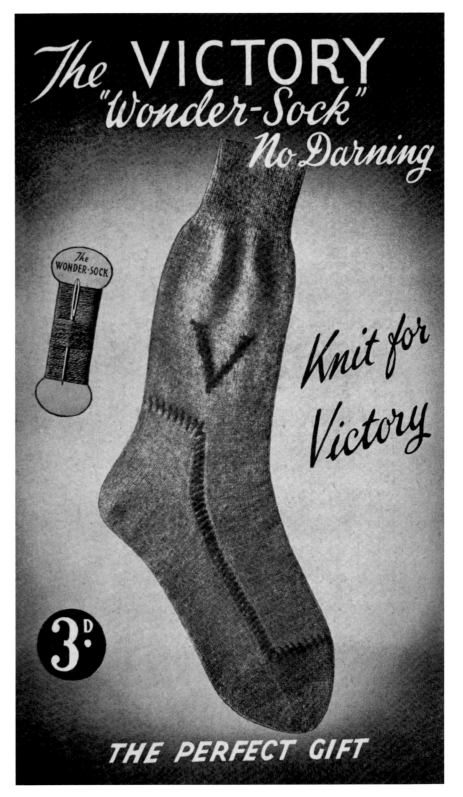

Garments to suit every member of the family can be found in this book. Pictured here is mother in a classic jumper, father in a Fair Isle pullover, and schoolgirl daughter in a pinafore skirt. Instructions for making are in the pages that follow.

complete

FAMILY KNITTING

illustrated

Clear and simple instructions
for knitting indoor and outdoor garments
for every member of the family

by
MARGARET MURRAY
and JANE KOSTER

Odhams Press Limited, Long Acre, London

Clothes are so expensive you must make them yourself when you can. This book is produced to help you solve your clothes problems. It proves that nearly every garment in the wardrobe can be made from a minimum of yarn with two needles and look as though it had been cut from fabric by a master tailor. *And* yarn is cheaper in coupons and money.[60]

The British government, meanwhile, promoted the 'Make Do and Mend' campaign as a means of conserving resources and curtailing demand for new materials. Summarized in a 1943 booklet produced by the Board of Trade, this wartime entreaty was featured throughout the press and women's magazines, with a 'Mrs Sew and Sew' character promoting sewing classes. The campaign encouraged civilians to unravel worn-out woollies and re-use the wool – thus contributing to the lack of knitted everyday wear available to researchers today. But although genuine examples of wartime and service knitting are rare in museums and private collections, the wealth of printed patterns from the time shows a multitude of well-designed, stylish and practical solutions to the circumstances (plates 36, 37 and 38). Even *Vogue Knitting*, in tune with the utility mindset, drew in its reins a little during World War II, reducing its paper size and exhorting readers to re-use yarn:

Look out those odds and ends of bright wools left over from the days before coupons. Unravel, wash and re-knit the old jumpers…use up the odd bits for bright contrast. Buy new wool if you must, but only if you must. And be doubly proud of the results of your ingenuity.[61]

37 Short sleeve jumper,
1942, Britain
V&A: T.27–1987
The main part of this jumper is
knitted sideways in a ridged
pattern of stocking stitch and
reverse stocking stitch, with
regular increases and decreases
forming a wave effect. The
unusual finish on the sleeves and
neck is created simply by casting
on 20 stitches, then casting
them off on the next row and
curling them round into a spiral.

No. 549
KNITTED IN
POLYNIT
SHORT SLEEVES
ONLY
Price 3^D

GoldenEagle

38 **Pattern leaflet**, Golden Eagle
Yarns, undated, probably late
1930s to early 1940s, Britain
Sandy Black collection
Favourite patterns were often
passed around and became well
used. This striking pattern leaflet
from Golden Eagle yarns
features the unusual sideways-
knitted design shown knitted up
in plate 37.

Vogue's 19th Knitting Book (1941) gave coupon values for every design and was at pains to explain the value of knitting your own garments: 'To buy a woollen cardigan or sweater weighing 10 ounces or more you must give up 8 coupons. Alternatively 1 coupon buys 2 ounces of wool…To knit them you need only spend 5 or 6 coupons.'[62] Given the high price of material, dresses were a key focus of ideas for making 'new frocks from old' by knitting insertions, collars, yokes and sleeves to 'turn last year's fabric frocks into something new'. As one housewife complained: 'Those who make their own clothes…are actually being penalized for their ingenuity, as it will often take more coupons to purchase material for a garment than to buy it readymade.'[63]

Vogue's 23rd Knitting Book (1943; plate 39), contains '16 pages of garments specially designed for smartness plus economy' to save precious coupons, from pretty sweaters in contrasting coloured wools to a crochet shopping bag. But, with further wool shortages and restrictions on trimmings in utility regulations – no turn-ups on men's trousers, for example – the designs are simpler and even more practical than those in *Vogue's 19th Knitting Book*.

Despite such efforts, haberdashery and wool shops surveyed in London and Worcester by Mass Observation (a social research organization started in 1937) at the start of clothes rationing in June 1941 reported reduced wool sales, with colours in short supply.[64] Initially one coupon could buy 2 ounces of wool, which was seen as expensive. Fine wools were favoured as they could go further – it was possible to make a fine two-ply jumper for 2 coupons. Many thought that wool for home knitting, and certainly wool for services knitting, should not be rationed at all and in July 1941, khaki knitting wool became coupon free. By 1942 wool for forces' knitting was allocated only to recognized organizations. One unfortunate consequence of this was that a prisoner of war might be 'robbed of one of his greatest pleasures – receiving gifts made by the hands of his mother, wife or sister'.[65]

Throughout both world wars, women's organizations played a significant role in mobilizing and

co-ordinating volunteer support in local communities (plate 41). Among those in Britain were the Women's Institute, which from World War I assisted the war effort on food, and the Women's Voluntary Service (WVS), which from 1938 helped supply clothing to the distressed. In 1941, with one million members, the WVS took on the distribution of ration books, as well as mending and tailoring for the forces – including teaching soldiers to darn socks. The WVS gained royal patronage in 1952, and had a uniform designed by couturier and utility designer Digby Morton. The government also recruited an army of 'Land Girls', who took over agricultural work from men who had gone to war; they were clothed in a practical uniform of corduroy breeches, khaki overall coat, fawn-wool ribbed stockings and a green jumper, often home-made. Land Girls were advised to 'keep one pair of stockings for best, and rotate the other pairs. Darn any areas which become thin as soon as possible.'[66]

Stockings were in extremely short supply and were one of the most important items for which women saved their coupons by home knitting. One Mass Observation respondent, a shop assistant, commented that stockings were 'a social necessity. I shall cut down luxuries and all the little extras. I have to buy stockings every week to look tidy.'[67] Others would rather do without stockings or paint on imitations, complete with seams, than substitute thicker wool ones for silk or rayon. The long-promised 'nylons' became available in Britain in 1946 as part of the utility scheme, but rationing of clothing and wool control continued long after the war ended: both were finally abolished in 1949.

In the years following World War II, the highly prized nylon stockings were expensive, and it was necessary to mend them – a service advertised as a way of earning extra money at home.[68] Such repairing of knitted items has a long tradition, as is evident in examples from a patched Coptic sock dating from the second to fifth centuries (see pp.10–11) to a pair of late-eighteenth-century men's breeches cut and sewn from black silk machine-knitted fabric, showing evidence of mending and darning all round the seat and crotch area, consis-

tent with horse riding (see pp.68–9). Indeed, in the seventeenth century, when hand-knitted silk or worsted stockings were extremely expensive and highly prized, it was commonplace to unravel stockings from the toe and knit on new feet – a practice that continued into the nineteenth century, when Jane Gaugain's manual provided instructions for re-footing stockings.

Home dressmaking and its attendant skills in re-using and mending reached a peak of popularity in the mid-twentieth century, and darning of socks was a familiar sight in the home until the 1960s. In affluent twenty-first-century western society, however, fashion has become highly pluralistic and the speed of change has dramatically increased consumption and production. Clothing now is far cheaper relative to income than it was just decades ago, when clothes were still kept and maintained for many years, continuing the thriftiness of wartime 'Make Do and Mend'. Now clothes are seldom mended, and the manual skills needed to accomplish darning have been virtually lost from the home environment. However, in contemporary textile practice, for artists such as Annette Messager and Celia Pym, darning has become the subject of their work, calling attention to past feminine skills (plate 40).

Post-war domestic knitting

Since the industrialization of knitwear manufacture, hand-knitting has steadily declined, becoming a craft hobby, but one that periodically undergoes a popular revival. A knitting craze started before World War I and continuing beyond, for example, inspired many popular songs. Weldon's and Leach's patterns for 'Jazz' jumpers, stimulated by the new era of carefree decadence, aligned colour patterning, including Fair Isle knitting patterns, with the jazz sensibility. By the 1930s Fair Isle was elevated to high fashion, and knitting was everywhere in public.

Following the massive service knitting effort for World War II, women could once again turn their needles to making something stylish for themselves. Cinema stars had taken up the knitting needles as publicity for the war effort on both sides of the Atlantic, and

39 *Vogue's 23rd Knitting Book*, September 1943
Sandy Black collection
Under the strapline 'Accent texture with colour', this bold red two-piece outfit of blouse and skirt has been cleverly styled to give the appearance of a dress, making a versatile outfit, and simplifying the knitting. The whole design is worked in a moss stitch variation, taking 18 ounces (594 g) of wool. The skirt is made in two simple pieces.

the influence of the glamorous Hollywood 'sweater girls' of the 1940s gave knitwear a popular boost, imbuing the form-fitting knitted sweater with sexual overtones. Knitting embraced the smart military-inspired tailored silhouette of the 1940s and later Dior's 'New Look' with nipped-in waists over voluminous woven skirts.

The 1950s were the heyday of fashionable knitting, as the volume of patterns and fashion records show. Following the austerity years of war and rationing, tailored dressmaker styles were gradually simplified and streamlined into sleek suits and tops that skimmed the hips. New synthetic easy-care materials became available to the home knitter, and the increasing number of women's and general magazines aimed at homemaking for women (and do-it-yourself for men) promoted a wide range of yarns and patterns. The *Knitting Wool Review* of 1958, a trade publication, lists over 600 brands and trade names of knitting wools (including a small number of yarns in nylon and Orlon): 'The range of man-made fibres for hand-knitting has also increased and several new brands have been introduced to cater for those to whom ease of laundering is of prime importance (see pp.146–7).'[69]

Several comprehensive volumes of stitch patterns and techniques have documented the breadth of hand and domestic machine knitting in the post-war period, providing permanent records of stitches that may have previously been handed down only by word of mouth or dispersed in individual patterns. These include *A Treasury of Knitting Patterns, A Second Treasury of Knitting Patterns* and *Charted Knitting Patterns* by the American feminist writer Barbara Walker, who, unable to find such a volume for her own use, produced between 1968 and 1972 these encyclopaedic books recording 1500 stitch patterns gathered from all over the world including North and South America, Europe and 'the Orient'.[70] Americans Susannah E. Lewis and Julia Weissman produced a compilation of innovative applications of standard machine-knitting techniques in 1986.[71] Elizabeth Zimmerman, born in England in 1910 but working in the US, devised original techniques

and methods including her 'percentage method' for sizing, and encouraged knitting in the round on circular needles. Her *Knitting without Tears* was published in 1971 and *Knitting Around (or Knitting without a Licence)* in 1989. Montse Stanley was born in Spain, where some of the earliest knitted artefacts are found, and her *Knitter's Handbook* of practical knitting techniques and know-how, first produced in 1986, became a standard work. Her passion for the subject and her research stimulated much academic interest in the history of knitting, and she established an important

40 Celia Pym, *Sweater Companion*, 2009, Norway and Britain
Developing the theme of wartime 'Make Do and Mend', Celia Pym is inspired to create new artworks through darning and repairing, referencing past skill and time taken. This piece was made from a discarded sweater. The artist notes: 'I work with process and ways of recording activities. Now I darn and am looking for holes in people's clothes and the stories that accompany them; repairing these holes and returning the mended garments. It is a way to briefly make contact with strangers. I am interested in the spaces the body occupies, the tenderness of touch and the ways in which we go about day to day life.'

41 Knitting for the war effort, 1939, Britain
'Britain is now a nation of knitters' proclaimed an article in *Illustrated* magazine on 18 November 1939 which also illustrated this group of women knitting 'for home and country' in a village hall. The good humour became harder to keep up as the war went on, but the camaraderie provided support and left a strong social legacy of community.

Knitting patterns from the 1960s to the 1980s

In the aftermath of World War II, knitting's economical, homely and comforting image slowly transformed as the years of austerity gave way to a new mood of optimism. Black-and-white, small-sized leaflets were replaced by larger, full-colour formats. Models became less coy, smiling and posing directly to the camera. After the sweater's sojourn in the glamorous Hollywood spotlight in the late 1940s, home knitting settled down into classic designs, but these coexisted with increasing attention to fashion trends. By the 1960s, simple shapes, closely skimming the body, were giving way to quicker knitting in bulky yarns, which were key to capturing the waning attention of younger knitters, for whom knitting appeared old-fashioned. Easy-care synthetic yarns became fully established and yarns and designs were transformed by colour and bold pattern, with space-dyed random effects becoming a hit in the mid-1970s, promoted initially as 'Instant FairIsle' and much easier to knit than the real thing. By the early 1980s graphic designs and quirky textures of all kinds found their way onto sweaters. Knitwear was again highly fashionable and appeared at all levels of the market from monthly fashion magazines to newspapers, weekly women's magazines, and in media and retail promotions, in addition to the regular output of the knitting yarn spinners. The industry eventually polarized between 'designer' patterns focused on natural yarns, intricate stitchery and the craft of knitting, exemplified by Rowan Yarns, Patricia Roberts and Kaffe Fassett, and the diminished family knitting market, dominated by synthetics and blended yarns, where knitting for babies and children preserved the traditions of centuries. A selection of patterns spanning more than 30 years is shown here.

TOP ROW, LEFT TO RIGHT:
Sirdar pattern 7773, late 1950s/early 1960s, Sandy Black collection; **'Knit with P&B 1964'**, 1964, AAD: EPH/5/15; **Patons pattern 8000 Supersonics**, 'America's newest fashion rage', 1960s, Sandy Black collection; *Vogue Knitting No. 68*, 1966, Sandy Black collection; *Stitchcraft*, March 1976, AAD: EPH/24/396; *Modern Knitting for Machine Knitters*, April 1977, Sandy Black collection; *Woolworth Knitting Magazine*, 5, 1974, AAD: EPH/24/366; **Rowan Den-m-knit**, 1992, AAD: EPH/10/1

SECOND ROW, LEFT TO RIGHT:
Stitchcraft, November 1960, Sandy Black collection; *Modern Knitting for Machine Knitters*, June 1960, Sandy Black collection; *Vogue Knitting No. 63*, 1963, Sandy Black collection; **Wendy pattern 1161**, 1970s, Sandy Black collection; **Patons pattern 2191**, 1970s, Sandy Black collection; **Patons hand-knitting collection**, Spring/Summer 1987, AAD: EPH/10/4; **King Cole mohair pattern 210**, 1980s, AAD: EPH/24/253; **'Knitting: Fashion for All the Family'**, *My Weekly*, 1985, AAD: EPH /24/379; **'Sandy Black shield sweater'**, Rowan Yarns, 1987, Sandy Black collection

THIRD ROW, LEFT TO RIGHT:
Stitchcraft, March 1960, Sandy Black collection; **'Easy Knit Classics'**, *Woman's Own*, October 1965, AAD: EPH/24/402; **Twilley's Patchwork pattern C841**, c.1970s, Sandy Black collection; **Patons Fair Isle pattern 6185**, c.1970, AAD: EPH/24/100; **'Folklore fun for all the folks'**, *Sandra*, February 1988, AAD: EPH/24/385; *Woman's Weekly*, 6 December 1988, Sandy Black collection

FOURTH ROW, LEFT TO RIGHT:
Heavyknit ponchos pattern 606, 1960s, AAD: EPH/24/61; **Emu Fair Isle yoke sweater pattern 4225**, 1960s, Sandy Black collection; **'Knitting in Synthetics'**, Coats booklet no.125, 1960s, Sandy Black collection; **Robin Family sweaters no.1061**, c.1970, AAD: EPH/24/115; *Patricia Roberts Knitting Book*, 1981, Sandy Black collection; *Woman Knitting Special*, designs for Princess Diana, 1984, Sandy Black collection; *The Knitwear Revolution*, Suzy Menkes, 1983; *World of Knitting for Hand and Machine Knitters*, April 1986, Sandy Black collection

BOTTOM ROW, LEFT TO RIGHT:
'Man Made Magic', *Daily Mirror* supplement, 1960s, AAD: EPH/2/24; **Patons pattern 9602**, 1960s, Sandy Black collection; **Patons 'The Aran Look' booklet no. 161**, c.1970, AAD: EPH/24/338; **Jaeger design for machine knitting**, 1972, Sandy Black collection; **Patons Fashion Knits 84**, 1984, AAD: EPH/24/34; **'Calamity' pattern**, *Patricia Roberts Knitting Book*, 1981; **Georges Picaud 'Anyone for Flowers?'**, Sandy Black pattern, 1981, Sandy Black collection; **'Fair Isle Fun' pattern**, *Sandy Black Original Knits*, 1982, V&A: T.65–1999

42 **The Beano**, 10 April 1982
Published at a time when hand-knitting was highly fashionable and visible (and Dennis the Menace striped jumpers were popular), this children's comic uses knitting to characterize 'the softies'.

43 **The Liverpool Look**, Patons & Baldwins pattern, early 1960s
Sandy Black collection
An example of the 'trickle-down' effect of popular styles to the home-knitting market, this pattern is for a collarless jacket inspired by the signature style created by Pierre Cardin for The Beatles, it is knitted in a 'continental stocking stitch' using twisted stitches for a firm fabric.

The Liverpool Look 1445–6[D]

P&B
PATONS · BEEHIVE

knitting collection, the Knitting Reference Library, now housed at the University of Southampton.[72] A visually rich volume of creative stitch techniques, *The Art of Knitting* by French textile lecturer Françoise Tellier-Loumagne uses photographic observation of the natural and man-made world as inspiration, encouraging readers to invent their own fabrics based on general principles and structures.[73]

The regular publication of single knitting pattern leaflets continued to reflect both everyday garments – school jumpers, baby- and children's wear, classic adults' sweaters – and contemporary fashions. Home-knitting yarns became heavier and patterns quicker to knit as social priorities changed through the 1960s and into the 1970s, culminating in super-thick yarns knitted on size 000 needles. Compared to the intricate stitchery and fine gauge of nineteenth-century knitting and the tailored patterns of the 1940s, hand-knitting had become far less skilful.

Meanwhile, the production of detailed instructions and patterns increasingly became a necessity for the majority of knitters in the West, as word-of-mouth traditions skipped generations and everyday knitting of essentials was replaced with knitting for pleasure, family gifts and fashion. Modern knitters in Britain and the United States appear to be the most dependent on written instructions, compared with other knitting traditions. In Continental Europe or Japan, for example, instructions are often much less detailed and rely on the confidence and skill of the knitter to be able to create garments from brief stitch instructions and a diagram, as in some of the earliest pattern manuals.

Over the 1960s, fashion diversified: younger, sharper, more playful fashions developed on the one hand, and hippie-inspired slouchy anti-fashions emerged on the other. As mass-produced clothing became more fashionable and desirable to those who associated knitting with austerity, home-knitting began to appear outdated. By the late 1960s, hand-knitting was likely to be ridiculed as old fashioned, and associated only with grannies and maiden aunts in the stereotypes of cartoonists and the media.

Not all was lost. The 1960s and 1970s young fashion revolution was echoed in home-knitting family patterns, with leaflets featuring, for example, the 'Beatles style'. Individual designers such as Mary Quant, Marion Foale and Sally Tuffin were commissioned to produce designs to inspire knitters (plate 45). Even so, by the late 1970s knitting was generally considered simply utilitarian and unfashionable.

The growth of a new wave of 'designer knitters' in the 1970s and early 1980s, however, positioned knitting at the heart of fashion once more. One outcome of the rise of synthetics and mass-produced clothing during the 1970s was a countermovement towards craft activities. Small-scale designer businesses emerged, particularly in Britain, which again produced knitwear by cottage-industry methods, calling on the hand-knitting skills passed down from previous generations (and more recent machine-knitting knowledge). Their hand-knitting patterns were featured in both the general women's weeklies – which had grown in number – and monthly fashion magazines such as *Honey* (launched in 1959) and the American *Cosmopolitan* (launched in the UK in 1972). The British version of French magazine *Elle* published a pattern almost every month, from its first issue in November 1985 until July 1993, by designers including Comme des Garçons, Joseph Tricot and Edina Ronay among many others (see p.130). Throughout the 1980s many designer pattern books were published in response to hand-knitwear's popularity in fashion, following the lead of Patricia Roberts, whose pattern books from the late 1970s created a high-fashion look for hand-knitting (see p.173). One key publication of this knitting boom was *Wild Knitting* – a compendium of designs from 25 designers published in 1979, which, with its irreverent approach to knitting, captured a new Zeitgeist (plate 44). Knitting may have remained an object for satire but it was undoubtedly both popular and fashionable.

But by the late 1980s, the relaxed look of hand-knitting had again fallen from favour, as fashion eschewed soft, knitted silhouettes for 'power dressing'. Fashion-led home knitting went into serious decline, returning

to the basics of children's clothes and babywear. Domestic machine knitting, however, which had gained in popularity in the 1950s and again in the 1970s, continued to thrive through local knitting clubs and groups where technical knowledge and patterns were enthusiastically shared.

When the tide turned against home knitting, one publication bucked the trend. *Vogue Knitting* had continued until the late 1960s and, after a twenty-year hiatus, was re-launched in 1982 as *Vogue Knitting International*, but published in the United States rather than

44 *Wild Knitting* (cover), 1979, London
NAL 43.P.79
This pioneering compendium of inventive and humourous designs from 25 contributors features colourful and imaginative knitwear in a wide range of materials, including sweaters, socks, dressing-up glamour, scarves, ties, jewellery and accessories such as knitted cigarettes. Sandy Black contributed two designs including an armadillo wrap.

JAEGER DESIGN FOR MACHINE KNITTING

45 Jaeger Design for Machine Knitting,
Sally Tuffin design, 1972
Sandy Black collection
This upbeat machine-knitted top is worked in rainbow coloured chenille. Sally Tuffin made her name with Marion Foale for the label Foale and Tuffin – part of the influential new wave of young British fashion designers in the late 1970s. The magazine *Harpers and Queen* featured this design and readers wrote in for the pattern.

46 Teatime in The Gingerbread House, 2007, Britain
This project of knitting a life-size house, furniture and garden was instigated by Alison Murray from Devon and was achieved with the help of over 500 knitters from around the UK and as far away as Portugal and Spain. It has been exhibited in many locations worldwide and raises money for charities along the way, demonstrating the community power that can be mobilized through knitting.

in Britain. It continues to be published at the time of writing.[74] Most of the traditional weekly women's magazines such as *Woman* and *Woman's Own* have now changed their format to, or been replaced by, celebrity titles.

Contemporary community knitting

In the United States in the 1980s, Ann Macdonald, researching her book on knitting, received responses from hundreds of knitters across the country to the question of why people (overwhelmingly women) knitted in the late-twentieth century:

> to save money – 'I wasn't about to pay $350 for a sweater I could make for $30!'
> to calm nerves
> to make gifts
> to earn money (usually a pittance)
> to help others – 'Our church group knits caps for children bald from chemotherapy'
> to keep busy and/or out of trouble – 'My strict Quaker mother figured if we knit we'd keep out of mischief'
> to be sociable – 'Our weekly Knit-Wits group of eight was formed twenty-two years ago, and we're like sisters.'
> to be creative
> to pursue the puritan work ethic – 'Knitting is such a relief from tension for me, but I'd have too much guilt if I just did nothing. This way I can both relax and *produce*.'[75]

The answers to her question about why more women knit than men included many stereotypes: 'Men are too restless to sit still…They're afraid of being called sissies…They don't really think about their clothes.'

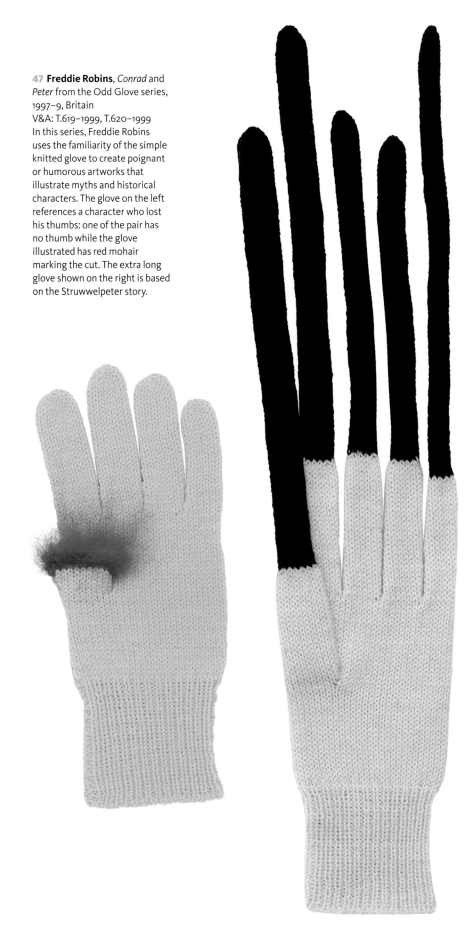

47 **Freddie Robins**, *Conrad* and *Peter* from the Odd Glove series, 1997–9, Britain
V&A: T.619–1999, T.620–1999
In this series, Freddie Robins uses the familiarity of the simple knitted glove to create poignant or humorous artworks that illustrate myths and historical characters. The glove on the left references a character who lost his thumbs: one of the pair has no thumb while the glove illustrated has red mohair marking the cut. The extra long glove shown on the right is based on the Struwwelpeter story.

Some changes in the role of men were also recognized, however – caring for children, doing the laundry and housework – which it was felt might lead to an increase in the number of men learning to knit.

At the beginning of the twenty-first century, the emphasis is on the social aspect of hand-knitting for pleasure. Hand-knitting has been rediscovered by a new generation of aficionados for whom knitting was not a familiar activity in the home, but rather something fun and creative with fast and tangible results from minimal equipment. It has captured the imagination while meeting unspoken needs for practical social engagement as an antidote to modern technological society. Paradoxically, new knitting groups meet in virtual spaces online as well as physically in public spaces to have fun, learn to knit, share their work and problems, and socialize.

The revival of knitting in both the United States and Britain has been notable for the increased involvement of men, especially in metropolitan areas. However, the roots of the American upsurge were planted in feminist soil. For example, the Stitch 'n' Bitch movement championed by Debbie Stoller when she was editor of feminist magazine *Bust* was a call to arms for women's solidarity. In contrast, the British 'guerrilla knitting' movement, started in 2000 by Rachael Matthews and Amy Plant with the Cast Off Knitting Club for Boys and Girls in London, was noted for its anarchic and eclectic modus operandi, finding social humour in staging alternative events in public spaces or those normally reserved for men.

Since the end of the twentieth century, knitting has increasingly been appropriated by artists as a political statement or for 'craftivism', especially in America, where it is often symbolically used in the art of gender politics.[76] Artists such as Lisa Ann Auerbach, Freddie Robins and Mark Newport subvert the traditions of the knitted sweater and extend them to the whole body, displaying great craft skill in the process (plate 46). A new genre of guerrilla public art, known as 'yarn bombing' or 'knit graffiti', has recently emerged, in which public objects such as statues, trees or buildings are 'tagged' with brightly coloured knitting and crochet and

48 **Craft Rocks** at the V&A, London, March 2004
The first 'Craft Rocks' event, organized in collaboration with Cast Off Knitting Club and UK Handknitting, saw many people having fun trying out knitting for the first time.

49 **Knitorama**, Rachael Matthews (London, 2005)
Sandy Black collection
Rachael Matthews founded Cast Off Knitting Club in London in 2000, pioneering the new wave of social knitting groups, famous for knitting in public places including the London Underground. This is one of the first of a new genre of knitting pattern books created with a large dose of irony and fun.

a large dash of humour. Knitting in public places has been regularly performed as an ironic and mildly subversive activity.

Group participation, inclusive attitudes and a sense of pride in making something by hand have rewarded a generation who had never previously learnt to knit. Recent interest in handcrafted objects for interior and decorative use has stimulated experimentation with tradition and created new applications for knitting in idiosyncratic and tactile furnishings. Charity knitting forms a major part of contemporary community knitting: people might combine to knit, for example, little scarves and hats for bottles of fruit juice in order to raise money for good causes, or join a major project such as 'Knit a River' (2006), which mobilized knitters throughout the world to raise awareness of people without access to safe water. The staging of participatory knitting events has also burgeoned, such as 'Craft Rocks' at the V&A (2004), which saw the museum filled with women and men learning to knit and make things (plate 48); the 'Knitted Wedding' (2005), a ceremony devised by Cast Off Knitting Club and held in a London art gallery, with knitters from across the UK and beyond

making knitted contributions to wedding outfits and food; and 'Knitting Nation' by Liz Collins (2006–8), a series of outdoor, large-scale machine-knitting performance events in Providence, Rhode Island, addressing issues such as gender politics. Such activities have stimulated a new wave of exhibitions, including *Knit 2 Together*, a travelling exhibition organized by the British Crafts Council in 2005, and *Radical Lace and Subversive Knitting* at the Museum of Arts and Design in New York (2007). It has also seen the publication of several tongue-in-cheek design-led knitting books, such as Rachael Matthews's *Knitorama* (2005)

(plate 49) and Mandy Moore and Leanne Prain's *Yarn Bombing* (2009).

Knitting humour continues unabated in the media, used with great irony and affection in advertising and retail promotion, where time-honoured stereotypes (such as the ill-fitting Christmas gift knitted by a well-meaning elderly female relative) are continually repeated. Appealing to a young audience of 'creatives', one internet email service ran a campaign showing a young man knitting with the slogan 'the new busy'. In its updated forms, the cultural heritage of knitting continues to run as a deep vein through society.

50 **Amy Twigger Holroyd**, 'Stitch Hacked', 2010, Britain
Amy Twigger Holroyd has developed a personal artistic practice she calls 'stitch hacking', i.e. subverting and customizing a commercially produced piece of plain or patterned knitwear. By carefully and laboriously reversing stitches she has reproduced the garment's label details including the logo in full textured detail. A subtle example of consumer customization and craftivism.

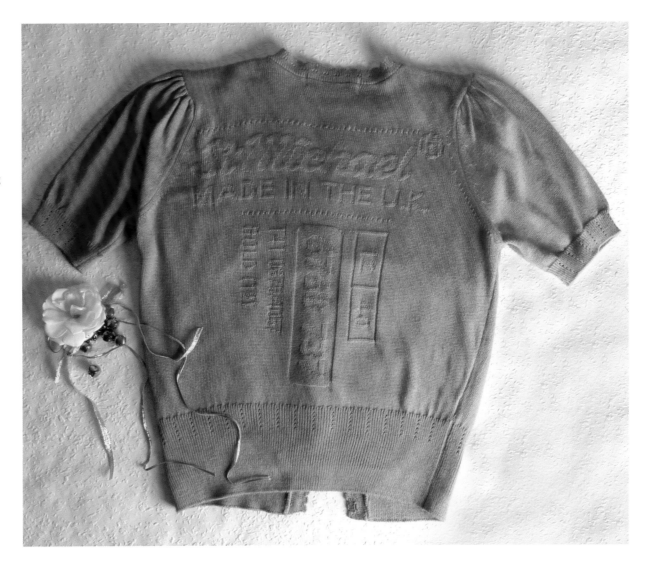

Classics to Couture:
Fashion Knitwear from 1900 to Now

Now in the trams and the buses they sits,
And they knits, knits, knits, knits,
Knits, knits, knits.
They buys the wool at
A guinea per pound,
And they gets a lot of little holes
And puts the wool around.
For all the girls are
Busy knitting jumpers,
Busy knitting jumpers all day long.

Can't you hear the jumper girls
Singing 'first two plain
And then two purl'.
Knit one, slip one,
Make a stitch and drop one,
Leave the needles on the chair.
So that Pa, with the hump's
Got to do the jumpers jump,
Singing 'jumpers, jumpers,
Jumpers everywhere.'

ROBERT WESTON AND BERT LEE, 'The Jumper Song', 1939

Rib sweater, photographed by John French for *Daily Express*, 6 September 1954
V&A: AAD 1979/9 JF2691
John French reflected the optimistic mood of the 1950s in his now iconic fashion imagery. Here a classic ribbed crew-neck sweater, industrially made and usually a menswear item, is given the John French treatment, becoming a stylish but timeless piece when worn with a belt.

THIS CHAPTER CHARTS THE EVOLUTION OF fashion knitwear through the twentieth century, from classic Pringle cashmere sweaters to the pioneering work of Elsa Schiaparelli, Vivienne Westwood's punk, the quintessentially British designer knitwear fashions that blossomed in the 1970s and 1980s, and contemporary eclecticism, combining craft skills with advanced technology. The sweater is a key element in this story, with sweater styles providing a shorthand for the prevailing mores and movements of twentieth-century fashion, transforming from underwear to outerwear, from menswear to womenswear, occasionally becoming glamorous, and now accepted as a staple of the everyday wardrobe.

While much twentieth-century knitwear shows continuity with historical garments, it has also been a focus for fashion innovation, often inspired by technical fabric developments, such as Dupont's elastane fibre Lycra, which spawned stretch knitwear and bodywear. At the turn of the millennium, modern machinery could knit the most complex structures to achieve any type of knitted fabric, with new developments in seamless industrial technology taking knitwear construction forward in the twenty-first century.

The modern definition of a sweater, jersey or pullover denotes a garment that is donned over the head. It is functional, versatile and comfortable. It has its earliest antecedents in seventeenth-century jackets (see pp.31–4), often knitted in the round as tubes, then cut to form a front opening; collarless knitted garments with sleeves that are completely open at the front were later named cardigans.[1] The forerunner of modern knitted sweaters is the dark blue 'guernsey' or 'gansey' made in Guernsey since Elizabethan times, which became a universal item worn by men working at sea and was adopted as official naval uniform in 1892.[2] The thinner sweaters produced on Jersey made the island's name synonymous with both the garment itself and the fine woollen stockinette from which it was made. The widespread adoption of the sweater into the twentieth-century wardrobe also has antecedents in two key concerns in the second half of the nineteenth century:

hygiene and outdoor pursuits. As health and hygiene became increasingly important in all aspects of life – including sanitation, household design and dress – the concept of 'rational dress' was promoted by feminist intellectuals, emphasizing plain, functional clothing and influencing a move from restrictive, decorative, multi-layered clothes to more relaxed fashions with a simplified silhouette (plate 2). (The movement also advocated a type of trouser, named after American dress-reform campaigner Amelia Bloomer, which gave unprecedented freedom of movement, in addition to drawing attention to the previously disguised, hidden or even denied sexual regions of women's anatomy. These knickerbockers came to be known as 'rationals'.) As one proponent wrote: 'Our garments should be garments with a meaning and a purpose. We should never contradict nature's simple lines by false protuberances or exaggerations. To be beautiful, clothes should by

their shape express the figure underneath.'[3] Dr Gustav Jaeger's Sanitary Clothing System (see pp.71–2), which strongly endorsed woollen underwear and outerwear for men and women for health reasons, shared similar concerns and had many followers (plate 1).

At the same time, healthy outdoor pursuits became fashionable, and young men increasingly took up sporting activities. By the 1870s male undershirts or vests, manufactured from stockinette fabric in wool, cotton or wool blended with silk, were transformed into outerwear as sports shirts with round necks or collars (see pp.68–71). Known as jerseys, they were widely adopted by athletes – from cricketers and footballers to rowers and rugby players – who often used striped and colour-block patterns as identification.

The growing emancipation of women resulted in their increased participation in sports such as golf, tennis and, most radically, cycling. In the 1880s the

LADIES' JERSEYS, AUTUMN 1888.

3 L&R Morley trade catalogue, 1888, Britain

These ladies' jerseys are very different from the simple garments now bearing that name and worn at the time of this image by sportsmen and boys. They are typical of late Victorian and early Edwardian style with decorated bodices. They are here made from industrially knitted jersey fabric (also known as stockinette) closely contoured to the body using folds and pleats. Outfits such as these were popularized by Lillie Langtry several years earlier.

This dress is described on page 2—the jumper on page 8.

4 **Leach's Knitted Jumpers pattern booklet**, 1920s, Britain
Sandy Black collection
This booklet has patterns for smart designs featuring soft and loose silhouettes in wools, silk and cottons. It also features advertisements for the new artificial silk yarns.

author Kate Gielgud wrote about changes to the usual tennis attire of serge skirts and blouses with starched linen collars, stating that friends 'introduced us to stockinette jerseys, woollen and light, which left our necks free, though we were not allowed to roll up our sleeves'.[4] As outdoor and leisure pursuits grew in popularity, the close-fitting fisher gansey, exclusively working-men's attire until the late nineteenth century, was audaciously adopted by women, who were emulated by their servants.[5] In 1878, the Princess of Wales and her children were photographed on the royal yacht wearing jerseys, starting a fashion trend.[6] The next year *Sylvia's Home Journal* commented: 'To wear fishermen's jerseys is the latest freak of fashion for ladies. With very little contrivance they fit very closely to the figure and when it is good, they are not unbecoming.'[7] Other famous figures also played a part in the popularization of jersey material in general: the figure-hugging two-piece 'jersey costume', imparting a svelte silhouette, was given a great deal of publicity when worn by the socialite Lillie Langtry in 1879–80. The daughter of the Dean of Jersey, Langtry was also known as 'the Jersey Lily' – an epithet that created further cultural and linguistic links between place, fabric and garment.

From the beginning of the twentieth century, the hosiery companies gradually moved away from knitting underwear towards outerwear production. Pringle first listed men's and boy's sweaters in their summer hosiery list of 1899, at which stage these sports garments were still a hybrid of underwear and outerwear. As demand for fashionable knitwear grew, the hosiery companies transferred their techniques to manufacturing jumpers and cardigans for a more discerning clientele who appreciated comfort with style. For example, in 1928 the Czech firm Pasold, manufacturers of knitted underwear and childrenswear, developed the White Bear brand of men's sweaters and cardigans, which, as noted in a history of the company, represented 'a radical departure from our customary type of product but fitted well into our manufacturing set up'.[8] As machine manufacturing developed and became mainstream, knitted goods became cheaper and more widely available.

Hand-knitting patterns reflected the changes in fashions. In the second half of the nineteenth century these had largely concentrated on practical items and household needs. In response to increasing demand for fashionable knitting among the growing middle classes, who enjoyed new leisure pursuits such as motoring, the first mass-market knitting leaflets were published in the first decade of the twentieth century. Marjory Tillotson's designs for Baldwin's from 1908 to 1920 began to ally knitting with fashion and the move towards simpler, less constricting clothing (see pp.125–6).

Following the constraints of World War I's ubiquitous 'knitting for the boys' campaign, when only drab military regulation yarns and colours were allowed, the rapid spread of the sweater fashion to all classes was assisted by the publication of low-priced knitting booklets and patterns in the growing number of popular women's magazines and needlework journals (plate 4). These new knitting patterns and attractive yarns allowed women to make themselves fashionable clothes cheaply, while the move away from cumbersome multiple layers made way for the new fashions of Paul Poiret, Coco Chanel and the *garçonne* style of the 1920s and 1930s. It was the jazz age of F. Scott Fitzgerald's *The Great Gatsby*, and long, lean 'jazz jumpers' with bold, colourful patterns (both home-made from patterns and shop-bought) helped to define the straight boyish silhouette or 'flapper' style (see p.102). The Fair Isle sweater fitted perfectly with this aesthetic (which almost camouflaged the human form), the contours of the body being draped with no more than a loose hip sash for emphasis (see p.110).

As the *garçonne* style and loose draped clothing became fashionable in the 1920s, the newly named rayon – originally known as 'artificial silk' or 'art silk' – became widely available, imparting a seductive shine and fluidity to garments at a more economical price than silk. The long rayon sweater formed a key part of the new sinuous look, the weight of the yarn giving a long-line silhouette to tunics and jumpers as they fell languorously from the shoulders. Rayon yarns were soon taken up by knitwear and hosiery manufacturers and proved popular while at the same time inspiring home-knitting patterns. A hand-tailored coat from the 1920s, made of cream wool and rayon, shows how the new shiny texture was employed as a contrast in an all-over jacquard pattern, inspired by Art Deco (plates 5 and 6). Warp-knitted fabric in rayon also provided a firm, smooth substitute for overprinting colourful 'jazz' patterns (V&A: T.309–1965).

During the 1920s and 1930s, key designers and personalities influenced the inclusion of the sweater in fashionable dress. When Edward, Prince of Wales, wore a hand-knitted Fair Isle sweater to play golf in 1922, it sparked a trend for the multicoloured style, which was advertised as a jumper and worn by both men and women in the increasingly emancipated 1920s. Coco Chanel's instinct for fashionable but relaxed clothing for herself spurred her to adapt everyday knitted woollen jersey, still most commonly seen in men's underwear, to create cardigan jackets, sweaters and skirts with soft silhouettes (plate 7). This was the start of 'sweater dressing' as knitted fabric was propelled into the foreground as a staple of fashionable outerwear.[9] Chanel worked with the French fabric manufacturer Rodier to develop a quality of wool jersey that would achieve the exact drape that she required, and went on to appropriate other items of men's clothing for women's fashion, including the cricket sweater, creating new classics on the way. The Chanel label still regularly features knitwear made by English, Scottish and Italian companies.

In the late 1920s, Elsa Schiaparelli adapted the distinctive surface and colour qualities of Armenian vernacular hand-knitting to create imaginative *trompe l'oeil* sweaters that entranced high society (see p.91). Her unusual designs, featuring a bow, a scarf, a handkerchief tied round the neck and even a skeleton inspired by African imagery, were instant fashion successes, elevating a humble handmade garment to new heights of fashion. The bow sweater held by the Victoria and Albert Museum, knitted around 1927, was donated by Schiaparelli herself following Cecil Beaton's pioneering exhibition *Fashion: An Anthology* in 1971.

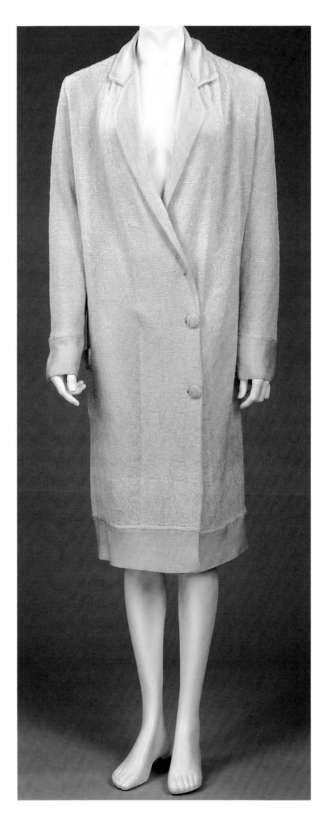

5 and **6 Art Deco coat and detail**, 1920s, France
V&A: T.15–1971
This tailored coat is hand-sewn and finished with bound seams, but the fabric is knitted by machine in double jacquard with a geometric design in wool and rayon. The edgings are made from double-knit fabric in rayon.

7 Coco Chanel with Lady Abdy,
May 1929
Chanel was the embodiment
of her own fashion philosophy
of relaxed and comfortable but
smart clothing. Here she wears
a version of her classic three-
piece suit consisting of cardigan
jacket, pullover and skirt, in
striped and patterned jersey
fabric specially created for her
collections. Her companion's
outfit features a similar
relaxed silhouette in
textured jersey fabric.

**8 Marilyn Monroe
wearing a sweater**, 1954
Marilyn Monroe in a typically
voluptuous publicity pose.
She regularly wore knitted
sweaters as part of her image,
both off- and on-screen –
as she did, for example, in
Let's Make Love (1960).

By the 1930s the basic sweater – round or V-neck with long or short, raglan or set-in sleeves – had taken its place firmly in both the feminine and masculine wardrobe. Its popularity overtook the knitted cardigan-jackets or 'sports coats' worn for golfing, motoring or walking that were based on the popular, masculine, country style of the Norfolk jacket. Golfing sweaters became a standard for casual wear, including the archetypal argyle-patterned diamond design, produced in cashmere or wool (see p.87). This classic sweater has often been revisited by designers: a 'deconstructed' version by Ritva (designed by Richard Smith and Mike Ross) in the 1970s was made as a signed art edition of 250 (V&A: T.17–2000: see pp.176–8). Knitwear fitted the bill for a casual but smart look, and the innovation of matching jumper and cardigan sets for women emerged as the classic 'twinset', which Pringle claim to have invented in 1937, and which is continually updated for contemporary fashion. In 1936, the writer Heinz Edgar Kiewe – also owner of Art Needlework Industries in Oxford, a shop that sold knitting patterns and needlework supplies until 1986 – discovered a sweater in a Dublin craftworker's shop that he went on to mythologize and promote as the Aran sweater. This twentieth-century commercial invention featured exaggerated textural relief patterns such as raised cables, honeycomb effects and bobbles, always knitted in natural cream or off-white.[10]

As the classics became established, the stage was set for more stylish knitwear. With the burgeoning of the film industry in the 1930s and 1940s, Hollywood stars became the new fashion trendsetters. The glamorous styles and provocative publicity images of such archetypal Hollywood 'sweater girls' as Lana Turner and Dorothy Lamour gave the basic sweater a new allure, simultaneously revealing and concealing a woman's contours, enhanced by sculpted shaping from padded bras worn underneath (plate 8). It was a look all women could aspire to, and it could be achieved with no more than a few balls of wool and a knitting pattern. The yarn companies excelled themselves in reflecting this glamour in the patterns published throughout the period. Hand-knitting patterns for twinsets, sweaters and cardigans became a key feature of such weekly women's magazines as *Woman's Weekly*, *Woman's Own* and *Woman*. Hand-knitting was so ubiquitous in the 1930s that, by the time the austerity of World War II took hold, women were able to clothe themselves and their families in practical but stylish clothes, working from the wealth of patterns and advice available in magazines, books and knitting-yarn-company leaflets (see pp.126–31). In 1939, a nationwide 'jumper craze' inspired popular songs such as 'The Jumper Song'.

Rationing of both clothes and wool in World War II served only to increase the number of knitters, to improve their resourcefulness and ingenuity and to confirm their perception of knitwear as fashionable clothing (see pp.138–41). As a result, the 1950s were the heyday of the sweater, whether home-knitted or ready-made, whether practical – for everyday wear or outdoor sports – or highly decorative and designed to be voluptuous. Evening sweaters had scooped or sweetheart necklines and were decorated with sequins or embroidery. Worn with a full skirt, these provided both the home knitter and the more affluent shopper with a touch of fashionable 'New Look' style.

To appeal to the growing middle classes and overseas markets, especially the United States, where the distinctive 'British' style was appreciated, Scottish companies such as Pringle and Ballantyne began to produce all-over beaded cardigans and highly intricate pictorial cashmere knitwear with designs of flowers or animals, utilizing the original handframe technique of intarsia (an expensive craft-based technique similar to tapestry weaving).

These classics have continued throughout the twentieth century to be part of the luxury knitwear repertoire, and are still produced in small quantities by Pringle, Ballantyne, N. Peal and others. For example, in the mid-1990s designers Clements Ribeiro, working with Scottish manufacturer Ballantyne, revitalized and re-coloured the cashmere sweater for a younger, more fashion-conscious market by using retro intarsia designs (plate 9). The traditional hand intarsia technique has, however, now largely been replaced by modern automatic machinery.

9 Clements Ribeiro intarsia sweater by Ballantyne, Autumn/Winter 2004 Ballantyne (now under Italian ownership) originated in Hawick, Scotland, in 1820 and established a reputation for exclusive knitwear patterned with intricate intarsia pictorial designs, building on the classic diamond argyle introduced in the 1930s. Sporting themes such as polo players vie with more feminine floral designs for complexity of detail. Many fashion designers such as Clements Ribeiro and Louise Goldin have worked with the company. The intarsia technique became part of the Ballantyne brand heritage, requiring painstaking manual work to follow hand-drawn charts on a hand-operated knitting frame in the same manner as early fancy stocking knitting.

10 Ralph Lauren, Fair Isle pullover, mid-1980s, USA V&A: T.421:2–2000 A casual style inspired by Scottish country weekends, worn as part of an outfit with a blue-striped white cotton shirt with frilled neck and cuffs and brown checked wool skirt. The machine-knitted Fair Isle design is pastels on natural ground, with a simplified OXO pattern in bands that repeat throughout the design, unlike true Fair Isle work.

In the United States, the 'Britishness' of classic knitwear was sufficient to sustain the reincarnation of the sweater in the quintessentially British style adopted by Ralph Lauren in the 1980s. He has said, 'My things, I've always thought, were in a lot of ways more English than the English.'[11] The distinctive knitwear for this label, including 'Fair Isle' slipovers and simple styles such as the cable sweater (plate 10), was originally designed and produced by designer Nancy Vale using outworkers in the UK.

11 **Juliette Greco**, 1965
Juliette Greco adopted the style of black polo-neck sweater, black trousers and black eyeliner from the early 1950s. Her association with jazz musician Miles Davis cemented the 'cool' credentials of this look.

As the decades passed, fashion became more pluralistic, with several styles coexisting across different social groups. The mid-1950s marked the beginning of a feminine style of refined casual dressing influenced by the United States, including simple sweaters in lively colours, worn with full skirts or ski-pants. Similarly, Italian style was a strong influence, particularly on menswear and casual wear in the 1960s, with a fine white or black polo-neck sweater replacing the shirt worn under a suit. Where the Italian knitwear industry had largely supplied the domestic market, the 1960s saw the country become the epicentre of knitwear design and quality production, based on its unique artisanal approach, with clusters of small local companies supporting and complementing each other. As part of Italy's post-war reconstruction in the 1950s, much of the skills base of people who had worked in older trades – such as the making of straw hats – was transferred into the operation of new knitting machinery.

The sweater as a key symbolic statement, almost an anti-fashion, is exemplified by the now iconic black polo-neck sweater, permanently associated with the avant-garde intellectuals, writers and poets of the French Left Bank, 'cool' jazz musicians such as Miles Davis, the 'beatniks' of the 1950s and 1960s and pop musicians such as The Beatles (plate 11). These associations were applied in fashion in the 1960s by innovators such as Pierre Cardin, André Courrèges and Mary Quant. The close-fitting, black, ribbed polo-neck sweater provided the perfect foil for their bold sleeveless tunics worn with opaque tights, highlighting a 'space age' silhouette. A similar anti-establishment statement was also achieved over the same period with the polo-neck's stylistic antithesis; the beatniks' 'sloppy Joe' sweater, hand-knitted in mohair or thick wool, signifying the new freedom of the teenager and the birth of youth and student culture.

In everyday wear, hand-knitting patterns at this time created parallel interpretations of the fashions of their day for the home knitter, emerging with their own special styles and designs. Throughout the 1950s and 1960s hand-knitting yarns became chunkier, in con-

12 Man's lumber jacket,
knitted from Mary Maxim
'Hoedown' pattern, late
1950s–early 1960s, USA
Sandy Black collection
Colourful motifs make a striking
design, to be worn with a smile. Based
on the original Cowichan heavyweight
patterned knitting, Mary Maxim
patterns could be knitted with either
raglan or set-in sleeves (as shown
here). The shawl collar and front edges
are in garter stitch with a metal zip.

trast to classic fine-gauge machine-made knitwear. Novelty patterns reflected the desire to knit garments as fast as possible: for example, Patons Supersonic knits used several yarns at once on thick needles. In the 1950s a fashion developed for thick-knitted jackets for men, incorporating bold motifs and imagery inspired by the great Canadian outdoors and sports, building on the Cowichan knitting tradition.[12] The label Mary Maxim provided patterns for these with graphic layouts using large-scale charts (plates 12 and 13). (In the first decade of the twenty-first-century, retro fashions returned to the thick, hand-knitted, patterned jackets

of Mary Maxim, but this time most were lined with fleece fabric for a practical hybrid garment with the look of hand-knitting.) By the 1960s, a new sophisticated lifestyle incorporated aspirational leisure travel, and the thick ski sweater, worn with sleek trousers, became part of this look.

In the context of high fashion, knitwear's place was assured: according to Jackie Modlinger, writing in the *Guardian* newspaper in the 1970s, 'In Paris every named designer now includes knitwear in his collection.'[13] The fashion designer Sonia Rykiel, for example, created her business in France in 1968, based on co-ordinated separates with the sweater as a key item – sexy, short, long, tight or voluminous, striped, graphic or feminine – earning the title 'Queen of Knits' in the 1970s from American *Women's Wear Daily*. Her elegant but informal ensembles often have unconventional elements such as mixed-weight yarns – fine wool with

heavy mohair – or extended frills outlining the silhouette, as in a blue outfit of co-ordinated knitted jacket, skirt and sweater (V&A: T.379: 1.2.3–2000). Rykiel's formidable presence in stylish knit dressing and fashion over 40 years was celebrated in 2008 with an exhibition at the Musée des Arts Décoratifs in Paris, and a fashion show for which 30 designers – including Jean Paul Gaultier, Martin Margiela and Alber Elbaz for Lanvin – produced tribute outfits. Intarsia-knitted graphic imagery, witty words, frills and bows grace the knitwear in collections now designed by Rykiel's daughter Natalie, which regularly return to the formula of timeless stripes (plate 14).

In the same era, other Italian and French designer labels, notably Missoni and Japanese émigrés Kansai (Yamamoto) and Kenzo (Takada), began to apply new colour, texture and proportion to high-fashion sweater dressing, often exploiting jacquard technology to the

13 Mary Maxim patterns, late 1950s (patterns patented in Canada in 1957), Canada
Sandy Black collection
This series of graphical knitting patterns included jackets for men and boys featuring outdoor themes and motifs, from bear hunting to oil drilling. Similar jackets became highly fashionable again in the first decade of the twenty-first century.

14 Sonia Rykiel, knitwear from Spring/Summer 2001
This typical collection of striped knitwear pieces played to the Rykiel signature, with impact created by multiple models in a rainbow of black and colour-striped T-shirt dresses, adorned with sequined lettering and rosettes at the hip.

full. Italian label Krizia, established in 1964, started the knitwear line 'Krizia Maglia' in 1967, and created a popular range of animal-inspired intarsia hand- and machine-knitted sweaters which became the signature of each successive Krizia collection. At the more commercial end of the fashion spectrum, the Italian firm Benetton focused on colour and universal appeal for its low-priced knitwear, which,from its beginnings in 1966 made basic knitwear accessible, fashionable and fun through the use of global branding and retailing.

In Britain, meanwhile, in arguably the most radical youth anti-fashion movement to date, punk style in the 1970s, included the ravaged-looking, open-mesh, roughly knitted sweater, more holes than yarn, in a warped updating of the original 'string vest' (plate 15). Thirty years later this style has reappeared in fashion, rediscovered by a raft of new designers. In the late 1970s and 1980s, a youth style known as 'casuals' adopted the knitted polo shirt or fine-gauge sweater with a sports-brand logo for a smart look, akin to the mods of the 1960s, but this time paraded on the football stands.

15 **Vivienne Westwood**, punk sweater, 1970s, Britain
V&A: T.94–2002
Loosely knitted in cotton and mohair yarns, these 'punk' sweaters made a huge impact in their time, and continue to be influential.

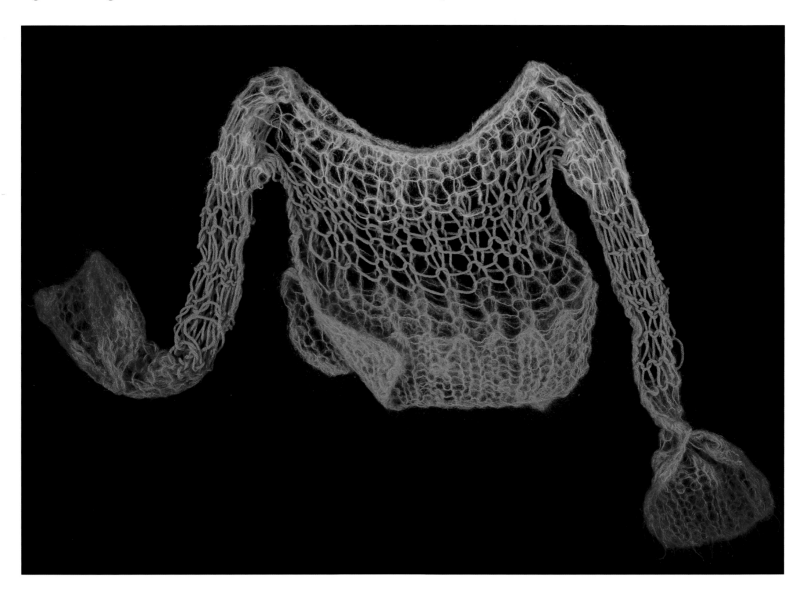

Continuing the move towards chunky yarns and looser fit seen in ski-inspired Nordic designs and new synthetic yarns, during the 1980s fashionable hand-knitted sweaters grew very large indeed. Based on a squared-off boxy shape, usually with drop shoulders and virtually no shapings, the emphasis was on colour and stitch patterning, using the sweater as a canvas to make a statement (V&A: T.210A–1990: see p.130, plate 29). It was a period when an oversized sweater became almost a dress: the sweater dress was invented and could be worn just with leggings. Radical British fashion designers incorporated knitwear and knitted fabrics as part of their palette of effects. BodyMap, for example, developed their own designs in stretch jersey and created a fresh approach, including fun hand-knitted pieces (plate 17). Vivienne Westwood turned to found materials and continued to challenge all norms with cut-up methods of making clothes, as seen in her 'Punkature' (Spring/Summer 1983), 'Hypnos' (Spring/Summer 1984) and 'Witches' (Autumn/Winter 1984) collections, which incorporated sweaters and skirts cut and pieced together from other old garments. Later in her career, Westwood reworked traditional sweaters in stripes and argyle-pattern variations, working with the 200-year-old knitwear manufacturer John Smedley (plate 16).

16 Vivienne Westwood,
'Buffalo' and 'Savages'
collections, 1982
Photographed by Carrie
Branovan for *The Face*, May 1987
The multicoloured oversized
wool sweater with bold jacquard
patterning from the 'Buffalo'
collection (see V&A: T.72–1992)
made a statement as part of a
multi-patterned and layered
collection. It is worn here with a
skirt, shorts and shoes from the
'Savages' collection
(Spring/Summer 1982).

17 BodyMap,
Autumn/Winter 1984
Photographed by Albert Watson
for *Vogue*, August 1984
BodyMap were one of the
pioneers of new wave body-
conscious dressing in the 1980s,
using newly developed stretch-
jersey jacquard fabrics. This
outfit is totally knitted, with
several different fabric weights:
a cotton jacquard cardigan
knitted on domestic machinery;
jersey jacquard frilled shorts; a
printed jersey T-shirt; extended-
finger gloves and striped jersey
leggings, all worn with tights
and socks by Mary Quant.

18 *Patricia Roberts Collection*,
1983
Patricia Roberts, a knitting
designer and editor, pioneered a
new stylish and fashion-conscious
approach to hand-knitting, with
the look and feel of an upmarket
fashion editorial. She published
several volumes of designs,
such as this one featuring a
patchwork Romany sweater
in shades of grey (see V&A:
T.486–1985).

19 Patricia Roberts, fruit
machine sweater, 1978
This sweater was a typical
example of the fresh approach
Patricia Roberts brought to
home-knitting patterns. Such
work heralded a new wave of
designer knitwear, combining
intricate stitch structures, use of
colour and mixed yarns. In this
particular textural design, there
are echoes of patterns from the
1940s, reinvented through
colour and humour (see V&A:
T.208–1985).

The British designer knitwear revolution

After the home knitting boom of the 1950s and the youthful fashion revolution of the 1960s, handmade knitwear declined as part of fashion, although a small number of designers, such as Mary Quant and Foale and Tuffin, produced patterns for the home-knitting market in collaboration with brands such as Jaeger (see pp.150–51, plate 45). Otherwise, hand-knitting remained largely separate from high fashion until a new generation of art-school-educated or self-taught designers took up the knitting needles or domestic knitting machine with a fresh approach and set new fashion trends in knitwear, based especially on the sweater.

Pioneered by British designers such as Patricia Roberts, Artwork and Martin Kidman for Joseph, the wider craft revival of the 1970s and 1980s transformed the hand-knitted sweater (at that time seen as dowdy) by incorporating multiple colours, intricate stitches and pictorial, graphic or rococo textural patterning. Old stitches and styles were brought together in new combinations and proportions, with added fashion flair. Traditional patterns were revived, re-coloured and brought into the fashionable arena by a wave of designer knitters, each with a special handwriting and signature style. The typical homely Aran sweater, for example, featuring relief patterns of cable and raised stitches in thick cream yarn, recaptured the imagination of these designers, perhaps seduced by its romantic mythology (see p.165). Likewise, several British designer knitters and commercial companies revisited the traditional Fair Isle sweater for machine production during the 1970s and 1980s. Sweater dressing became the height of fashion, with export markets in the United States, Japan and Europe.

Known as a 'knitter's knitter', Patricia Roberts was at the forefront of the new wave of British designer

knitwear. Her most well-known designs incorporate highly intricate stitchwork in multiple colours combined with often humorous or childlike graphic imagery and three-dimensional effects (plates 18 and 19).

The sweaters designed by Artwork in the 1980s epitomize the fashion for hand-knitwear. Artwork were the husband-and-wife team Jane Foster and Patrick Gottelier, who began their business in 1977, combining fashion-design and industrial-design backgrounds respectively. Artwork became known for graphic-patterned knitwear, often inspired by Foster's research in the V&A collections. Working mainly with outworkers in Cornwall and elsewhere, they made up the hand-knitted garment pieces centrally. They started with heavy-gauge sweaters, and later introduced their own woven separates to complement the knits, also experimenting with industrial production. Artwork also revived beaded knitting (albeit at a greatly enlarged scale) in their Egyptian collection of Summer 1981 and used printing on intarsia knitting in several designs. From 1984, they were particularly known for designs in denim yarn, sometimes complete with studs and fringing, creating a second line, George Trowark, for these non-seasonal, more traditional clothes (see p.109, plate 7). Although there were periods when production was transferred to east Asia, this proved unsatisfactory, and Artwork returned to its hand-knitting roots. One of the most longstanding of the British designer knitwear companies, Artwork continued to operate until 2008.

From the late 1970s through much of the 1980s hand-knitted and decorative sweaters featured regularly in the monthly fashion glossy magazines as high fashion news. Fashion editors commissioned patterns from knitwear designers, and patterns often appeared in fashion titles *Honey, Elle, Over 21* and *Company* as well as such traditional women's weeklies as *Woman* and *Homes and Gardens* (see p.150). *Vogue Knitting* relaunched in the United States in 1982, and many designers published their own pattern books, including Patricia Roberts, Kaffe Fassett and Sasha Kagan. A few, including this author, also developed their own

20 Artwork, knitwear, Spring/Summer 1985
Artwork developed their own personal style of printed imagery on handmade knitwear, reviving a practice generally applied to factory-made knitting, as in printed cardigans from the 1950s. For their Spring/Summer 1985 collection, the theme was classical Greece. Prints were designed by Timney Fowler and printed by Roger Riley. Here, thick cotton yarn is intarsia-knitted in abstract blue-and-white blocks and over-printed in a black design, worn with matching printed cotton skirts. A similar intarsia-knit top in white and a blue intarsia cardigan (detail) are held in the V&A (V&A: T.162–1985; T.162A–1985).

exclusive yarns and knitting kits (V&A: T.65–1999), often working with Rowan Yarns, who produced regular designer pattern booklets. The move into knitting yarns and kits by designers enabled the fashion-conscious to make their own knitwear or turn to the skills of previous generations of hand-knitters – usually their grandmothers, their mothers being of a generation that had not seen knitting as a useful skill, preferring shop-bought clothing.

One lasting legacy of the avalanche of designer knitwear and publications at this time was their undoubted influence on the major knitting-machine manufacturers, leading to the production of more complex mass-produced sweaters. The development of electronic stitch control with programmable pattern preparation replaced slow mechanical systems, opening up a whole new world of patterning and stitch possibilities.

21 Susan Duckworth
Cabbage Rose sweater,
Autumn/Winter 1985, Britain
V&A: T.311–1985
Hand-knitted in wool and mohair, this sweater is typical of Susan Duckworth's painterly approach to colour and pattern, skilfully merging many colours. Her creative process starts from picking up 'two needles and a bag of yarn'. She is particularly known for her intricate floral designs in natural yarns. Handmade knitwear with bold motifs was in great demand in the mid 1980s, especially in the United States.

The new technological capability was in turn fed by a ready-made series of colourful design inspirations and found steady demand from a waiting mass market that could not afford the prices of artisan-made cottage-industry production. (The high price of materials and labour meant that a typical designer sweater would retail at around £300 in a London store).[14] The influence of the British designer knitters and major Italian companies such as Missoni and Krizia can be seen in the output of more mass-market labels such as Inwear, French Connection, Les Copains and Sportmax, which were able to translate intricate designs into simplified but visually striking jacquard production, at the same time pushing the boundaries of colour and yarns to include textured qualities such as chenille. More recently, as sophisticated and versatile technology has become commonplace, elaborate knitwear designs have become the norm, demonstrated in labels such as Crea Concept, She's So and Catherine André.

Despite the technological advances that the British designer knitters inspired, manual craftwork was key to the success of their innovative designs. Whether their pieces were made by hand on needles or on domestic machines, hand manipulation could achieve highly individual relief and pattern effects that were beyond the capabilities of the industrial production then available in the UK. So although the British designer knitters operated on many levels, from 'knitters who are fashion designers with knitting as part of their total style' to 'those who are first and foremost knitters'[15], most of their businesses were based on the skills of home knitters, knitting by hand or domestic knitting machine, who could still be found in sufficient numbers and with the appropriate level of skill to make cottage-industry production viable. Unless companies could be persuaded to experiment with new ideas and yarns, knitwear businesses such as Ritva and Crochetta were reliant on such cottage-industry production.

At the extreme end of such hand craftsmanship, some designers made one-off creations.[16] Two unique art pieces designed and knitted by Claire Boyd in 1973 are testament to the innovation that could be achieved

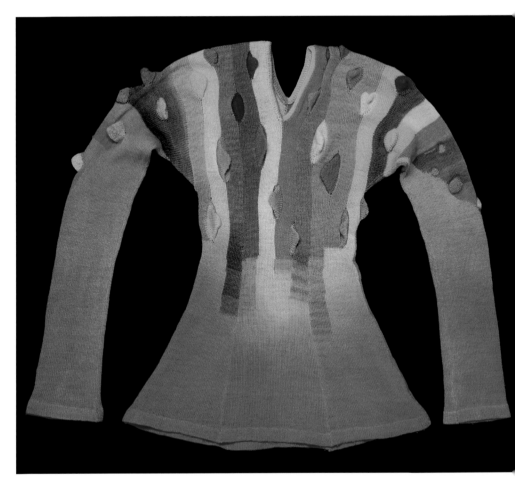

by an individual designer-maker. Boyd studied woven textiles at Camberwell College of Arts in London, then, as a postgraduate at the Royal College of Art (RCA), worked with stretch-knit fabrics that respond to the movement of the wearer with sound. At Angela Flowers Gallery in London in 1973 she exhibited a series of sweaters that focused on changing shapes and silhouettes, coming to life in movement on the body (plates 22 and 23).

A fresh approach to the artist's convention of limited editions was applied to sweaters by the company Ritva, which was started in 1966 by husband-and-wife team Ritva and Mike Ross and continued as a label until around 1980. Ritva Ross was an ex-model and had studied graphic design; Mike Ross studied fine art at the RCA and had opened a shop in Chelsea selling imported

22 Claire Boyd, 'Animal Skin' sweater, 1973, Britain
V&A: T.336–1985
Claire Boyd's sweater is striking in both colour and design. It is intricately crafted in pure wool that was first dyed in narrow strips to grade the colour dark to light, then reknitted into the garment and finally overdyed in sections to shade colour over the entire sweater in different directions. The colour moves across the pieces in unexpected ways to give a chaotic but also naturalistic effect.

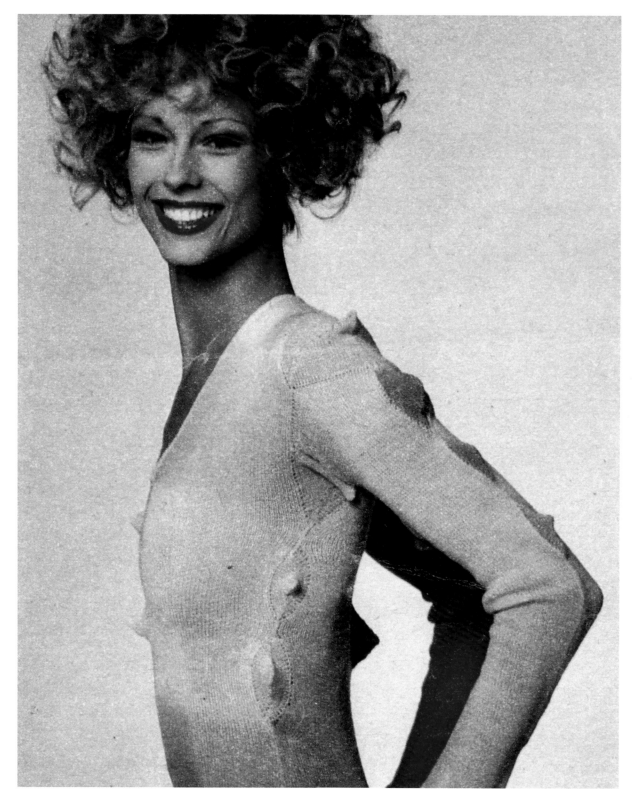

23 Claire Boyd, 'Animal Skin' sweater, 1973,
Photographed by
Clive Arrowsmith for the
Observer Magazine, 13 May 1973
One of the unique sweaters
exhibited at the Angela Flowers
gallery, this was knitted on a
simple domestic knitting
machine and created a new and
changing silhouette when worn.
Art sweaters such as this were
highly unusual and innovative in
the early 1970s and could only be
made using manual methods.
Each sweater variation had a
different colouring and pattern
of 'blips' and some featured
patterns of holes.

memorabilia. Like most of the small designer-knitwear businesses, the company started from a small studio, using outworkers and able to operate an almost bespoke service by adapting a small sample range. Ritva designed co-ordinated knitted ensembles, often with crochet squares, from knitted minidresses to jumpsuits and two-piece outfits with sideways-knitted flared panelled skirts, in tune with the lean silhouette and changing youthful fashions of the time. The designs caught the eye of the press and were featured in *Nova* and *Life* and sold to fashionable boutiques in London and the United States. One press cutting ran 'Together knits add up to total warmth and cat-like comfort'.[17]

Mike Ross started a men's knitwear line, 'The Ritva Man' in 1970, inspired by the 'Homerun' sweater he made for his American baseball team, but the Ritva brand is best known for its innovative 'Artist Collection' sweaters, designed in collaboration with several contemporary artists including David Hockney, Allen Jones, Elisabeth Frink and Patrick Hughes. Featuring colour-block knitting with applied embroideries of the artists' designs and a signed edition number, the sweaters sold for $96, and each was framed so it could also be hung on the wall. The sweaters are in simply shaped V-neck or round-neck styles with set-in sleeves, in acrylic yarn knitted on single-bed domestic machines with flat-knitted hems or 'mock rib' edgings (plate 24). The company was highly influenced by Pop Art and also created graphic knits of fish, lips and cartoon-like characters. Ritva also undertook sweater commissions for musicians, including the Rolling Stones (*Goat's Head Soup* tour) and Paul McCartney's Wings, and for films such as *A Clockwork Orange* and *The Shining*. The *Clockwork Orange* sweater featured the film's well-known face logo and was made in an edition of 150 for sale in Los Angeles at $110.

These Ritva sweaters epitomize an adventurous era of do-it-yourself production in which the concept was paramount but the production quality was, of necessity, fairly basic. Neither of the owners was trained as a fashion or textiles specialist: rather, they were dependent on limited resources and individuals making in their own

24 **Ritva,** artist sweaters, early 1970s, Britain
V&A: CIRC.182–1972, CIRC.185–1972, CIRC.183–1972
These are three of Ritva's artist sweaters with appliqué embroideries: one by Allen Jones (target with leg), one by David Hockney (American scene Pico Boulevard), and one by Elisabeth Frink (eagle). The edition number can clearly be seen embroidered on the back neck, together with the plethora of labels used. In November 1971, *Nova* magazine said: 'Wear it. Frame it. Hang it on the wall. Take it down. Leave it to someone in your will. Sell it for more than you bought it. For it's a very special sweater – a wearable work of art.'

homes. The plethora of labels put into the back of each of the 'Artist Collection' sweaters was a testament to the handcraft-based small-scale production of such British knitwear companies, which were influential beyond their own means and reach and collectively made a new movement in fashion knitwear.

While the boom in designer knitwear in the 1970s and 1980s was uniquely British, the popularity of knitwear at this time saw high fashion designers elsewhere making design statements through themed catwalk shows in which exotic decorative influences were paramount. Jean Paul Gaultier's collections of this period exhibited strong cross-cultural themes, from the seventeenth century to the 1940s and modern dystopias, incorporating at the same time overt sexuality and cross-dressing. Gaultier's Autumn/Winter 1985 catwalk paraded men as peacocks, dressed in ornately patterned multicoloured jacquard pieces directly inspired by Persian carpets (plate 25), whereas the women were dressed in pinstriped suits. Another typical

25 **Jean Paul Gaultier,**
carpet coat, Autumn/Winter 1985, Italy
This 'carpet coat' is unisex. Created from a large rectangular piece of knitted wool jacquard with no front shapings or fastenings and straight slits for armholes, it is knitted as an exact copy of a carpet in a non-repeating all-over design (a considerable technical feat), finished with cream cotton tassel edging on the cuffs. Seen in a contemporary fashion shot, it looks as if the model has just plucked the carpet from the floor. (see V&A: T.377–1985).

26 Jean Paul Gaultier, bronze-lurex and black-lycra-jersey outfit, 1987, Italy
V&A: T.147: 1+2–2000
This zipped bomber jacket and high-waisted zipped skirt in textured jersey fabric is the result of Gaultier's collaboration with Courtaulds Courtelle Yarns, who sponsored an annual student knitting competition for 10 years. Students designed jersey fabrics, inspired by a briefing from Gaultier, who created pieces especially for them. This 'blister' fabric outfit (81% acrylic, 19% polyamide) was promoted in *Vogue* in October 1987.

Contemporary Socks and Stockings

Socks are fun! Echoing the daringly patterned women's stockings of the end of the nineteenth century, novelty designs abound in contemporary knitted socks. Whereas colour patterns such as argyles and tartans were the preserve of sporting wear when they first began to adorn men's socks in the mid-nineteenth century, they can now be found on clothes for all occasions. No longer discreetly hidden but playfully revealed, socks and stockings are designed as conversation pieces in a vast array of detailed graphic patterns, the fine gauge providing a blank canvas limited only by imagination.

Since the late 1970s, technology has played a major part in this new flowering of designs for socks, with specialist computer-controlled hosiery machines offering a versatility in handling patterning that is not always found in larger-scale knitting manufacture. Much innovation has been pioneered in Japan, where socks are on regular display indoors because shoes are routinely removed. Examples such as a range of intricately shaped socks featuring an inventive use of the sock heel – sometimes worked in layers – show a typical technical exuberance. Noted for their intricate and attractive designs, the Japanese company Antipast creates a wide range of hosiery, including long stockings and socks in a multitude of creative and colourful designs with floral, geometric and narrative themes. Recalling the heyday of handframe knitting, such hosiery maintains the development of the industry while cherishing past traditions.

LEFT TO RIGHT:
Haat by Makiko Minagawa, Issey Miyake Inc., stocking with geometric overall design, made without heel in nylon, heat set to shape, 2007, Japan
Sandy Black collection

Antipast, four stockings with floral and geometric designs, in wool with nylon patterning, 2007–9, Japan
Sandy Black collection

Bernhard Wilhelm, two stockings in cotton and nylon with all-over design of names, 2000, Austria
Sandy Black collection

Four socks for children in cotton with nylon and elastane, featuring 3D crocodile, dragon, duck and Father Christmas designs, sold in Sock Shop, mid-1990s, Britain
Sandy Black collection

Three ankle socks in transparent and brightly coloured nylon, striped and with fish motifs, sold in a US drugstore for $1 a pair, late 1990s, China
Sandy Black collection

example of Gaultier fashion in knitwear is a highly textured bronze-lurex and black-jersey outfit of zipped bomber jacket and high-waisted zipped skirt (plate 26).

As fashions changed and power dressing took over the female wardrobe, after the mid-1980s handmade knitwear saw a sharp decline. With the expansion of hard-edged high fashion by international brands, designer knitwear companies were challenged by increasing competition from the commercial knitwear that their own innovations had helped to improve, and many closed. Those that survived had to be distinctive, often focusing on intricate design and colouring in high-value yarns such as cashmere. Designer labels such as Shirin Guild and Shi Cashmere (see p.195) catered for an older, moneyed clientele, utilizing volume in over-sized and often coarse-gauge machine-made knitwear to create sophistication and minimalism for a wide range of body shapes. Guild (of Iranian background) created signature sweaters inspired by the drape of clothing from non-western cultures and made from unusual materials such as bamboo, linen and paper yarns as well as cotton and wool (e.g. V&A: T.891–2000). Although the sweater styles were simple, the proportions were unusual: a sweater might be a metre wide, consequently having a deep V-neck and tiny sleeves, or might double as a dress, challenging UK producers to find machinery wide enough for the specification.

During the 1990s the craft of hand-knitting was revitalized by high fashion designers such as Yohji Yamamoto and Julien MacDonald to create couture knitwear with elaborate handwork. Others used both old and new technology side by side, notably influential Japanese designers Issey Miyake (in collaboration with textile engineer Dai Fujiwara; see pp.185–7) and Yoshiki Hishinuma, embracing knitting technology to experiment with new forms for knitwear working in three dimensions (plate 59).

Coming into the present day, high-street knitwear has been transformed by technological advances, now routinely including a high level of design and many unsung design details, such as darts knitted in to create three-dimensional shaping (plate 27). Complex trim-

27 Peter Pilotto, sports-inspired knitwear, Spring/Summer 2011, Britain
A highly engineered knitted outfit by London-based designers Peter Pilotto shows a sophisticated used of fashioned knitted structure for visual impact. The vertical two-colour effects are achieved through the plating technique, used in a ribbed structure that has been shaped with knitted 'darts' to move around the contours of the body, emphasizing knees and breasts. The horizontal banding is formed by alternating stripes of stocking stitch and reverse stocking stitch to create textural ridges, with integrated pockets.

28 Crea Concept, knitted dress and wrap, Autumn/Winter 2009, France
The Crea Concept brand, created in 1999, specializes in layered knits and wovens, sometimes combined in one garment. Precise technical detailing for contemporary knitwear dressing creates fluid draped silhouettes and heavier, textural surface.

mings, edgings, braids and fine patterns are all evident, as are more ambitious shapes, including drape-fronted cardigans. The sweater, however, remains integral to fashion and a basic garment capable of infinite variation. Today, classic machine-made sweaters in cashmere are regularly included in high-fashion collections (for example Prada, Armani, Balenciaga), while the oversized hand-knitted sweater has periodically created dramatic couture in the hands of Dior, John Galliano, Alexander McQueen and Yohji Yamamoto.

As knitwear technology and design continue to evolve, each leading the other at different times, variations on the sweater and the cardigan remain staple garments in the fashionable wardrobe. Hand-knitted, heavy-gauge and fine-gauge knitwear items exist side by side, and designers have taken advantage of the fact that (almost) any design can now be manufactured industrially to extend the repertoire to more innovative designs. As one journalist put it, 'Knitwear has become interesting' (plate 28).[18]

Fashion and knitwear exhibitions

The effect of the 'designer knitwear' revolution in making knitting a major trend in the UK and elsewhere in the 1980s was reflected in the advent at this time of the first specialist knitwear exhibitions, hitherto virtually unknown. Two exhibitions are notable: the British Craft Centre's *The Knitwear Revue* (1983) and *Knitting: A Common Art* (1986–7), a Crafts Council touring exhibition. In the following decade, three further knitting exhibitions took place across Europe: *Mil Anys de Disseny en Punt*, a major historical survey at the Textile Museum of Terrassa (1997); and, both exhibiting contemporary work, *Slipstitch: New Concepts in Knitting* at the Dutch Textile Museum, Tilburg (2000), and *The New Knitting*, an exhibition that toured the UK and Ireland in 1997 and 2000–2.[19] Knitting as an arts practice became popular at the turn of the new millennium, inspiring two institutional exhibitions: the Crafts Council's *Knit 2 Together* (2005) and *Radical Lace and Subversive Knitting* at the Museum of Modern Art in New York (2007). Each of these exhibitions imparted a different emphasis in its positioning of knitting and knitwear between craft, history, community, art and fashion.

The V&A made its own key contributions to early exhibitions of knitting with *Knit One, Purl One* (1987), a seminal exhibition of historical and contemporary knitwear from the collections, and a Kaffe Fassett exhibition in 1988. In 1994, the controversial exhibition *Street Style: From Sidewalk to Catwalk, 1940 to Tomorrow* broke accepted V&A policies by displaying non-elite clothing worn by subcultural groups, demonstrating the different ways in which dress is performed in a diverse society with conflicting values, needs and interests. One exhibit was a completely knitted outfit comprising a patchwork of recycled Aran sweaters, designed and made in 1993 by Sarah Ratty of Conscious Earthwear (plate 29). Interestingly, the pieces exhibited have both a history and a prognosis: they are on the cusp between anti-fashion and fashion. They attracted the attention of the more adventurous fashion press, including *i-D*, where Ratty is quoted as saying, 'The '90s is a time to use *everything* we do, including how we dress, to express our fundamental beliefs, hopes and dreams, affirming to others the vision of the world we want.'[20]

Radical fashion and radical knitwear

The V&A exhibition *Radical Fashion* (2001) brought together eleven of the most internationally acclaimed fashion innovators from the UK (Alexander McQueen, Hussein Chalayan, Vivienne Westwood), France (Azzedine Alaïa, Jean Paul Gaultier), Japan (Issey Miyake, Comme des Garçons, Junya Watanabe, Yohji Yamamoto), Belgium (Maison Martin Margiela) and the United States (Helmut Lang) in an exposition of ideas that have changed the direction of fashion and challenged established perceptions. All have developed innovations in knit construction as part of their total concepts. The significant presence of knitwear within the exhibition is especially notable, as each designer curated his or her own section and art-directed the photo essays in the accompanying book. Much has been written about these designers and their overarching influence through the latter part of the twentieth

29 **Sarah Ratty for Conscious Earthwear**, Aran outfit, 1994
Photographed by Ben Gold
Sarah Ratty's outfit comprises a poncho-style skirt, tank top, coat and hat. Ratty's eco-philosophy led her to recycle used materials, and these designs, although roughly made by interlocking old Aran sweaters otherwise destined for landfill (obtained from Oxfam), had a raw and fresh fashion appeal. Ratty continues to champion eco fashion through her Ciel 'eco-philosophy' fashion collection. See V&A: T.670/671/672–1993 and T.207–1994.

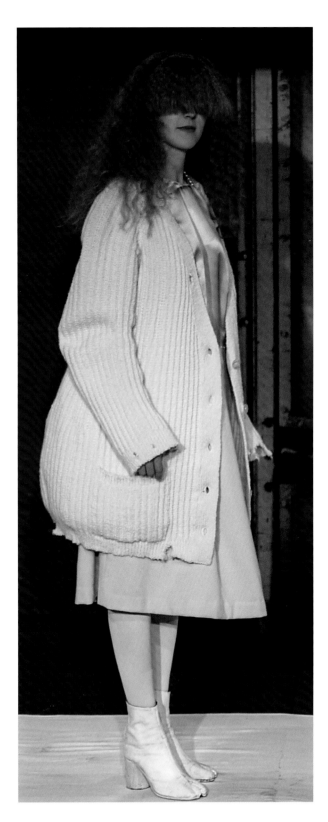

30 **Maison Martin Margiela**, Autumn/Winter 2000
This oversized cardigan was moulded to a large tailor's dummy (notional 'size 78'). The effect is bizarre but wearable – a new way of playing with scale. The collection also included sweaters that had been similarly designed.

century, and the *Radical Fashion* exhibition provides a forum in which to consider their work.[21]

Maison Martin Margiela showed pieces from Autumn/Winter 2000 and Spring/Summer 2001 in presentations that took as their motif the notion of scale and the mechanics of grading in pattern-cutting. All pieces were based on a notional 'size 78' in which the proportions of patterns had been scaled up by 148% from the norm of size 42, inspired by an 'outsize' tailor's dummy from the 1930s. The results were applied to overcoats and dresses, jeans, jackets and heavy- and fine-gauge knitwear such as classic men's cardigans. A regular feature of Margiela collections, knitwear is always subverted to be out of true, with, for example apparently torn-off edgings (carefully engineered), or mismatched or asymmetrical construction. The over-sized sweater shown at *Radical Fashion* was moulded to the form of the large dummy so that 'when worn by a woman of smaller size it will retain its enlarged form'.[22] The results were surprisingly wearable, but with the offbeat proportions and effects for which Margiela is renowned (plate 30). The theme of scale has recurred throughout Margiela's work and was explored, for example, in the collection 'A Doll's Wardrobe' (Spring/Summer 1995), inspired by clothes for Barbie dolls.

From his considerable 30-year oeuvre, Issey Miyake chose to display the revolutionary knitted garments from his A-POC ('A Piece Of Cloth') line – a manufacturing innovation launched in 1999 in collaboration with textile engineer Dai Fujiwara. This involved the production of industrial warp-knitted tubular fabric with an embedded layout of garments that could be released by cutting and needed no finishing processes – complete knitwear direct from the machinery. In 2001, the A-POC concept was very much in its early stages, having had three presentations: 'Just Before' (Spring/Summer 1998), 'King and Queen' (Spring/Summer 1999) and the plain 'Baguette' designs (Spring/Summer 2000) (plates 31 and 32). Much had still to be explored and progressed with this new and experimental form of computer-based total creation, from yarn to garment. However, the 'Baguette' designs, the first really commercial A-POC

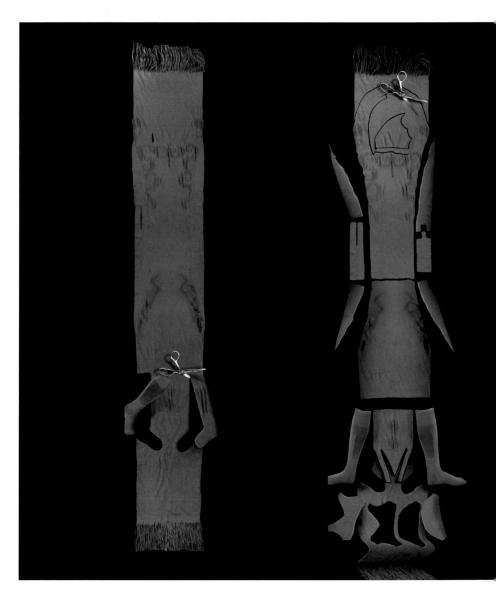

line, so called because they could be cut anywhere, are still in production.

In addition to the all-in-one warp knits that began the project, the A-POC concept was soon applied to radical woven textiles. These are similarly engineered in the weaving, creating new forms that utilize double cloth so that embedded pattern and garment pieces are ready to cut out and assemble.

After more than a decade, the engineering and design development of A-POC has matured, although new design concepts are continually evolving. Known as 'A-POC Inside', it is now integrated into all Miyake lines, including 'Pleats Please'. From 2008 to 2011, Dai Fujiwara had total charge of the Issey Miyake creative direction – the ultimate accolade to his ingenuity and creativity (plates 31 and 32).

Jean Paul Gaultier's installation for *Radical Fashion* comprised a number of dresses drawn from his 1997–2000 couture collections. These included a highly intricate hand-knitted woollen ball gown worn over a

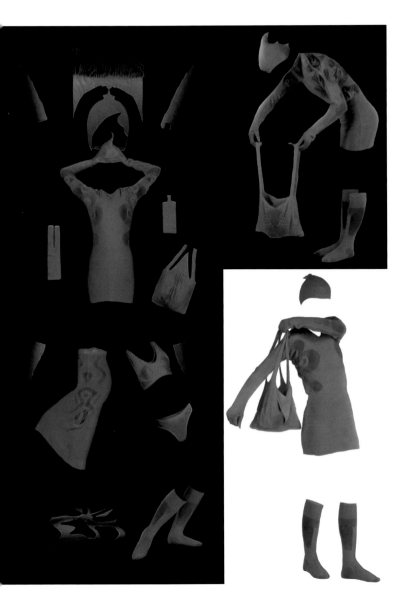

**31 Issey Miyake with Dai
Fujiwara**, A-POC 'Queen'
Collection, Spring/Summer 1999
Courtesy of Issey Miyake Inc.
A computer animation explains
step by step the revolutionary
concept of A-POC, the scissors
releasing a series of garments
from what looks like a flat piece
of cloth, worn by an invisible
model. The cloth, made on
industrial machinery, is in fact a
flattened tubular-mesh, warp-
knitted fabric, strategically
joined along pattern lines
according to a computer
program that forms seamless
garments when cut away and
opened out.

net skirt. Worked seamlessly in knit and crochet, its
skilful construction could be appreciated in the round
– an opportunity not normally afforded by catwalk
presentation, photography or display cases. The three-
dimensional conception of this dress, with intricate
but homely stitches completely integrated with the
form, takes on a certain poignancy in combination
with the humble woollen material.[23] It is reminiscent
of the couture knitwear of the immediate post-war era
(see p.92), and the painstaking lace knitting of the

**32 Issey Miyake with Dai
Fujiwara**, A-POC 'Baguette'
Collection, Spring/Summer 2001
Courtesy of Issey Miyake Inc.
The plain but stretchy fabric –
cotton or wool with nylon and
elastane – creates comfortable
clothing. The outer fringes reveal
its warp-knitted one-step
manufacturing process, the result
of cutting out the pieces along
predetermined lines created as
part of the flat layout.

Shetland Islands (see pp.56–7), celebrating skills that have largely disappeared. Gaultier had designed similar, albeit simpler, dresses for Régine Chopinot's ballet *Le Défilé* in 1988, and he continues to use hand- and machine-made knitwear and printed jersey.

Azzedine Alaïa holds a major place in the history of fashion knitwear: his sculpting of the body in stretch-knitted fabrics and his revealing 'bandage' dresses made extraordinary use of the elastomeric fibre Lycra in knitted fabrics, creating groundbreaking, sexy, body-conscious silhouettes. One of the bandage dresses was shown in pride of place in *Radical Fashion* among other form-fitting couture dresses. Popular with celebrities and models such as Grace Jones and Naomi Campbell, these clothes captured the 1980s movement towards body-building exercise and influenced trends in stretch sportswear (plates 33 and 34). Alaïa used a particularly high proportion of Lycra (up to 30 per cent) to create the corset-like quality of his clothes, sculpting and accentuating the female form, with each couture piece 'built' and fitted to the individual. One example dating from 1985 and working with stretch-viscose double-jersey fabrics in a mosaic of multiple panels demonstrates Alaïa's consummate skill in the construction of tailored knitwear. In emerald green, it consists of a long-sleeved leotard or 'body' – a garment that fastens at the crotch for a lean, smooth silhouette – with a buttoned shirt-collar neckline and a matching pair of knitted high-waisted ski pants, worn with a belt (plate 34). The wearer's body is therefore fully covered yet simultaneously revealed in a second-skin outfit. The 'power' silhouette of the 1980s is imparted by the insertion of stiff shoulder pads. Alaïa continues to sculpt with knitted fabrics in his couture line.

Comme des Garçons' display in *Radical Fashion* focused on the 'Optical Shock' (Spring/Summer 2001) collection: lightweight Op Art-inspired printed red-and-white fabrics in polyester and cotton wrapped and shaped using contrast strips of camouflage fabrics. The V&A holds one of the seminal designs by the founder of the Comme des Garçons label, Rei Kawakubo: the so-

33 **Azzedine Alaïa**,
bronze body, 1985
Photographed by Peter
Lindbergh for *Vogue*,
December 1985
Vogue described Alaïa's body-
conscious clothes as 'part of
his ideal body plan: shoulders
strong, waists whittled, deeply
belted, jerseys sliced and
seamed to emphasize noble
proportion', enabling the
'goddess body to become a
distinct possibility'. The model
photographed wearing the
garment called a 'body' reflects
this aspirational ideal.

34 **Azzedine Alaïa**,
body detail, 1985
V&A: T.376/A–1985
The knitted body was a new,
sleek, all-in-one outerwear
garment, similar to the dancer's
fitted leotard. This example is
part of an outfit with matching
knitted ski pants. Two mock dart
lines are embedded in the
knitting through 'fully fashioned'
shaping, the movement of stitch
loops creating visible lines and
decorative holes.

called 'lace' sweater and skirt ensemble that formed part of her Winter 1982 collection (plate 35). Here, in contrast to the regularity of a machine-made garment, hand-knitting enabled the uneven placing of the holes. Kawakubo is famously quoted as saying, 'I like it when something is *off* – not perfect. Hand-weaving is the best way to achieve this. Since it isn't always possible, we loosen a screw of the machines here and there so they can't do exactly what they're supposed to.'[24] So significant was this raw, unfinished look that this and other collections (and those of Kawakubo's contemporary, Yohji Yamamoto) initially attracted opprobrium from the fashion press, who felt the clothes embodied a 'bag lady' or 'post-Hiroshima look'.[25]

In the Autumn/Winter 2002 catwalk show entitled 'Free Knitting', Kawakubo's entire collection was made from around 50 knitted fabrics, capitalizing on the malleability of knitting – the perfect medium to achieve her distorted silhouettes, which pulled coats and jackets right around the body. The classic sweater and cardigan figure regularly in many guises within the diffusion Comme Comme and Robe de Chambre ranges, using the signature vocabulary of layering one silhouette on top of another or juxtaposing and superimposing two contrasting fabrics, pattern pieces or garment layers.

'I'm not a couturier, I'm a cutter,' is the quote from Yohji Yamamoto that opens his visual essay in the *Radical Fashion* catalogue, although he has deliberately shown during couture week in Paris.[26] Among the dresses on display in his section of the exhibition was the spectacular oversized bridal outfit with hat held up by bearers that formed the finale of his Autumn/Winter 1998 fashion show.

Known for his enveloping and dramatic silhouettes, often enlivened by flashes of strong colour, Yamamoto is renowned for uncompromising but beautiful clothes, using masculine detailing and tailoring for the female form and often featuring bold graphic or floral imagery on his menswear. Occasionally, hand-knits appear on the catwalk in heavy-gauge coats or cardigans for both women and men. However, it is the Y's line that excels in terms of knitwear. Season after season, collections

35 Comme des Garçons, 'lace' sweater and skirt ensemble, Autumn/Winter 1982
V&A: T.167&A–1985
This entirely black outfit comprises a heavy-gauge (4 sts and 5 rows to 2.5 cm) woollen hand-knitted sweater, worn with a heavily gathered and layered cotton-jersey skirt with uneven horizontal pleating. The body panels have deliberate random holes, made by neatly casting off and casting on groups of stitches over the entire garment. Smaller holes are worked horizontally like oversized buttonholes, the larger ones gradually shaped diagonally over a number of rows. The sweater is made in two main V-shaped pieces, one over each shoulder, creating overlapping diagonal strips, with ribbed sleeves and welts sewn on. A separate diagonally shaped piece is attached at one side to the lower front to hang below the welt.

36 Yohji Yamamoto, ensemble from Y's collection, Spring/Summer 2004 Manipulation of traditional knitwear garment panels and shapes is a strong feature of the Y's range, which is handmade on a small scale using manual machinery. This range featured loosely fitting trousers made from cardigan panels, with sleeves for legs and an extra sleeve enabling multiple ways of wearing.

comprise asymmetrical sweaters, cardigans and gilets in Shetland or merino wool, perhaps with an elongated upper shoulder area to crumple and distort when worn, or mismatched seams that twist the lines. The Spring/Summer 2004 Y's collection included radically unconventional fine-knitted pieces constructed from multiple sweater and cardigan parts, enabling them to be worn in several ways – a Yohji Yamamoto signature (plate 36). Yohji Yamamoto's career and work over more than 30 years was celebrated in an exhibition at the V&A in 2011.

Junya Watanabe originally designed the Comme des Garçons Tricot line in Japan, then started working under his own name with Comme des Garçons in 1992, realizing his truly radical vision in knitwear as a regular part of his own collections. His exhibit for *Radical Fashion* typified his use of asymmetry and technical processes to achieve a geometry that appears impossible to wear. His section included the complex fabrications of the 'Techno Couture' collection (Autumn/Winter 2000), in which honeycombed puffballs of interconnected polyester chintz framed the body in the manner of an expanding paper toy or lantern.

Watanabe went on to create puffed-up 'Michelin Man' outfits and black-leather and gilt-chain outerwear pieces for Autumn/Winter 2009, complemented by spiral-strip knits in cardigans and tops, black mohair and gold-lurex jacquard-knit cardigans and pure gold-lurex cardigans and tops of a type not seen since the 1970s and 1980s. For the Autumn/Winter 2008 season, the geometry of the circle was perfectly realized in knit cardigans, sweaters and tunics by complex fashioning and unusual construction, playing with and subverting the standard offering in knitwear. Heavy dogstooth and checked tweed coats with multiple layers were perfectly imitated in black-and-white jacquard-knit fabrics, prompting a double-take to see whether they were knitted or woven.

In addition to being included in *Radical Fashion*, where she exhibited signature tartan outfits, Vivienne Westwood was subsequently accorded a major retrospective exhibition at the V&A in 2004. Because of the 'Britishness' of her inspiration, knitwear has played a greater role in Westwood's image than that of many other designers, from her first loose mohair sweaters to the regular reinvention of classic cashmere and argyle-patterned knitwear (made by John Smedley), as seen in the 'Harris Tweed' collection (Autumn/Winter 1987). Hand-knitting is a particular Westwood favourite, representing signature looks in several catwalk shows, in particular in the 1994 seasonal collections 'Café Society' and 'On Liberty'. She uses corsets and 'bum cushions' to accentuate completely hand-knitted outfits with eccentric, colourful and complex raised patterns. Westwood's stated 'favourite dress of all time', which she has worn regularly, is an intricate brown-wool hand-knit from 'On Liberty' in an undulating lace 'shale pattern' with flowers and leaves knitted in relief.[27] 'Storm in a Teacup' (Autumn/Winter 1996) included a bizarre (even by Westwood standards) hand-knitted dress in multicoloured yarns worked in the same shale pattern in stripes, incorporating heavily textural colourful novelty yarns. This skilful use of knit techniques contrasts with earlier punk pieces in which cheap stockinette fabric (used for cleaning cars) was roughly overlocked with heavy fleece fabric and re-purposed pinstripe gabardine to create instant skirts. The Vivienne Westwood collections continue to incorporate variations on classic industrial knits.

Jersey fabrics in daywear

Knitted jersey fabrics, first produced after the introduction of circular knitting machines in the early nineteenth century (see Timeline), are now found in all types of fashion, from everyday clothes to designer fashion and couture. In cotton or wool, knitted jersey is practical, comfortable and predictable in its behaviour; in silk or viscose it is fluid and highly malleable. Those couture designers whose creative method is to sculpt with fabric draped on the stand in three dimensions utilize fluid jersey fabrics as an expressive medium, especially for eveningwear.

Claude Montana's fishtail dress from 1985 (V&A: T.363–1989), for example, with its complex cut and many sculpted panels, epitomizes the characteristics of single jersey fabric, which is soft and drapes well. In contrast, double jersey has much more 'body', especially when made from wool, and can be precisely tailored and moulded. Classic 1990s designs from Yves Saint Laurent (V&A: T.311.1/2–1997) and Calvin Klein (V&A: T.243.1/2–1997) illustrate the tailored fit that can be achieved. It is these sculptural qualities of bonded wool double jersey that Pierre Cardin and Mary Quant were able to utilize in the 1960s in dresses and tunics that stood away from the body to create their own distinctive silhouettes (plate 38). In the same era, Biba designer Barbara Hulanicki used lightweight-wool double-jersey jacquard fabric extensively in outfits such as a leopard-patterned trouser suit from 1970 (plate 37). She also specialized in long, romantic jersey dresses with full gathered sleeves and near-circular skirts.

Synthetic double-jersey fabrics such as Crimplene – the brand name of a fabric made with Courtelle acrylic fibre – became widely available in the 1970s, and began to usurp wool for suits. Cardin went on to develop Cardine – his own synthetic jersey fabric, which he was able to mould into innovative three-dimensional shapes.

Casual sportswear and the body-conscious 1980s

During the fitness boom of the 1980s, cotton jersey found its place in everyday casual sportswear, particularly in the ubiquitous single-jersey T-shirt and fleecy-backed double-jersey sweatshirts. In the same way that Chanel had earlier adopted wool jersey (single and double), innovative designers such as Mary Quant and Katharine Hamnett turned to wool and cotton double jersey for sporty looks. Norma Kamali's skater-inspired outfit comprising full-skirted top and ribbed sweatpants captures a designer's interpretation of the Zeitgeist (V&A: T.311/A–1984).

The introduction of elastomeric Lycra into knitted jersey fabrics in the mid-1980s soon moved from exercise wear to mainstream fashion. The body-consciousness prevalent at this time is encapsulated in a complex patchwork body suit from 1990 by British designer Pam Hogg (V&A: T.149–1994), cut and sewn from many colours of stretch single jersey in polyester and cotton. A Lycra-jersey body suit by Issey Miyake from around the same time incorporates synthetic leather panels reminiscent of body armour (V&A: T.228–1992).

The cotton sweatshirt gained tremendous popularity in both men's and women's casualwear as a practical and cheap easy-care garment, usurped only in the late 1990s by the polyester 'fleece', constructed using a different technique of pile jersey knitting. The derivation of these pieces and their manufacture is evident from the fleecy lined woollen underwear worn in the eighteenth century by Thomas Coutts (see pp.69–70), showing both continuity and technical innovation over the centuries.

Since the late twentieth century, the term 'sportswear' has taken on a wider meaning, particularly in the United States, to embrace much more general casualwear, as distinguished from the increasingly technical active sportswear market. Knitted fabric continues to be a mainstay of contemporary sportswear and casual style, with many unnoticed technical features and functions creating new standards of design and technology.

Knitwear dressing

In Britain, knitwear development in the first half of the twentieth century tended to concentrate mainly, although not exclusively, on upper-body garments, worn as casual 'separates'. This changed, however, with the influence of developments in Europe. In France, Italy and Spain, from the 1960s, fashion designers such as Sonia Rykiel, Missoni, Kenzo, Laura Biagotti and Anna Molinari distinctively worked with a total knit silhouette, using knitwear as well as jersey fabrics for both body-conscious looks and enveloping draped outfits. As jersey enables simplified pattern cutting for softer tailoring, they used the cut-and-sew methods applied to woven fabric. To create constructed knitwear, garment pieces are either knitted to shape – 'fully fashioned' – or made as garment 'blanks' (unshaped garment-length fabrics) with integrated welts from which garment shapes are cut and overlocked together. In the United States, designers such as Bonnie Cashin and Donna Karan developed a wearable style utilizing both fashioned and draped knitting.

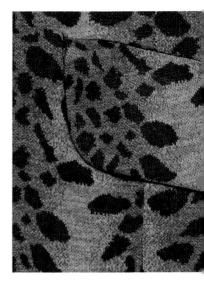

37 Barbara Hulanicki, Biba trouser suit, c.1970, Britain
V&A: T.36:1/2–1999
The narrow-legged, wide-bottomed trouser was a signature shape of Biba's innovative trouser suits, which were renowned for such decorative fabrics as flowered chintz or leopard-patterned wool jacquard, shown here. This photo of Barbara Hulanicki, designer and founder of Biba, wearing her leopard-patterned jersey jacket, was taken in the offices of the large Biba department store in Kensington, London, at the height of its success.

The fashion for layered knit dressing developed in the 1970s and early 1980s. As the *Observer* commented in an article entitled 'Piling it On', 'The fashion-watching woman is already well aware that she should be looking layered this winter.'[28] British designers Mary Farrin and Crochetta emerged in the early 1970s at the time of the fashion for maxi skirts, creating looks that covered the entire body in knitted fabric, many produced by cottage-industry methods on domestic knitting machines (plate 40). The volume and weight of fabric worn together at this time seems inconceivable in the early-twenty-first century, when centrally heated homes are the norm and climate change is raising ambient temperatures in the northern hemisphere.

The malleability of knitted fabric compared to woven is highly attractive to many designers, in whose hands and imagination knitwear occasionally takes on a more experimental form. Volume and drape become the leitmotif, rather than stretch for fit and comfort as in classic knitwear. Shi Cashmere, the label designed by Iranian Shayesteh (Shi) Nazemi and based in London since 1981, is known for its unconventional approach to knitwear, slicing expensive cashmere fabric lengths 2 metres wide into voluminous shapes swathed around the body. Trained as a fashion designer and not in knitwear, Nazemi nevertheless set up her own small knitwear factory in Scotland to produce her collections, having started by using knitters working at home. One critic wrote of the clothes in 2006: 'The radical simplicity of their architectural shapes is an addictive combination of the wildly luxurious and the abstemious.'[29] (plate 39)

The complexity of layers and patterns typical of layered knit dressing at this time can be seen particularly brilliantly in the knitwear created by Bill Gibb in collaboration with his artist friend Kaffe Fassett, who was later commissioned to design fabrics of exquisite colouring for the Missoni label. Fassett and Gibb met while Gibb was at the Royal College of Art in London from 1966 to 1968, and it was on a fabric-buying trip to Gibb's native Scotland that Fassett was inspired to knit by the colours of the Scottish wools from Holm Mill in Inverness. Gibb left the RCA before graduating to set up a Kensington boutique with three others; it lasted only briefly but set Gibb on the road to becoming the 'golden boy of British fashion'.[30] When Gibb gained a contract to design for wholesale label Baccarat, Fassett designed the knitted swatches while Gibb developed innovative styles and silhouettes that were radically different from the fashions and classic knitwear of the time.[31] Their first work together produced an award-winning collection of patchwork, tweeds and knits for Baccarat for Autumn/Winter 1970.

In 1972 Bill Gibb Ltd was formed, dressing fashion icons and celebrities of the 1970s – including Twiggy,

38 **Mary Quant**, pink dress, 1966 Photographed by David Montgomery for *Vogue*, April 1966
This typical Quant 'Ginger Group' dress, worn here by Twiggy, was made in bonded jersey fabric with wool face and nylon backing and cut in deceptively simple lines that evoked young girls' dresses, as did the Peter Pan collars and above-the-knee length. The dress is similar to V&A: T.86–1982 from 1966.

39 **Shi Cashmere**, cashmere outfit, 1984, Britain
This flame-red cashmere outfit consists of three unusually constructed and capacious pieces of knitwear: a draped crossover top with long sleeves, a folded 'harem' skirt and a large poncho. See V&A: T.46A&B–1989.

40 **Mary Farrin** modelling her own knitwear designs in a promotional photo shoot, 1974
This is an example of the maxi skirt fashionable in the early 1970s, machine knitted in a tweedy acrylic bouclé yarn.

Bianca Jagger and Elizabeth Taylor – in a modern-day couture practice, creating one-off extravagant gowns. This was a new wave in fashion, in which Gibb and his contemporaries, including Barbara Hulanicki and Ossie Clark, were inspired by the glamour and decadence of the 1920s and 1930s. A rich focus on fabrics and prints created voluminous skirts balanced with fitted waists or empire lines and an emphasis on movement and fun. In keeping with the post-hippy romantic mood, fabrics, embroideries and knitwear were specially commissioned, reflecting Gibb's love of historical and decorative imagery.

Unlike many of his contemporaries, and as a result of his close collaboration with Fassett, Bill Gibb made knitwear a major element of his work. This created the opportunity for a distinctive look to be developed in another medium in addition to the prints. Samples were knitted by Mildred Boulton using both hand-knit and domestic machine-knit techniques. A typical ensemble might consist of a sweater, waistcoat, skirt, cardigan or djellaba/poncho, scarf and hat, all in care-

fully coordinated patterns and colours to create an interchangeable wardrobe. Building on the success of the knitwear, the domestic machine-knit production was with some effort translated into industrial production by Goulds of Leicester, owned by Harry Green, who is said to have 'burst out laughing when he saw the samples'.[32] At a time in the 1970s when the contraction of the British textile industry and rise of offshore production was beginning to take hold, the labels were able to proclaim proudly 'Made in England'.

The knitwear was certainly original, exuberant and totally different from anything Gibb's contemporaries were designing. One outfit from the Autumn/Winter 1975 'Moon and Buddha' collection consists of a kimono-style coat and scarf with rounded, overlooked edges and jacquard Buddha-patterned binding with added purple, navy and pale green (plates 41 and 42). The Spring/Summer 1976 designs featured a bold but finely detailed 'Scottish paisley' pine-cone motif with garlands, factory-knitted in double jacquard (plate 43). Several photographs of the time show Gibb wearing his own knitwear designs, especially from the 'Byzantine' collection of Autumn/Winter 1976. Gibb's interest in knitwear continued through several different incarnations that the business went through in an attempt to survive financially. In 1980–81 he designed exclusive knitwear collections for Harrods and many home-dressmaking offers for the *Daily Telegraph* and women's magazines such as *Homes and Gardens*, with complementary knitwear patterns by Kaffe Fassett. During the peak of hand-knitting publishing in 1987, Gibb produced *Hollywood Knits* – a book of 20 knitting patterns based on Hollywood stars – both 'sweater girls' and male pin-ups – including Marilyn Monroe, Greta Garbo, Dorothy Lamour and Errol Flynn. Fassett and Gibb continued to work together until Gibb's early death in 1988.

Meanwhile, since publishing his first knitting pattern with *Vogue Knitting* in 1969, Fassett had built up a keen following, particularly during the 1980s home knitting boom. In his distinctive brand of knitwear he painted with colour, yarn and rich pattern using simple shapes (plate 44). His book *Glorious Knitting* celebrated

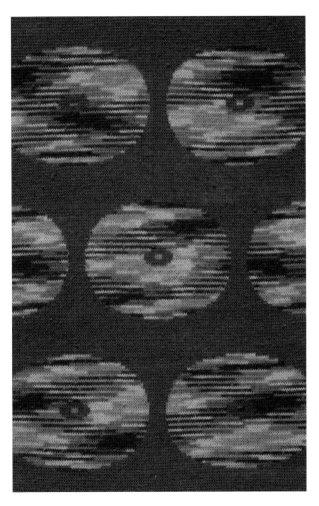

41 Kaffe Fassett, knit fabric design for Bill Gibb's 'Moon and Buddha' collection, Autumn/Winter 1975, Britain V&A: T.434:2–1995
The bold use of both colour and large-scale motif in this design provides visual impact. The fabric is industrially knitted in wool double jacquard on a grey ground with the moon motif knitted in space-dyed yarn shading from pale to dark grey, and yellow to orange.

this painterly approach with stunning photographs of inspirational artefacts and became a best-seller. Essentially a painter, textural designer and colourist working collaboratively with fashion designers, Fassett never marketed his own knitwear designs in the same high-fashion context as Gibb's, but they became a key part of the British 'designer knitwear' boom that democratized fashionable knitwear in the 1980s. He was accorded a solo exhibition of his knitwear at the V&A in 1988.

The two- and three-colour jacquard technique used in Gibb and Fassett's knitwear was a breakthrough in British production of the time – the many colour changes were unprecedented – but soon became a standard knitting technique across the industry. This is in marked contrast to the colour intricacy of knitwear produced in

42 Bill Gibb, 'Moon and Buddha' Collection, Autumn/Winter 1975
Photographed by David Bailey for *Vogue*, September 1975
Several garment styles made up this collection, knitted in wool double-jacquard fabric in cut-and-sewn construction. The signature use of variegated coloured yarn by Kaffe Fassett can be clearly seen within the oval motifs, knitted in space-dyed yarn in grey with yellow, orange and brown on a grey ground. The pictured outfit consists of jacket, wide trousers and scarf.

Italy and France since the late 1970s by Missoni and Kenzo, which often utilized four, five or even six-colour jacquard techniques to give richness and unique depth of colour to the work.

Arguably the most important name in total knitwear dressing, Missoni has celebrated many milestones in more than 50 years as a family enterprise.[33] Ottavio Missoni, an athlete during the 1948 Olympics, had already begun to create knitted jersey tracksuits for the Italian team by the time he married Rosita Jelmini in 1953. She had grown up within a family business making shawls and fabrics, and they soon set up their own knitwear business together in Gallarate, northern Italy, by adapting the production of shawls using old warp-knitting machinery inherited from Rosita's family. The pair went on to establish the unique Missoni look, achieved through a signature total-knit concept using layers of multiple patterns and a kaleidoscope of colours – a style that captivated the international fashion press in the late 1960s and early 1970s (plate 46). The early championing of Missoni by fashion writer Anna Piaggi, US *Vogue* editor Diana Vreeland and the trade paper *Women's Wear Daily* all helped to establish Missoni as a label and Milan as a fashion capital. The *Daily Mail* wrote in 1973: 'Buyers from all over the world flock to purchase their clothes and others attempt to copy them. Fairly unsuccessfully, because they are really more like works of art.'[34] The Missonis considered themselves artisans, 'outsiders in the world of fashion', and the work 'our way of expressing the emotions we receive from the world, from travel, from reading; from people, from art, from music'.[35]

Their creative colour combinations rely on a unique colour palette of yarns being available, and colour palettes vary with each collection, sometimes earthy in tone, other times with brighter colours or highlights, but also occasionally making strong use of black-and-white in bicolour patterns in distorted stripes and blocks. In the early years especially, the collections began with the fabrics, not the silhouettes. Little of the knitwear made by Missoni is fully fashioned, and inspiration for colours, patterns and materials would always come

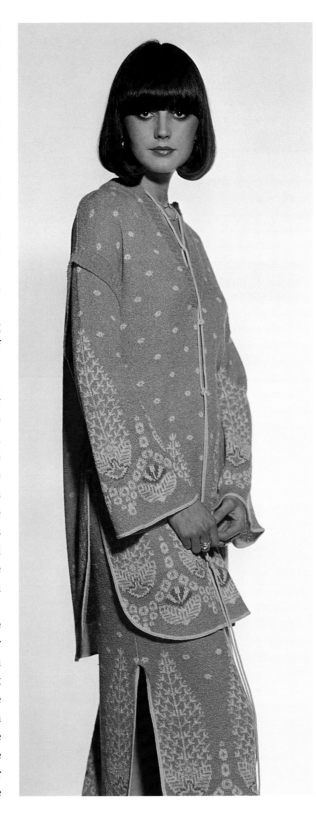

43 Bill Gibb, pink outfit, Spring/Summer 1976 Photographed by Terence Donovan for *Vogue*, March 1976 This four-piece set comprised cardigan, jacket, skirt and scarf, which could be worn all together or separately (see V&A: T.435:1-4–1995). Here, the skirt and jacket are shown. The outfit is knitted from a yarn of textured acrylic and nylon, making the suit light enough for a summer season. The 'Scottish paisley' motif recurred in different forms for both winter and summer seasons.

44 Kaffe Fassett, coat, 1979 V&A: T.354–1980 Kaffe Fassett's hand-knitted textiles were often created directly on the needles, blending and contrasting colours with an artist's eye. Early designs were sometimes reminiscent of ancient maps. This photograph shows a detail from the back of a multicoloured striped wool coat with voluminous rococo sleeves.

come before fashion drawings. One of the Missonis' innovations was to take the heritage of 'space dyeing' – a technique of dyeing yarns which creates multiple colours in one length, previously applied in the family business of Rosita's grandparents – to create multi-coloured embroideries and adapt it to yarns used for knitting the entire garment. This slow technique worked on hanks of yarn produces variegated and slightly irregular patches of colour, resulting in the experimental and exciting multicolour effects which had such an impact in the early '70s. Space dyeing has continued to be a speciality of the company, contributing significantly from the outset to the distinctive Missoni handwriting (plate 45). As the Missonis' son Luca recalls:

Computers [now] give you the opportunity to change a design very fast. With the jacquard [systems] we used at the end of the 1970s it was tough to make the tiniest change in the pattern. Once you decided that you loved a particular pattern, it was easier to adapt the fashion to it than change the design.[36]

In order to create the total-knit 'put-together look', as the American press called it, Missoni mixed together many different weights and structures of knitted fabric, all produced on their own factory premises at Sumirago in Lombardy – a village off the tourist map, now almost entirely dedicated to the Missoni company. There, older machines like the warp-knitting machines used by Rosita's family now vie with state-of-the-art computerized flat-bed machines to produce everything from open-mesh fabrics and jacquard patterns to complex uneven stripes, checks and chevrons, and multiple geometric and zigzag patterns. These knit fabrics are made up entirely by tailoring cut-and-sew methods into structured coats and jackets and softer sweaters, dresses and skirts – the full gamut of clothing.

Inevitably, both the company founders and the typical Missoni customer grew older over the decades, but a second generation of designers emerged in the mid-1990s: the Missoni's youngest son, Luca, and daughter Angela, responsible for menswear and womenswear respectively, revisited the archive and refreshed the archetypes for the twenty-first century, moving forward with body-conscious women's designs and quirky men's knitwear, appealing to a younger market. Luca Missoni is now in charge of the Missoni archive, curating and protecting the future heritage of a unique business. Although their continuity of vision remains outside fashion, sometimes, as in the late 1990s, the Missoni look becomes mainstream again. The early patchworking technique has been revived in the modern clothing (plate 45) and latterly in 'new tapestries' created by Tai Missoni as artworks. Woven fabrics have been incorporated into collections for printed dresses, for example, but these are always in a minor role compared to the knits and jerseys. The stripes, jacquard patterns and Raschel zigzag knits remain archetypally Missoni (plate 46).

Jersey eveningwear by British designers

Since the 1960s, the fluidity of knitted jersey in silk or viscose has become the signature of many British eveningwear designers. While many fashion designers who came to the forefront in the 1960s and '70s, including Missoni, Krizia, Kenzo, Kansai, Sonia Rykiel and Bill Gibb, made bold use of colour and pattern fabrication in medium-weight knitwear, others, such as Jean Muir, Yuki and John Bates, focused on the fluidity of knitted jersey fabrics in silk or viscose. For these designers the sculpting, moulding, draping and manipulation of monochrome lengths of fabric took precedence over pattern and construction within the fabric itself. Since the mid-1990s, a different approach has appeared as a new wave of designers, especially Julien Macdonald and more recently Mark Fast, have radicalized the concept of eveningwear through the medium of knitting. They have designed constructed knitwear which, like the creations of Azzedine Alaïa previously, celebrates and reveals the female body, while at the same time provoking new arguments regarding contemporary culture and the politics of the body.

John Bates was one of a group of influential designers – including Mary Quant, Ossie Clark and Marion Foale and Sally Tuffin – who emerged to reinvigorate British fashion in the 1960s. He was particularly known in the mid-1960s for designing clothes for pop stars and actresses, notably Diana Rigg of *The Avengers* – a stylish cult television programme (still popular today). Bates designed for the Jean Varon label from 1959 and his John Bates label from 1974. His clothes, using large volumes of highly decorated cloth, appealed to a bohemian clientele who liked to be distinctive: drama was key. A dress in very fine black silk jersey from 1979, for example, consists of a backless top with military-style padded shoulders and beaded silver epaulettes, minimally connected to a skirt with a pointed train and finished with a beaded tassel (plate 47). This outfit revealed and concealed the wearer's body in a highly audacious manner.

Sheer exuberance in dressing up for evening is captured in fluid jersey outfits in silk or viscose by Yuki – a

45 Missoni, patchwork coat, Autumn/Winter 2002
This 'coat of many colours', fashioned from a patchwork of different multicoloured jacquard fabrics, represents in one garment an archive of typical graphic patterns and textures in bright colours (see T.260–2004). It is seen here modelled for the V&A's 'Fashion in Motion' series of fashion promenades through the museum in November 2003, when a selected retrospective collection of Missoni garments was shown.

46 Missoni,
beach playsuit and wrap, 1968
Photographed by Patrick Rouchon
for *Grazia*
Joyous colours are worked in the
distinctive Missoni zigzag stripes
which are formed on specialist
warp knitting machinery. Although
designed in 1968, these outfits have
a timeless quality. The same fabric
structure is still produced and re-
coloured for Summer collections in
rayon or cotton and adapted for
Winter in wools.

Japanese-born designer (full name Gnyuki Torimaru) who trained in textiles, then studied tailoring at London College of Fashion in the 1960s. He subsequently worked with British couturier Norman Hartnell and in Paris with Pierre Cardin before starting his own label in London in 1972. Known for his draped jersey silhouettes, he designed outfits that appeared simple but were created with careful precision and could be worn by women of all sizes. Signature pieces include a large, square-cut pierrot-style evening coat, trimmed with marabou feathers at the collar and edges (1977, V&A: T.1–1979), and, from the same year, an all-in-one pants suit draped at the front from a halter-neck, with volumes of fabric enveloping the body (V&A: T.266–1989). Later work in the 1980s (plate 48) moved away from jersey to focus on pleated polyester pieces. Yuki's business in the UK closed then reopened in 1984 but continued in Japan until the late 1990s.

Compared with Yuki's extravagant creations, which often used many metres of draped and gathered silk jersey, Jean Muir's ready-to-wear dresses are more restrained. They are, however, supremely crafted around the body, her signature top-stitching effect providing subtle emphasis and definition. In a career that spanned from 1966 to 1995, Muir's work reveals an evolving timelessness. She concentrated on a few key fabrics, such as viscose matte jersey, suede and wool crêpe, which were developed like an artist's palette to create an easy-to-wear and flattering quality that has been described as 'liquefaction'.[37] One fabric defined her work, however. As Muir's one-time personal assistant and biographer Sinty Stemp has said, 'While Jean Muir worked with a range of materials, it was her work in matte jersey – a fabric she practically made her own – and particularly her jersey dresses, that would make her legendary.'[38] Actress Joanna Lumley, an early model for Muir and a lifelong fan of the clothes, has commented, 'They don't dictate – it's you looking beautiful in a dress, not just you in a beautiful dress'(plate 49).[39]

Muir herself was matter-of-fact about the fashion business, saying, 'We are a wholesale company making clothes, we do not sell to individual people,' and empha-

sizing the importance of technical aspects: 'Accuracy and system are as imperative as in any engineering process!'[40] Initial sketches were sent to Paris, where a French *toiliste* made the first patterns, which Muir personally fitted twice.[41] She famously tried all the toiles on herself to check the drape and movement of the garment patterns.

A long, fluid, black evening dress in silk jersey from Autumn/Winter 1995 (plate 50) is typical, comprising numerous narrow top-stitched panels suspended from a beaded collar, each panel flaring sharply at the hem to create movement and volume when worn. In addition to monochrome eveningwear, Muir is known for flashes of bright colour and bold prints that were translated into abstract patterns for intarsia knitwear. She also designed other styles of knitwear, all made in Scotland using cashmere and other quality yarns (plate 51).

Muir was passionate about design and education, publishing her 'Manifesto for Real Design' in the *Sunday Times Magazine* in 1994, and serving as Master of the Faculty of Royal Designers for Industry for the Royal Society of Arts (RSA). She wrote: 'Making is the most natural thing in the world…One has to hope that, once and for all, the academic snobbery about skills, craft and design will cease. Three-dimensional thought is a different *kind* of intelligence.'[42] Muir's philosophy and methods were captured in a television documentary in 1992. She died in 1995, but her company continued for several years, finally closing in 2007. Nevertheless, Jean Muir clothes and her ethos of quality and understated design are still cherished.

The mid-1990s, a period of recovery from recession in the UK, saw the production of some highly glamorous eveningwear. While hand-knitting had been revitalized in the previous decade, technological developments had continued in industrial knitting. As machinery became more sophisticated, with computer-aided design systems endless possibilities were opened up for designing textures and surfaces within jersey fabric. These were used to great effect by American-born designer Ben de Lisi. Having moved to London in 1982, de Lisi staged his first London catwalk show in 1995 and

47 John Bates,
jersey, evening dress, 1979
V&A: T.190–1980
John Bates developed clothes for dramatic entrances and exits (such as a bird of paradise embroidered djellaba, V&A: T.772–1995). His couture eveningwear became ever more daring and revealing by the late 1970s, as this dress shows. It was displayed on this especially designed mannequin, with a cocktail hat by Frederick Fox as part of a 1979 exhibition of British fashion by Simpsons of Piccadilly in London.

48 Yuki, catsuit and snood,
Autumn/Winter 1986
Photographed by Norman Parkinson for *Vogue*,
October 1976
Jerry Hall is here provocatively photographed wearing a pleated Yuki silk-jersey catsuit atop an Aston Martin car. Yuki designs used volumes of silk or viscose jersey, which often revealed rather than camouflaged the body, especially in movement.

quickly came to prominence. Focusing on eveningwear, he dressed film stars such as Kate Winslet for high-profile events, using knitted jersey in such a way that the fabric structure itself rather than the volume or drape creates the interest. One striking dress (plate 52) features a jacquard rose motif repeating diagonally around the garment, which is simply cut as a fitted sleeveless shift with low back and knotted sash and is lined in cream jersey to reveal the transparent pattern effect over the body. De Lisi has said, 'The most difficult thing is to create pure beautiful clothes.'[43] He was the first designer to collaborate with high-street store Debenhams and

49 **Jean Muir**, outfit, Autumn/Winter 1975
Photographed by Michael Barrett
Joanna Lumley models a brown viscose jersey outfit of tunic and culottes, worn with a cloche hat designed by Graham Smith. Lumley was one of Jean Muir's first house models, starting in 1964 with Muir's predecessor label Jane and Jane, and continues to wear and champion the clothes, which have become 'vintage' pieces.

50 **Jean Muir**, evening gown,
Autumn/Winter 1995
V&A: T.218–1996
A long, fluid, black evening dress
in silk jersey from the final
collection Jean Muir designed
herself is typical of her design
aesthetic. Narrow top-stitched
panels are suspended from a
beaded collar, each panel flaring
sharply at the hem to create
movement and volume when
worn. The keyhole front
opening, outlined in top-
stitching, creates provocation in
an otherwise demure design.

has worked on interior design for hotels as well as becoming a television presenter and commentator.

Working between the two extremes of hand-knitting and constructing in jersey fabric, young knitwear designer Julien Macdonald started to produce handmade lace dresses using hand-operated domestic knitting machines in 1994. He was invited, while still studying at the Royal College of Art, to work with Karl Lagerfeld at Chanel and designed a number of gossamer-fine lace dresses for the Chanel Spring/Summer 1997 show. Because of the Chanel connection, top models were flown in to appear in Macdonald's graduation show in 1996, and his fine-knitted lace-panelled dress in black and bronze with train (plate 53) was worn by Helena Christensen. He went on to build his own glamour eveningwear label, dressing celebrities such as Kylie Minogue and Shirley Bassey for the red carpet in revealing and daring designs, and became a star of London fashion week with spectacular showmanship.

In a move that some saw as surprising given his reputation as a knitwear designer, in 2000 Macdonald was invited to be creative director of Givenchy, following in the footsteps of Alexander McQueen. Although he was young, Macdonald's practical knitting ability – learnt at college in Brighton, at the RCA and while working for other designers – enabled him to demonstrate what he wanted on the machines to the highly experienced technicians he worked with in the French and Italian knitting companies. After three years at Givenchy, Macdonald returned to his London base, continuing to show not just knitwear but also a range of sharply tailored high-octane eveningwear, which won him two British Fashion Council awards for glamour. In 2006, Macdonald was awarded an OBE for services to fashion, and he continues to build his brand.

Knitting in twenty-first-century fashion

During the first decade of the twenty-first century, fashion designers continued to explore the diverse qualities and endless permutations of knitwear through both technical innovation and handcraft. Several designer

labels have rapidly achieved a cult status for innovative knitwear in this time: Sandra Backlund from Sweden for her intricate hand-knitting; Louise Goldin for her futuristic and powerful constructed knitwear; Mark Fast for his body-conscious womenswear and Sibling for radicalizing classic men's knitwear for a new generation. As information now flows almost instantly around the globe, it is possible for an individual designer-maker to have a major influence on fashion while remaining him- or herself a microbusiness. Backlund is one such designer. She is a product of a complex education, first studying art and art history, then textile handicrafts, then teacher training, preparatory fashion studies and finally three years of fashion as a mature student at Beckman School of Design in Stockholm. All this set Backlund apart from her contemporaries, and she always 'wanted to do her own thing'. She started her small business in 2004, and her art-piece creations – meticulously hand-knitted sculptural garments built in three dimensions around the body – almost single-handedly inspired a fashion for wildly oversized, heavy hand-knitted pieces (plate 58). These have been emulated in both high fashion and the mass market, especially making a statement on the catwalk.

Backlund makes each complex piece individually, inventing as she goes along. She says, 'Knit is creative, it invites you to improvise, but another side of it is precise, counting, and you need to be patient.'[44] Although she has previously worked with many materials, including hair, wool has become her main medium, and she uses it to achieve a 'collage' technique by changing direction, leaving stitches on safety pins, sculpting, then sewing panels from the inside. Working from a personal aesthetic of beauty, she consciously dresses and undresses different parts of the body, revealing the interaction between vulnerability and protection. In 2007 she won the top prize at the prestigious Hyères Festival of Fashion and Photography held annually in France.

As more companies took up the 'big knitting' concept, from 2008 Backlund began to explore new areas. After working seven long days a week on hand-knitting (echoing the subsistence knitting of previous eras), Backlund investigated a move into production using the expertise of an Italian knitwear factory and for Spring/Summer 2010 succeeded in creating pieces that retained her signature style but were repeatable (plate 54). She says:

> It was of course a big step for me to go from working alone in my studio, inventing pieces while doing them myself by hand, to suddenly be working with a team of experts within a field of knitwear that I never before have had the chance to get to know. I was overwhelmed by all the possibilities I saw and, even though I will never give up doing my hand-knitted pieces, I now see how to develop my collections in ways that I never thought were possible.[45]

Backlund's experiences illustrate the divide that exists between the craft knitter and those working in industry. The processes of industry inevitably consume and reinterpret designs according to the manufacturing systems of the period. The designer's skill is in guiding and negotiating that interpretation into something that corresponds to their original vision while at the same time tuning this vision to mass-production

53 Julien Macdonald, lace dress, 1996
V&A: T.24: 1/2–1997
The intricate, multipanelled dress is knitted on a hand-operated domestic machine, fully fashioned to shape, in viscose yarn. It is not easy to knit faultlessly in such a complex design – the front bodice alone comprised nine contoured panels.

realities. The divide is successfully bridged when both designer and technician have been challenged but neither feels the compromise has been too great.

In contrast to Sandra Backlund, knitwear designer Louise Goldin embraced advanced knitting technology early in her career, sculpting knitted fabric into distinctive and inventive silhouettes, both body-conscious and futuristic. The computer screen is Goldin's medium of interpretation for designs in a combination of diverse materials, textures and volumes, but she favours double-jacquard fabrics to give substance to the pieces (plate 55). However, her confident mixing of weights, gauges, structures and shapes in a patchwork of visual elements was developed from original experimentation on manual knitting machines, where she could be in full control.

Goldin graduated from Central St Martins in 2006 with a collection that combined layers of fine knitwear with macramé work for immediate visual impact. After doing work experience with Julien Macdonald and others, she built her expertise during a period designing knitwear for Brazilian label Tereza Santos. Goldin initially collaborated with a knitwear manufacturer in Brazil to produce many of her fabrics and garments, but she has since moved to Italian manufacturers.

Unlike many designers, Goldin relishes the technical processes of industrial knitting and has learnt to use the specialist programmes involved and the art of communicating with technicians to achieve her vision. Hers is a fashion-led approach to knitwear, in which the fabrication is the servant of the design concept. A series of short films of the processes involved in producing Goldin's Autumn/Winter 2009 collection were broadcast in 2008–9 on the influential fashion website Showstudio.[46]

Attention to technical detail is an important factor in the garments. For example, for Goldin's Spring/Summer 2011 collection, sportswear-inspired leggings included intarsia-knitted transparent sections carefully shaped in body-contouring squares rather than simple stripes. Goldin has since been commissioned to design knitwear for the Versace label. She is determined to continue with her all-knitted collections, fusing both high and low technologies and developing her ambition to be the 'next generation Missoni'.[47]

After graduating from Central St Martins in 2008, Canadian-born Mark Fast quickly rose to prominence for his body-conscious openwork stretch cobweb dresses, especially when he sparked controversy and debate through his promotion of larger-sized models on the catwalk in 2009. The main collection is completely handmade in his London studio on domestic knitting machines, using a labour-intensive technique based on knitting with small groups of needles in turn. Yarns are always elastane combined with nylon or viscose, and the dresses require a body to give them form and make sense of the complex structures. A second line, the Faster by Mark Fast range, was launched in 2010; it is made in Italy using seamless industrial technology. This transition means the knitwear is producible on a larger scale while incorporating Fast's signature openwork mesh effects (plate 56).

Having created knitwear for some of the top designer names in fashion, including Alexander McQueen and Lanvin, the trio of designers that make up the label Sibling launched their radical men's knitwear brand in 2008. Joe Bates, Sydney Bryan and Cozette McCreery subverted the conservative men's knitwear market by introducing shocking pink, sequins and heavily textured embroidery to classic knitwear styles (plate 57). Further collections have incorporated new interpretations of Fair Isle looks with graphics such as skulls and lettering, and the 'Knit Monster' – a showpiece all-over knitted bodysuit incorporating a balaclava head-piece complete with punk mohican decoration. In 2010, Sibling designed a capsule women's range of cardigans for UK high street store Topshop, 'Sister by Sibling'.

Innovation in knitwear moves on steadily, fuelled by individual design creativity and technological advances but – as in other areas such as product design or architecture – radical shifts occur periodically. New forms of knitwear are created that blend technical knowledge of knit structure with a conceptual vision, and often a strong dose of humour, arousing ripples of excitement and a new interest in the genre.

54 Sandra Backlund, dress,
Spring/Summer 2010
Photographed by Peter Gehrke
After creating her signature
handmade 'big knitting' pieces,
where volume and silhouette are
key, the challenge for Backlund
was to translate these concepts
into industrially produced
lighter-weight pieces requiring
little manual processing. This
dress is one of the results.

55 Louise Goldin, dress,
Autumn/Winter 2008
Louise Goldin develops strong
silhouettes for confident
women, often using
asymmetry and padding,
patchworking several fabrics
together. Industrially knitted
jacquards, designed around
the body, are key to many of
her complex manipulations.
Goldin now designs knitwear
for the Versace label.

56 Mark Fast, openwork dress, 'Faster' collection, Spring/Summer 2011 Photographed by Fiona Garden The Faster collection, comprising ballet-inspired dresses, all-in-one bodysuits, tops, underwear, tights and leggings, reveals an ability to successfully translate a manually produced concept into a commercial product in collaboration with Italian manufacturers.

57 Sibling, sequined leopard-print twinset, 2008 Taking the classics of knitwear and subverting them with modern irony, Sibling have established a radicalized but wearable concept for contemporary menswear. Each collection is themed around different traditions, incorporating graphic intarsia, jacquard and embroidered designs with structured knit textures.

Knitwear in Designer Fashions

Knitwear now frequently makes its appearance on the catwalk as a statement in its own right. There are eternal variations on iconic knitwear staples such as cable stitches, argyle patterning, Fair Isle and Nordic designs. In 2010, Dolce & Gabbana's D&G label showed reindeer and star-patterned knitwear, cable-knit body suits and Nordic-patterned cocktail dresses in knitted and printed matching fabrics. Junya Watanabe adapted Fair Isle and cable-knit fabrics to tailored men's jackets for his Autumn/Winter 2011 menswear collection. The phenomenon of 'big knitting' has consistently grown, stimulated over a number of years by designers including Yohji Yamamoto, Bless and Sandra Backlund. Others, such as Missoni and Julien Macdonald, have complemented signature body-conscious silhouettes with heavier knits, seen for example in the Winter 2010 and 2011 seasons. Most 'big knits' are hand-knitted on needles in bulky yarns, echoing the new millennium trend in which knitting has become 'cool'.

Tailoring shapes on the industrial knitting machine is now feasible at moderate prices. The soft engineering that creates integral darts, complex shapings and edgings – a long way from the basic standardization of the 1960s and 1970s – is almost taken for granted. Nevertheless, innovation often stems from individual designers 'playing' on their manually operated machines to inspire more commercial production processes. As a result, mainstream knitwear design is today far more adventurous and technically complex. Fabric volume and drape create new silhouettes, with the flexibile knitted fabric moulding around the body. Graphic imagery, often humorous, continues to be interpreted in intarsia knitwear for both menswear and womenswear by designers such as Sonia Rykiel, Antoni and Alison, Yohji Yamamoto, Sibling and recent graduates Hannah Taylor and Yang Du. Knitting design is set for a bright future as more designers take confident new approaches to the classic knitting genre, which continues to display endless versatility.

Pictured is a small selection of looks from the international catwalks, ranging from tight to loose, plain to colourful, reinvented classics to sculptural heavy knits.

Clockwise from top left

Julien Macdonald,
Autumn/Winter 2010

D&G, Autumn/Winter 2010

Alexander McQueen,
Autumn/Winter 2010

Prada, Autumn/Winter 2010

Sonia Rykiel,
Spring/Summer 2008

Junya Watanabe,
Autumn/Winter 2011

Junya Watanabe,
Autumn/Winter 2011

Proenza Schouler,
Autumn/Winter 2011

Missoni, Autumn/Winter 2010

Giles Deacon,
Autumn/Winter 2007

Mark Fast, Spring/Summer 2009

Postscript

AS TECHNOLOGICAL DEVELOPMENTS and digital processes take hold in all aspects of design and manufacturing, knitting is shedding its old-fashioned image, assisted by innovations such as three-dimensional complete garments and Issey Miyake's groundbreaking 'A-POC' manufacturing technology. The shaping of even a seemingly humble sock heel – turning a corner in a material in the most economical manner – represents a complicated feat of soft engineering. It is gradually becoming apparent to non-specialists that the links between technical capability and emerging knitwear design are interdependent. Now technologically sophisticated knitwear production is available in every high street and designer store: intricately formed, unusually shaped or trimmed, perhaps deconstructed or wrapped, fashioned in endless new ways to redefine knitwear once more for the twenty-first century.

From the work featured in the last chapter, it can be seen that knitwear has played a significant role in both everyday clothing and high fashion, but it is perhaps always destined to be seen in parallel to fashion. Its place in society and culture is, however, assured as the different spheres of life in which knitting features continue to expand, occasionally intersecting as a site for new developments and ideas. In some respects, knitting has come full circle from the skills of medieval hand-knitting, via its early mechanization, to the computer-controlled digital processes of today, arriving at a point where hand-knitting – whether for pleasure, artistic expression or fashionable effect – exists side by side with mainstream knitwear manufacturing and its hidden technologies, now taken for granted.

From its humble domestic roots to pioneering technology, the knitting industry has burgeoned, but not without some economic and social turbulence. Knitted artefacts clearly express technological, design, social and economic aspects of history. Wear and tear and the traces of the hand reveal the human stories behind such objects, from the splendours of the aristocracy to the humblest everyday clothing.

58 Sandra Backlund, sweater, 'Diamond Cut Diamond' collection, 2006
Photographed by Carl Bengtsson
An example of Sandra Backlund's signature 'big knitting' – oversized and handmade knitwear that inspired a new trend in large-scale wrapped and sculptural knitwear.

59 Yoshiki Hishinuma, *Casablanca*, 2005
The potential for designers to take a highly creative approach to knitting technology is demonstrated in Yoshiki Hishinuma's art piece, which can also be worn as a cape. In contrast to the one-piece tailored jacket shown on page 74, here Hishinuma experimented with three-dimensional knitting construction on the Shima Seiki industrial machine to create a non-standard piece inspired by the form of a lily, taking the seamless industrial knitting technique into new dimensions.

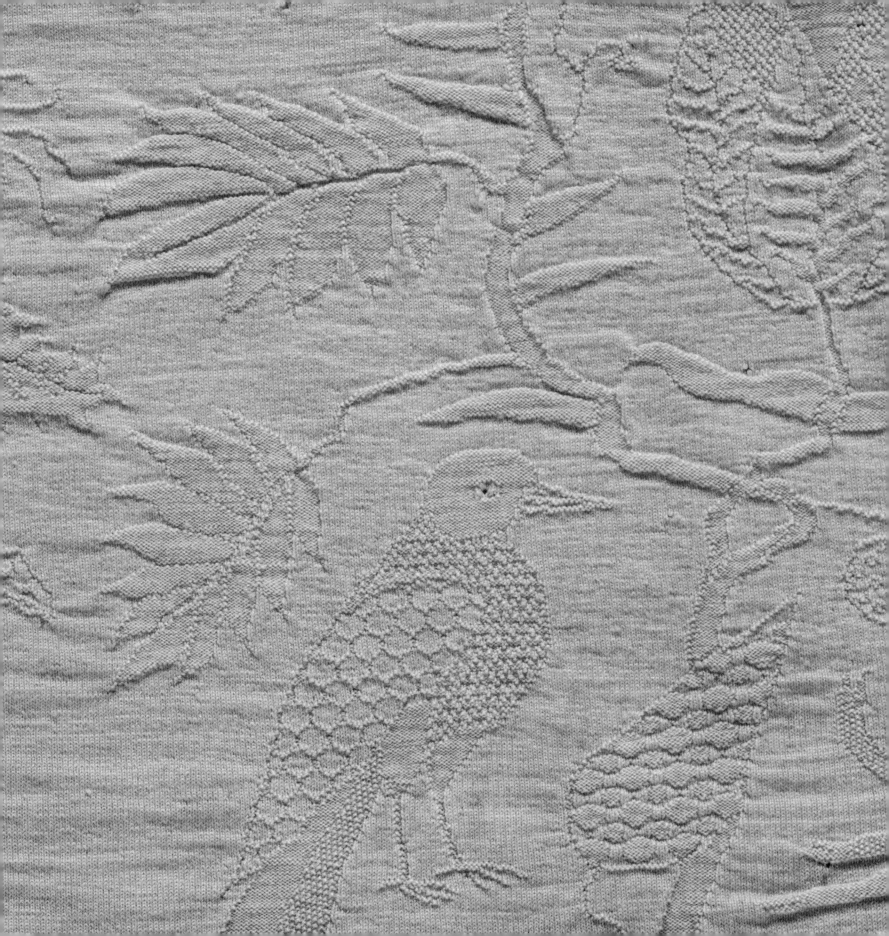

Timeline

Two-colour knitting

Complex construction

Peg Frame demontrator

Lee's stocking frame

Twelfth to Sixteenth Centuries: From Hand- to Machine-knitting

The origins of hand-knitting cannot be dated exactly. A high level of skill is evident in the knitted objects and fragments dating from the twelfth century. Hand-knitting in the round (four or five needles) and flat (two needles) used for gloves, caps, stockings etc. Knitting needles made from bone, metal and wood

1535 onwards: Peg frame-knitting documented in straight and circular formation, using hand techniques to wind yarn and form stitches

*c.***1589:** William Lee's stocking frame invention, using bearded needles. Simple eight-gauge stockinette

Knitting in the round

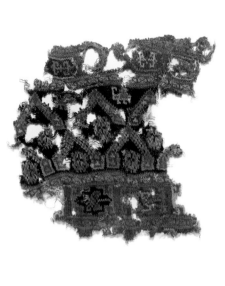

Multi-colour knitting

Seamless stockings

Stocking frame

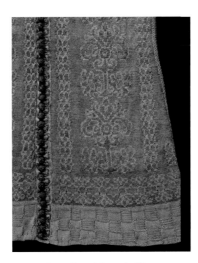

Brocade and damask effects

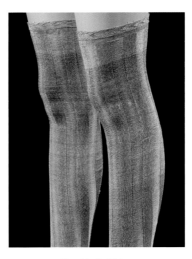

Hand-knit ribbing

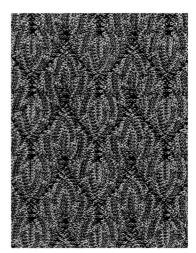

Complex warp-knit

Seventeenth to Eighteenth Centuries: Technical Invention

Early knitting machines emulated the stitches and fabrics produced for centuries by hand-knitting, including stocking stitch, damask patterns, ribbing, colour patterns, circular work and lace. Knitting sheaths used to speed up commercial hand-knitting

1620–1750: Stocking frame development. Finer fabrics up to 30-gauge, colour-stripes

1750–1810: Knitting industry expansion. Continuous improvements made to the manually-operated stocking frame to create a wider range of fabrics. Development of rotary-powered machines and warp-knitting technology. Industrialization of yarn spinning to improve quality and supply of yarns

1758: Machine-made ribbed fabrics created with Jedediah Strutt's Derby rib attachment (second needlebed)

1767: Hargreaves' spinning jenny

1769 onwards: Plating technique for embroidery and brocade effects, figured (patterned) lace meshes

1771–83: Arkwright's Mills

1775 onwards: Mesh fabrics and vertical stripes, plain and zig-zag, made by new technique of warp-knitting (Crane, Britain). No hand-knit equivalent

1776: Eyelet lace transfer stitches, tuck stitch fabrics developed

1779: Crompton's spinning mule

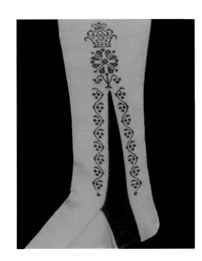

Plated decoration

Eyelet transfer lace

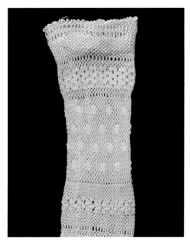

Warp-knit lace

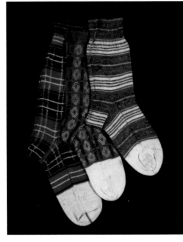

Industrially-knit seamed socks

Circular knitting

Mass production

Griswold circular

Nineteenth Century: Industrialization and Mass Production

Transition from manual towards powered flat and circular industrial-knitting machinery, operated in factories from the middle of the century. Small manually-operated circular and flat knitting machines used for stocking knitting in domestic setting and in factories

1805 onwards: Automatic colour and pattern fabric designs using Jean-Marie Jacquard's (France) weaving technique of punched-hole cards integrated into knitting machine control

1816: First small diameter circular knitting machine 'Le Tricoteur' (Marc Brunel, Britain) for tubular knitted stockinette

1845: Large diameter steam-powered circular knitting machine (Peter Claussen, Belgium). Commercial development of stockinette (jersey) fabric for cut and sewn garments. Continuous development of circular knitted jersey fabrics

1849: Latch needle patented by Matthew Townsend (Britain) giving speed and cost reductions, especially in circular knitting

1857: First patent for inverted V-bed formation (Eisenstuck, Germany). Developed by Dubied (Switzerland), Stoll (Germany) and many others

1857–63: Automatic fully-fashioned shaping on flat rotary-driven machines developed by Arthur Paget, then William Cotton (both Loughborough, Britain). Simultaneous knitting of multiple stockings and shaped garment pieces enabled mass production

1863: Small-scale flat knitting V-bed machine Lamb's 'Family Knitter' (USA)

1878: Griswold small diameter sock knitting machine (USA and Britain), able to shape heels and toes. Later versions comprised a separate dial for ribbing

1892: Plain/Purl patterned knitting, e.g. garter-stitch and moss-stitch based fabrics made on (manually operated) purl-stitch machine by Stoll (Germany)

Intarsia stocking with embroidery

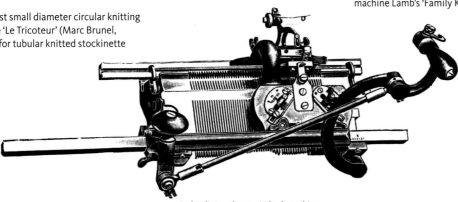

Dubied's Lamb-type V-bed machine

Stoll automatic shaping

Circular jersey

Missoni warp-knit

Miyake warp-knit

Twentieth Century: Advanced Technology and Versatility

Continuous improvements in weft- and warp-knitting, technical design and production capabilities. Hand-knitting for leisure using needles made from plastics, aluminium, wood and bamboo.

1900–73: Automation of flat V-bed knitting machines, using mechanical control. Produced a wide range of fabrics (e.g. double jacquard, fully fashioned, tuck stitch, ribs, slip stitch, transfer lace). Machine builders included Stoll (Germany), Dubied (Switzerland), Scott and Williams (USA), and, from 1962, Shima Seiki (Japan). Intarsia knitting still produced manually on hand frames

1948 onwards: Warp-knitting technology for meshes, 'crochet' openwork laces, interior and industrial fabrics further developed by Karl Meyer (Germany)

1956: Caperdoni invented new warp-knitting system using tubes, the Waltex machine, as used by Missoni company for zig-zag striped and fancy fabrics

c.1960s onwards: Continuous development of industrial circular knitting machine and patterned fabrics including double jacquard

1970: Seamless gloves requiring no finishing process produced on first automatic glove-knitting flat V-bed machine by Shima Seiki (Japan)

1975: Electronic control of flat machines developed by Stoll (Germany). Versatility of machinery creates a greatly increased patterning scope such as large-scale jacquards. First electronic pattern preparation unit with visual display introduced in 1978

1995: Wholegarment knitting system with additional needlebeds by Shima Seiki (Japan) enabling knitting of complete garments requiring minimal finishing

1997: Seamless bodywear. Santoni (Italy) develop 'body-sized' tubular knitting machinery from hosiery industry

1999 onwards: Tubular warp-knitting for seamless bodywear. See garments by Issey Miyake Inc (A-POC Inside), Cifra and Santoni (Italy)

Waltex warp-knitting machine

Jersey jacquard

Wholegarment

Notes

1 History, Tradition and Mythology

1 Such techniques include sprang, braiding, tablet weaving and nalbinding (looping using a single threaded needle, also known as knotless netting). See Glossary.

2 For further discussion on the origins of knitting and its relationship to earlier techniques see Turnau (1991), pp.13–15; Rutt (1987), pp.23–32; also, for comparison, Thomas (1987).

3 Speiser (1983).

4 This complex technique utilizes many warp threads, held on a warp beam similar to weaving looms, each thread feeding into hooked (bearded) needles held in a needle bar to form chains of loops in a vertical direction, which each intermesh with adjacent threads. It does not have an exact equivalent in handcraft work, although it is used to replicate netting, lace and crochet-style fabrics industrially. See Timeline and Glossary.

5 Described by Mary Thomas in her classic *Knitting Book* (London, 1987), first published in 1938.

6 Rutt (1987), p.31.

7 Levey (1969), pp.183–205; Levey (1982), pp.34–40.

8 Burnham (1972), pp.116–24. For nalbinding and knotless netting, see Nordland (1961); M. Hald, 'Ancient Textile Techniques in Egypt and Scandinavia: A Comparative Study', *Acta Archaeologica* (1946), vol.17, pp.49–98.

9 However, Turnau (1991), p.14, cites fragments of garments that may have been knitted that were found in Nubia and originating from the sixth and seventh centuries in the private collection of Dr Walter Endrei, Budapest. Mary Thomas (1987), p.91, tantalizingly shows a fragment of geometrically patterned two-colour knitted silk with crossed eastern stitches dating from between the seventh and ninth centuries, from the Fritz Iklé collection in Switzerland, but this is now lost. See also Levey (1969), p.185, citing a 1948 report for the Basel Museum, and Rutt (1987), p.32.

10 Others can be found in Washington, DC, New York and Detroit. Louise Bellinger of the Textile Museum, Washington, DC, wrote in 1954 that they could have originated in India: L. Bellinger, 'Patterned Stockings, Possibly Indian, Found in Egypt', *Textile Museum Washington, DC, Workshop Notes* (Dec. 1954), no.10, cited in Levey (1969), p.185. However, Rutt countered this theory, stating 'the foundation of her argument falls away now we know that all old Egyptian stockings were knitted from the toe up'. Both Rutt and Turnau show images of these cotton stockings and fragments featuring narrow or wide bands of geometric motifs and Arabic inscriptions. Rutt states the fragments may be stockings or bags and 'there is no proof that they were knitted as flat pieces, but no convincing evidence that they were not'. Rutt (1987), p.33; Turnau (1991), p.15.

11 This area has a thickness and change of knitting direction consistent with either a seam or a rough 'knitting up' of the stitches. Here the seamline is at the side of the leg, close to the heel insertion point.

12 Rutt described this fragment as knitted in a technique he refers to as 'compound knitting', a term defined, in correspondence with the V&A, as deriving from a curator in Gothenburg, to describe knitting into the second course below, rather than the course below. (This term is also referred to in his article 'Knitted Fabrics from China. 3rd Century BC', *Journal of Textile Institute* (1991), vol.83, pp.411–13). However, I can find no evidence of such a technique in this fragment. A remarkably similar knitted fragment is found in Sweden in the Lamm collection in the museum at Lund. Rutt (1987), pp.37–8, has a photograph of this fragment, including back view, dated to the fourteenth century.

13 Rutt (1987), p.37.

14 Early examples of everyday medieval knitted items include a mitten and a child's vest in the Museum of London.

15 Finely knitted in silk, the cushions' insignia are worked in two-colour patterns in all-over geometric chequerboard placement: Rutt (1987), pp.39–44; Stanley (1997), pp.45–6; also Stanley (2002), pp.25–33.

16 A group of relic purses in Switzerland being one exception: Rutt (1987), pp.50–54; also Turnau (1991), p.18.

17 Rutt (1987), p.50.

18 Turnau illustrates six sets of knitted liturgical gloves, examples of which can be seen in museum and church collections across Europe, demonstrating similar features and colours. The English caps were more commonplace and were found in more significant numbers: Turnau (1991), pp.231–3, ills. 37–42.

19 Turnau (1991), p.16, p.18.

20 A similar pair of gloves (unlined) in the Whitworth Museum, Manchester, shows the same monogrammed cartouche motif, but with identical lettering orientation on left and right gloves. This unlined glove appears to have a similar sewn edge-to-edge seam on the outer palm, but a cut and sewn seam for the gauntlet.

21 There are a number of examples in the V&A and other museums, particularly the Museum of London. Caps of a similar kind have also been excavated in Germany: Turnau (1991), p.120.

22 For the fourteenth-century fragment, see E. Crowfoot, F. Pritchard and K. Staniland (2001), pp.72–5. For the 1488 statute, see Hartley and Ingleby (2001), p.6; Buckland (1979).

23 P. Stubbes, *Anatomie of Abuses* (London, 1585).

24 Buckland (2008), vol.36, pp.40–45. Also Levey (1969), pp.188–9.

25 However, for the Basque beret, one of the earliest productions of industrial knitting from the 1950s, triangular wedge-shaped sections are knitted in a technique called *flèchage* to form a sideways-knitted circle of fabric. This construction is used for commercially made berets, such as those made by Kangol since 1938 and supplied to the army during WWII. These are knitted, felted and blocked in a manner similar to medieval caps but require one seam to join the beginning and end of the knitted circle.

26 See Joan Thirsk's classic article, which discusses the spread and development of the stocking hand-knitting trade in England: Thirsk (1973), p.64. Others, however, regard this as a conservative estimate and put the figure higher, based on three pairs per year.

27 Cunnington and Mansfield (1969), p.114.

28 Joan Thirsk suggests this was half their true worth of £8: Thirsk (1973), p.54. See Chapter 2.

29 Philip Stubbes, cited in Hartley and Ingleby (2001), p.7; Rutt (1987), p.70. According to Stubbes, the price of a pair of these British handmade silk stockings was 20 shillings, compared with 8 or 9 shillings for worsted and between 1 and 2 shillings for coarse woollen stockings: Stubbes cited in Thirsk (1973), p.59.

30 Thirsk (1973), p.54, 72; Levey (1982), p.34.

31 The width of the tops is gathered in by rapidly decreasing stitches immediately before a change to ribbing, which would have helped keep the stocking up, before the leg shaping is commenced in stocking stitch. The heel is turned and the toe shaped and finished by three lines of fully fashioned decreasings.

32 Knitting a gored stocking took significantly longer than knitting plain stockings: the separation for heel flaps was begun much higher and the top part of the foot was gradually narrowed by an inch, taking advantage of the hand-powered process: Henson (1970), p.104.

33 According to Felkin, Josiah Crane patented an adaptation of the frame for 'shading, brocading and flowering in gold, silver etc' in 1769, which needed the help of a drawboy (in a similar manner to the draw loom for weaving). This was later improved by the important addition of a thread carrier, enabling 'most rich waistcoat pieces' to be produced: Felkin (1967), p.107.

34 The technique was well known for darning knitting by the mid-nineteenth century. See, for example, *Plain Knitting and Mending in Six Standards* (1876) pp.32–3; Mrs Warren and Mrs Pullan describe its early use as a decorative technique of 'knitted embroidery' in *Treasures in Needlework* (London, *c*.1855), p.337.

35 Felkin asserts that by 1750 'hose embroidered by the insertion of threads forming a pattern by hand while the stocking was in process of manufacture' had ceased to be made: Felkin (1967), p.434.

36 Felkin (1967), p.434.

37 Felkin (1967), p.108. See also image in Farrell (1992), p.32.

38 Henson (1970), p.166.

39 Green and yellow vertically striped woollen stockings dated late eighteenth century in the Museum of London have separate shaped sole and toe pieces made in tightly knitted white cotton: Museum of London no. 53.101/19.

40 According to Jeremy Farrell, '19 out of every 20 pairs made were black': Farrell (1992), p.60.

41 Farrell (1992), p.62.

42 Farrell (1992), p.63.

43 Margaret Simeon in *The History of Lace* states that, following the development of crochet 'in the early nineteenth century…fine knitting was also used as a new way of making lace, or at least an open lacy fabric that could be used as a substitute' (London, 1979), p.107. A story of lace knitting being introduced in Shetland in 1837 is told in Rutt (1987), p.171. For needlework manuals, see Chapter 3.

44 See Felkin (1967), pp.143–55 and Henson (1970), pp.352–6 for a full account.

45 Other examples of shirts with partial front openings can be found in museums including Nordiska Museet, Stockholm, and the Danish Nationalmuseet in Copenhagen. Their all-over geometric patterning in blocks of plain and purl stitches, when knitted in silk, gives a light-reflecting rich damask effect. Light-coloured cotton or wool yarns are similarly effective in pattern. Evidence for a seventeenth-century woollen knitted shirt is proposed by Ruth Gilbert of the former Textile Conservation Centre, Winchester, who recently studied knitted fragments found at Lindisfarne in 1888: Gilbert, (2008).

46 An infant's jacket held in the Museum of London shows clear traces of the circular knitting technique, the changing position of the marker stitch for the beginning of each round appearing as a faint diagonal line: Museum of London number A21989c, dated seventeenth century. As further evidence of the circular knitting technique, an uncut infants' jacket of this construction exists in the collection of the Knitting and Crochet Guild in Yorkshire.

47 An uncut version identical to this jacket was sold at Sotheby's on 24 September 1980: information from V&A acquisition records and subsequent note, which also mentions a photograph of the uncut version, but its whereabouts is unknown.

48 Buck (1996), p.74.

49 Riello and Parthasarathi (2009), p.114.

50 North and Hart (1998), p.20.

51 Ruth Gilbert, studying at the University of Southampton, lists 33 jackets or panels across the UK (9), France (1), Spain (5), Denmark (3), Sweden (1), Italy (1), the Netherlands (1), United States (7), Austria (1), Germany (1), unknown (2): personal correspondence, November 2007.

52 North and Hart (1998), p.184.

53 Quoted in F. Hinchcliffe, *Knit One Purl One* (exh. cat., Victoria and Albert Museum, London, 1998), p.4.

54 Knitting historian Irena Turnau is of the opinion that there was a large production of patterned silk waistcoats, and the relationship of these to 'similar garments sewn from patterned silk [woven] materials' was 'just as knitted carpets were to the more expensive figural tapestries': Turnau (1991), p.126

55 Gilbert identifies 5 of the 20 garments she has studied as having tubular sleeves: Gilbert, personal correspondence 2007.

56 One must therefore dispute Rutt's assertion that 'we have no clear evidence' that 'some brocaded waistcoats were hand-knitted': Rutt (1987), p.82

57 Lewis (1986), pp.129–48.

58 Henson (1970), p.326, p.327

59 Josiah Crane's invention, described in note 33 above, could have produced the needle selection necessary to achieve knitting in two colours in a row. However, the lower parts and cuffs are worked in plain-and-purl chevron damask, with garter-stitch narrow side edgings. It is possible these areas could have been knitted using turn-stitch machine methods or knitted by hand and 'run on' to the needles to complete the colour knitting, as is still practised in high-quality fully fashioned knitting.

60 Turnau shows that the assortment of knitted items required to qualify as a master evolved in tandem with the demands of fashion, as stockings became more economically significant: Turnau (1991), p.32; Rutt (1987), p.73.

61 Turnau and Ponting (1976), pp.7–59.

62 The carpet has the initials HIC beside the date 1781 and is a close copy of a carpet made in Strasbourg in 1777 by one Jean Henri Fischbach, now in the Musée de l'Oevre Notre Dame: Turnau and Ponting (1976), p.20. The V&A carpet was personally purchased in 1962 by Eric Pasold of the Pasold knitwear firm and placed in the museum in 1977.

63 The only similar item that is known is a petticoat with a variety of abstract patterns within a diamond grid sold at a London auction in 1981: V&A records RF file ref. T.177–1926.

64 By comparison Turnau and Ponting (1976) mention an unusual masterpiece dated 1725 (number 22 in the catalogue) and knitted by nuns, where the imagery is 'completely unsymmetrical with a most odd collection of animals'.

65 Levey (1982); see also Felkin (1967), p.141, who describes a 'fishing-net machine', which received the Society's award of 50 guineas in 1796, demonstrating that thirty years later new inventions were still in demand. The Society became The Royal Society for the Encouragement of Arts, Manufactures and Commerce in 1908 and is now known as the RSA.

66 Levitt (1986).

67 Rutt (1987), p.119; O'Connell Edwards (2010), p.21.

68 The hand-coloured charts featured in volume 3 of Jane Gaugain's *Lady's Assistant* (Edinburgh, 1845) could also be applied to such beaded patterns in addition to worsted work (see p.126).

69 Macdonald (1988), p.15.

70 *Pearsall's Illustrated Handbook for Knitting in Silks* (London, 1900), endpaper.

2 Livelihood and Industry

1   Walker (1814), p.89.

2   See, for example, Harte (1997).

3   D. Defoe [1724–6], (abridged 1971), p.207, 513.

4   J. Thirsk, 'The Fantastical Folly of Fashion: The English Stocking Knitting Industry 1500–1700', in *Textile History and Economic History*, ed. N.B. Harte and K.B. Ponting (Manchester, 1973), pp.50–73.

5   Cunnington (1970), p.181.

6   Quoted in H. Barty-King (2006), p.11.

7   Act of Parliament 6 Geo.III c.29, cited in Rath (1976), pp.140–53.

8   A. Young, *Tour of the North* [1770], cited in Hartley and Ingleby (2001), p.63.

9   Rath (1976), pp.140–53.

10 O'Connell Edwards, (2007), pp.44–7.

11 S.A. Mason, *The History of the Worshipful Company of Framework Knitters* (Leicester, 2000).

12 Rutt (1987), pp.167–8.

13 Henshall and Maxwell (1951–2), pp.30–42.

14 Quoted in Fietelson (2006), p.28.

15 Fryer, (1995), p.25. The enquiry was held in Edinburgh.

16 Ann Sinclair, paper on Fair Isle knitting presented at Pasold Symposium on Knitting in Scotland, National Museum of Scotland, March 2008.

17 Fryer (1995), p.71.

18 From an 1871 account of Shetland by Robert Cowie, quoted in Rutt (1987), p.173, and Fryer (1995), p.70.

19 Fryer (1995), p.70.

20 A 1914 report on Fair Isle hosiery by W.R. Scott, part of a larger 'Report to the Board of Agriculture for Scotland on Home Industries in the Highlands and Islands', states, 'The first beginnings of the industry came when a Spanish galleon belonging to the Armada, and said to have been the flagship of the Duke of Medina Sidonia, was wrecked at Fair Isle in 1588. The islanders were taught the art of knitting by some of the surviving sailors'; *The Economic Journal*, vol. 25, no. 98 (June 1915). Scott was in turn citing a text by J. Wilson, *A Voyage Around the Coasts of Scotland and the Isles* (Edinburgh, 1842), p.411. A carbon-copy document of the report is in V&A records relating to Fair Isle gloves and mittens, T.80 & 81–1916. See also Norbury, (1962), pp.10 and 173, repeating the story. Rutt (1987), pp.176–9, discusses its inaccuracy at length.

21 For example, Fair Isle beret dated c.1900, TEX 2004.439; Fair Isle seaman's cap, 1916, TEX 7740, Shetland Museum and Archives.

22 In 1987 educationalist Mary Harris of the Institute of Education in London created an exhibition, *Common Threads*, highlighting the inherent mathematics within textile practice, utilizing examples of knitting and children's socks to illuminate mathematical principles of repeat and symmetry. This exhibition is now housed at the Constance Howard Textile Centre at Goldsmiths College, London.

23 Starmore (1990), p.20.

24 Freeman (1990), pp.24–32.

25 Fryer (1995), p.136.

26 V&A records and author interview with Annie Thomson's daughter Ann Sinclair, September 2010.

27 This description of Lee comes from economic historian Stanley Chapman: Chapman (2002), p.1.

28 Henson (1970), p.45.

29 N. Harte, 'Wm Lee and the Invention of the Knitting Frame', in *Four Centuries of Machine Knitting*, ed. J. Millington and S. Chapman (Leicester, 1989).

30 Defoe (1971), p. 465.

31 Thirsk (1973), p.72.

32 Wells (1972) p.95, p.78.

33 A typical nineteenth-century frame shop can be seen at Ruddington Framework Knitters Museum, Nottingham.

34 As a trade union leader, Gravenor Henson played a significant role in this period, as he later recounted in his *History*: Wells (1972), p.95. 'Cut-and-sewn' production eventually became predominant in the hosiery industry.

35 *Report of the Commissioners Appointed to Inquire into the Conditions of the Framework Knitters, Part II, Nottinghamshire and Derbyshire*, 1845, quoted in Weir (1998) p.24.

36 Wells (1972), p.112.

37 Palmer (1984), p.28.

38 Lewis (1986), pp.129–48.

39 According to Marilyn Palmer, 'by 1800 the stocking frame had reached the limits of its versatility, being able to knit forty distinct types of fabric': Palmer (1984), p.12.

40 Wells (1972), p.75.

41 William Cotton of Loughborough first patented his rotary-powered straight-bar automatic fully fashioned machines in 1864, representing a transition from hand power to industrial high-speed mass production. The machines were a direct descendant of William Lee's early frames.

42 However, there were exceptions: Stanley Chapman states that in the mid-eighteenth century 'in Nottingham 200 women were working stocking frames': Chapman (2002), p.14.

43 'The Flying Wheel', 150th anniversary publication by I&R Morley, published to coincide with their exhibit at the British Empire Exhibition, Wembley, London (1924), p.22, Ruddington Framework Knitters Museum Archives, Nottingham.

44 See description of fleecy machine knitting technique in Glossary.

45 Levitt (1986), p.206.

46 See Cunnington and Mansfield (1978), plate 45.

47 A knitting pattern for knee warmers and other items of underwear such as long underpants featured in every edition of Patons and Baldwins *Woolcraft* manual, including the updated and revised 25th 'original' edition published in 2001 (see also Chapter 3): Rutt (1987), p.146.

48 Cunnington and Mansfield (1978), p.124; see p.130, jersey fabric 'coat shaped wrapper' by Robertson, Higgins and Lowe, 1885.

49 Jaeger (1897), pp.118, 153.

50 A.E. Garrett, item 1327/15, Jaeger Archive, Westminster Archive Centre, London.

51 A.E. Garrett, 'Why Wool?', leaflet, 1933, item 1327/16, Jaeger Archive, Westminster Archive Centre, London.

52 W. Vaughan, *An Essay, Philosophical and Medical, Concerning Modern Clothing* (Rochester, 1792): 'The last part of my Essay concerns a Proposal for Stockings to be made with Toes, as Gloves are with fingers'; p.110.

53 Jaeger (1897), p.123.

54 Barty-King (2006), p.85.

55 Great Exhibition, Report of the Jury, Class XX, Clothing and Goods of Immediate Personal and Domestic Use, National Art Library, Victoria and Albert Museum, London, also available online at www.royalcommission1851.org.uk.

56 First introduced into Australia by settlers in 1788, Spanish Merino sheep thrived and an export trade soon developed, the first bale of Australian wool arriving in England in 1807. While the term 'Merino' also refers to the breed of sheep, 'Merino' refers to a wool/cotton-mix knitting yarn.

57 For example, Courtaulds was taken over in 2000 by American conglomerate Sarah Lee, who then resold it in 2006.

58 Levitt (1986), p.205.

59 Ibid, p.205.

60 See also L. Johnston, *Nineteenth-Century Fashion in Detail* (London, 2005), pp.12–13.

61 Barty-King (2006).

62 Schiaparelli (1954), p.60.

63 Jane Koster, 'For Two Pins – Fashion Designing for Hand Knitters', lecture for The Wool Education Society at the Royal Society of Arts, Adelphi, London, 22 January 1957, published by the International Wool Secretariat, Department of Education, London.

64 'The Fashion for Hand Knitteds', *Harper's Bazaar* (November 1951), p.57.

65 See ibid.; Hinchcliffe (1985); Koster (1957).

66 Maria Luck-Szanto, company portfolio, 1975, V&A: Maria Luck-Szanto Archive, vol.1, p.2.

67 Maria Luck-Szanto, 'Resume on the Invention of a Tailor Knitting Machine', V&A: Maria Luck-Szanto archive, vol.2, p.27.

68 Macqueen and Szanto applied for a joint patent in 1956 for 'Improvements in or relating to Knitting Processes and Knitting Machines'. This was subsequently changed, being made solely in Macqueen's name, as he was developing the machine in practice with engineering firms, but, an agreement was drawn up to protect Maria Luck-Szanto's interests.

69 'The Macqueen Tailor-Knitting Technique', *Hosiery Trade Journal* (October 1960), pp.96–103.

70 K. Macqueen, 'Cybernetics and Haute Couture', *New Scientist* (28 February 1963), pp.450–53.

71 M.W. Betts and F. Robinson, 'Whole Garment and Integral Garment Knitting and its Application in the De-Skilling of Garment Assembly', *Knitting International* (August 1976), pp.31–6.

72 Part of the early WHI Archive, including knitting patterns, knitwear and incomplete garments, is now held at the London College of Fashion.

73 Press release dated 2 October 1947, issued by the WVS, WHI Archive, London College of Fashion.

74 Lady Reading, press cutting, no publication name, WHI Archive, London College of Fashion.

75 Minutes of WHI board meeting dated 10 October 1949, WHI Archive, London College of Fashion.

76 Menkes (1983), p.8. Sandy Black's 'Vase of Flowers' angora coat features on the cover.

77 David Spencer, in his key reference work *Knitting Technology*, acknowledges that 'Micro-electronic technology, computer programming and major advances in shaping techniques have enabled the major part of his [Macqueen's] far-sighted dream to be realized': Spencer (2001), p.225.

3 Knitting in the Home

1 Travellers such as Daniel Defoe (himself a wholesaler in the hosiery trade), William Howitt, John Aubrey and Celia Fiennes provide informative accounts of the economic and social aspects of rural industry around the British Isles, before industrialization: Defoe [1724–26], (abridged 1971); J. Aubrey, *Perambulation of Half the County of Surrey* (London, 1673); W. Howitt, *The Rural Life of England* (London, 1844); C. Fiennes, *The Illustrated Journeys of Celia Fiennes 1685–1712*, ed. C. Morris (London, 1982).

2 Hartley and Ingleby (2001), p.17.

3 T. Pennant, *A Tour of Wales in 1773* (London, 1778–81), cited in Rutt (1987), p.162.

4 Howitt, (1844), quoted in Hartley and Ingleby (2001), pp.81–2; J. Thirsk, 'The Hand Knitting Industry', in eds Millington and Chapman (1989), p.13.

5 Macdonald (1988), p.7.

6 Ibid., p.3.

7 Ibid., pp.8, 9.

8 Irena Turnau asserts that references in literature to folk knitting before the seventeenth century are rare, and nothing older than the seventeenth or eighteenth century is found in European museums: I. Turnau, *The History of Knitting Before Mass Production*, trans. A. Szonert (Warsaw, 1991), p.163.

9 Both Sheila McGregor and, more recently, Annemor Sundbø, trace the stitch patterns and techniques used in Scandinavian and Norwegian folk costume, from seventeenth-century jackets to the well-known Norwegian Selbu and Setesdal knitting, in Sundbø's case through the medium of her 'rag pile' of discarded sweaters: McGregor (1984); Sundbø (2001a) and (2001b).

10 The knitting writer and collector Montse Stanley amassed an extensive postcard collection, now at the University of Southampton, showing knitting from Holland, the Balkans, Sardinia, Sweden, Germany, Macedonia, the French regions of Bretagne, Auvergne, Breton, Normandy, the Pyrenees, Limousin, and Alsace, plus Biscay and Lerwick in the Shetland Islands.

11 See illustrations in Hartley and Ingleby (2001), pp.57, 58, 60.

12 See Gravelle LeCount (1990).

13 Letter dated 7 September 1977 to Kathleen Kinder by Lily Crooks. Documents from V&A AAD RF file for T.47–1989.

14 Thompson (1955); M. Wright, *Cornish Guernseys and Knit Frocks* (Penzance, 1979); Pearson (1984); Compton (London, 1985).

15 Starmore and Matheson (1983), pp.11–12.

16 Mrs Noble, quoted in Pearson (1984), p.45.

17 Lt. Col. W. Marshall-Fraser, quoted in Thompson (1955), p.19.

18 The technique is described by Sheila McGregor (1984) pp.22–8 and (with slight differences) by Sokalski (1993), pp.51–2.

19 Refer to www.vanhaintyo.fi.

20 This popular epithet came from Robert Southey, who wrote 'They er terrible knitters e' Dent', in *The Doctor* (1834–7), as cited in Hartley and Ingleby (2001) p.78.

21 Rutt (1987), p.193.

22 A. Svenson and R. Warren, *Sock Monkeys (200 out of 1,863)* (New York, 2002).

23 Rutt (1987), p.76.

24 Hartley and Ingleby (2001), p.18.

25 *The Knitting Teachers Assistant Designed for the Use of National Girls' Schools* [1838], ed. E.M. Corbould (London, 1877); R.J. Cattlow, *Directions for Plain Knitting for the Working Classes and Schools* (Cheadle, 1846). See also L. Floyer, *Plain Knitting and Mending in Six Standards* (1876). All are cited in E. Potter, 'English Knitting and Crochet Books of the Nineteenth Century', *The Library: Transactions of the Bibliographical Society* (May/June 1955), pp.24–40.

26 Humphrey (2006), pp.17–18.

27 Macdonald (1988), p.151.

28 Ethel M. Dudley, *Knitting for Infants and Juniors* (London, 1914).

29 E.P. and C.A. Claydon, *Knitting without Specimens: the Modern book of School Knitting and Crochet* (London, 1914), preface.

30 J. Robertson, 'Knitting Lessons in Primary Schools May be Cut', *Shetland Times* (3 May 2010), Available at www.shetlandtimes.co.uk/2010/05/03; H.J. Marter, 'Knitting Goes from School Curriculum', *Shetland News* (7 May 2010), available at www.shetland-news.co.uk/2010/May/news, accessed 20 October 2010.

31 Rutt (1987), p.137. Harvey (1985), p.64, says the queen knitted four scarves 'to be given to the four most distinguished private soldiers in Colonial regiments serving in the Boer War (1899–1902)', with names.

32 Humphrey (2006), p.53. Humphrey compares pinballs from the V&A Museum, London, Fitzwilliam Museum, Cambridge, Castle Museum, York, and Ackworth School with the embroidered medallion samplers at Ackworth, pp.53–9.

33 Harvey (1985), p.57.

34 J. Gaugain, *The Lady's Assistant*, vol.1, 4th ed. (Edinburgh and London, 1841), p.16.

35 Ibid., Preface.

36 Rutt (1987), pp.111–38, 234–8.

37 For a full account , see Bonney (2008–9), pp.4–9.

38 F.M. Ford, *A Call* (1910), reprint (Manchester, 1984), p.67.

39 Rutt (1987), p.113.

40 Gaugain from vol.III of *The Lady's Assistant*, preface p.v (Edinburgh, 1846).

41 M. Tillotson, *The Complete Knitting Book*, 5th ed. (London, 1948), p.198.

42 Similarly, in Europe, companies providing yarns for the textile industry also produced yarns and patterns for the hand-knitting market to meet growing demand, including Lana Gatto, Filpucci and Loro Piana in Italy. Catering just for the home knitting market were others such as Anny Blatt, Pingouin and Georges Picaud in France and Woll ID in Germany.

43 Keighly (1989), p.32.

44 Ann Talbot, 'Emphasis on Embroidery', *Stitchcraft* (May 1937), p.8.

45 Rutt, however, points out one or two historical errors and inconsistencies: Rutt (1987), e.g., p.93.

46 J. Norbury, 'Design in Knitting' (lecture given to the Wool Education Society, The Royal Institution, London, 9 October 1952), published by the International Wool Secretariat (London, 1952).

47 The Women's Library, London. Information from exhibition 'Women's Magazines' 2009.

48 F. Klickman, *Popular Knitting Book* (London, 1921), Preface.

49 *Woman's Weekly* (1 February 1936).

50 Braithwaite (1995).

51 Eve Sandford, quoted in ref. AAD 6/1-1988, Archives of Art and Design, V&A, London.

52 Candee (1988), pp.62–92.

53 Leaflet, Ruddington Framework Knitting Museum archive, 1930s, Nottinghamshire.

54 K. Kinder, '400 Years of Domestic Machine Knitting', in *Four Centuries of Machine Knitting*, ed. J. Millington and S. Chapman (Leicester, 1989), pp.69–72.

55 Bulletin of the Associated Field Comforts, Hamilton, Ontario, April 1917, held in collection of McMaster University, Hamilton, Ontario, available at http://pw20c.mcmaster.ca, retrieved 15 November 2009.

56 The soldiers' replies are kept in the McMaster University Library in Hamilton. See 'Socks for the Boys: Marion Simpson and the Knitters of the First World War', available at http://pw20c.mcmaster.ca, accessed 15 November 2009.

57 'Knitting for the RAF', pattern booklet, ref.608.AH.0056, National Art Library, V&A, London.

58 M. Murray and J. Koster, *Practical Knitting Illustrated* (London, 1940), p.34.

59 M. Murray and J. Koster, *Knitting for All* (London, 1941), p.254.

60 M. Murray and J. Koster, *Complete Home Knitting* (London, 1942), Foreword.

61 *Vogue's 23rd Knitting Book* (London, 1943), p.5.

62 *Vogue's 19th Knitting Book* (London, 1941), p.5.

63 Quoted in 6.6.41 F39 Housewife, Mass Observation diaries, Special Collections, The Library, University of Sussex, Brighton.

64 File 18/4/B, Mass Observation Shop Interviews, London 17–23 July, Worcester 1–6 July 1941, Special Collections, The Library, University of Sussex, Brighton. Rationing of clothing was introduced on 1 June 1941.

65 23.4.41, Mass Observation diaries, 'Grumbles', Mill Hill, London, Special Collections, The Library, University of Sussex, Brighton.

66 W.E. Shewell-Cooper, *Land Girl: A Manual for Volunteers in the Women's Land Army* (London, 1942). See also A. de la Haye, *Land Girls: Cinderellas of the Soil* (exh. cat. Brighton Museum, 2009).

67 18/3/C F35C, shop assistant B, Mass Observation, July 1941, Special Collections, The Library, University of Sussex, Brighton.

68 See Handley (1999), p.50. Sketchley 'the dry cleaners' employed girls specifically for knitting up the ladders in nylons.

69 *Knitting Wool Review* (1958), p.30.

70 Walker's books greatly expanded the early work of Marjory Tillotson and Mary Thomas without the corresponding garment designs that might so easily have dated.

71 S. Lewis and J. Weissman, *A Machine Knitter's Guide to Creating Fabrics*, Lark Books (Asheville, North Carolina 1986). Although the technology of domestic machines has become more sophisticated and now gives much greater patterning scope, the creativity of these designs was exceptional for the time and illustrated the potential of the craft.

72 In 1997, Stanley co-curated a major exhibition at the Textile Museum in Terrassa, Spain, covering the last thousand years of knitting design, using both her own and the museum's collections: *Mil Anys de Disseny en Punt* (exh. cat., Centre de Documentació i Museu Tèxtil, Terrassa, 1997).

73 Tellier-Loumagne, trans. S. Black (2005).

74 However, the association with *Vogue* no longer pertains, and the title *Vogue Knitting* although retained in America, has now changed to *Designer Knitting* for the UK.

75 Macdonald (1988), p.xx–xxi.

76 A term eliding craft and political activism coined by artists such as knitter Betsy Greer to recognize the resurgence of craft as it relates to socially engaged art practice. In December 2009 the Arnolfini Gallery in Bristol staged an exhibition entitled *Craftivism*, and in November 2011 the journal *Utopian Studies* (Oxford Brookes University) published a special issue on Craftivism.

4 Classics to Couture

1 The use of the word cardigan to denote a woollen jacket worn informally derives from the Earl of Cardigan (1797–1868), who is said to have worn such a garment around the time of the Crimean War. This is disputed by Rutt (1987), p.135.

2 See Rutt (1987), p.132.

3 Louisa Starr, cited in Wilson and Taylor (1989), p.62, quoting from Susannah Handley, 'Aesthetic Dress 1910–1939' (BA thesis, Brighton Polytechnic, 1983).

4 Kate Gielgud, quoted in Wilson and Taylor (1989), p.55.

5 Adburgham (1961).

6 Levitt (1986), p.126; Rutt (1987), p.134.

7 Cited in Adburgham (1981), p.192.

8 Pasold (1977), p.208.

9 Wilson and Taylor (1989), p.87.

10 Kiewe propounded ancient links between Celtic patterns and Aran knitting, and went on to promote the style at Art Needlework Industries, which sold knitting patterns and needlework supplies until 1986. Popular films such as *Man of Aran* (1934) and the documentary drama *Edge of the World* (1937) helped to establish the romance of island life, but the men in the films all wear dark-coloured ganseys. See H.E. Kiewe, *The Sacred History of Knitting* (Oxford, 1967), illustrations 46, 47, 60 etc following p.114. See also Rutt (1987), p.194.

11 M. Gross, *Genuine Authentic: The Real Life of Ralph Lauren* (New York, 2003), p.37.

12 For further discussion of Cowichan knitting, see Miekle (1987) and Rutt (1987), pp.206–8.

13 J. Modlinger, 'Knitmistresses', *Guardian* (15 May 1973).

14 In the author's own business, for example, an angora coat went on sale at Saks Fifth Avenue, New York, for $1000 after the store mark-up of 150–300%.

15 S. Menkes, *The Knitwear Revolution* (London, 1983), p.10.

16 An example is *Sheep in Wolf's Clothing* (1986) by Judith Duffey in the Whitworth Art Gallery, Manchester.

17 'Knit Two Together and Double the Fashion', undated magazine tearsheets, Ritva archive, V&A AAD/2001/2/4.

18 Imogen Fox, 'Interesting Jumpers', *Guardian* (16 November 2007), p.21.

19 The 2000–2 exhibition toured the London College of Fashion, The Harley Gallery, Nottinghamshire, and Hawick Museum, Scotland, with an accompanying catalogue published by the London College of Fashion.

20 Sarah Ratty, quoted in 'What Next?', *i-D* (May 1991), p.34.

21 See Black (2002), pp.90–117.

22 Quote from label text in *Radical Fashion* exhibition, V&A Museum, 2001. Documents from V&A AAD file.

23 Black (2002), p.43.

24 Rei Kawakubo, quoted in Koren (1984), p.117.

25 Ibid, p.114. However, in the *St James Fashion Encyclopedia*, fashion curator and writer Richard Martin's 50-year fashion chronology of just one page length lists Rei Kawakubo's 'lace sweater' as the sole entry for 1982, alongside entries such as Dior's 'New Look' for 1947: *St James Fashion Encyclopedia*, ed. R. Martin, rev. ed. (Detroit, 1997), Introduction, p.*x*.

26 Yohji Yamamoto, quote from *Radical Fashion*, ed. C. Wilcox (exh. cat., Victoria and Albert Museum, London, 2001), p.136.

27 Vivienne Westwood, quote from *Radical Fashion* (2001), p.136.

28 A. Boyd, 'Piling it On', *Observer* (8 December 1974), p.23.

29 Lisa Armstrong, Introduction to Shi Cashmere catalogue (London, 2006).

30 Rew (2003).

31 Baccarat was initially set up by Claire and Monty Black to support designers by providing them with production capability.

32 Ibid., p.61.

33 There have been a number of exhibitions of Missoni's work, including *Workshop Missoni: Daring to be Different* in Milan and London in 2009: see *Workshop Missoni: Daring to be Different* (exh. cat., Estorick Collection, London, July–Sept 2009, curated by Luca Missoni).

34 K. Samuel, quoted in Tutino Vercelloni (1994), p.27.

35 Rosita Missoni, quoted in Tutino Vercelloni (1994), p.14.

36 Author interview with Luca Missoni, July 2009.

37 A. Fraser, essay in *Jean Muir* (exh. cat., Leeds City Art Galleries, 1980), p.7. Lady Antonia Fraser is referencing seventeenth-century poet Robert Herrick.

38 Stemp (2007), p.11.

39 J. Lumley, quoted in ibid., p.121.

40 Ibid., pp.17 and 19.

41 Author interview with Joyce Fenton-Douglas, former studio manager and design director at Jean Muir, September 2010.

42 J. Muir, 'Manifesto for Real Design', *Sunday Times Magazine* (6 March 1994), p.5.

43 Ben de Lisi, speaking at London College of Fashion, Conversations in Cool series, 6 February 2008.

44 Author interview with Sandra Backlund, 15 September 2008.

45 Sandra Backlund, quote from press release, September 2009.

46 Entitled *Unravelled*, the series of films was broadcast in ten episodes from December 2008 to February 2009; available at www.showstudio.com/archive.

47 Author interview, 21 September 2010.

Further Reading

A. Adburgham, *A Punch History of Manners and Modes* (London, 1961)

A. Adburgham, *Shops and Shopping* [1964] (London, 1981)

H. Barty-King, *Pringle of Scotland and the Hawick Knitwear Story* (Fakenham, 2006)

S. Black, *Knitwear in Fashion* (London and New York, 2002)

H. Bonney, 'Polka Knitting', *Text (Journal of the Textile Society)* (2008–9), vol.32, pp.4–9

B. Braithwaite, *Women's Magazines: The First 300 Years* (London, 1995)

A. Buck, *Clothes and the Child: A Handbook of Children's Dress in England 1500–1900* (Bedford, 1996)

K. Buckland, 'The Monmouth Cap', *Costume* (1979), vol.13, no.9, pp.23–37

K. Buckland, '"A sign of some degree" – the Mystery of Capping', *Text (Journal of the Textile Society)* (2008–9), vol.36, pp.40–45

D. K. Burnham, 'Coptic Knitting: An Ancient Technique', *Textile History* (1972), vol.3, pp.116–24

R. Candee, 'Domestic Knitting in the Factory Age: Anglo-America Developments of the "Family" Knitting Machine', *Textile History* (1988), vol.29: 1, pp.62–92

S. Chapman, *Hosiery and Knitwear: Four Centuries of Small-Scale Industry in Britain c.1589–2000* (Oxford, 2002)

R. Compton, *The Complete Book of Traditional Guernsey and Jersey Knitting* (London, 1985)

E. Crowfoot, F. Pritchard and K. Staniland, *Textiles and Clothing 1150–1450* (Woodbridge, 2001)

V. Cumming, C.W. Cunnington and P.E. Cunnington, *The Dictionary of Fashion History* (Oxford, 2010)

C.W. Cunnington and P. Cunnington, *Handbook of English Costume in the Eighteenth Century* [1964] (London, 1970)

C. Cunnington and A. Mansfield, *English Costume for Sports and Outdoor Recreation* [1969] (London, 1978)

D. Defoe, *A Tour Through the Whole Island of Great Britain* [1724–6], abridged (Harmondsworth, 1971)

J. Farrell, *Socks and Stockings* (London, 1992)

W. Felkin, *History of the Machine-Wrought Hosiery and Lace Manufactures* [1867], centenary edition (Newton Abbot, 1967)

A. Fietelson, *The Art of Fairisle Knitting* [1996] (Colorado, 2006)

J. Freeman, 'The Crafts as Poor Relations' in *Oral History, The Journal of the Oral History Society* (Autumn 1990), vol.18, no.2, pp.24–32

L. Fryer, *Knitting by the Fireside and on the Hillside: a History of the Shetland Hand Knitting Industry* (Lerwick, 1995)

R. Gilbert, 'Not so much Cinderella as the Sleeping Beauty: Neglected Evidence of Forgotten Skill', *Proceedings of North European Symposium for Archaeological Textiles X*, Copenhagen, 2008

M. Ginsberg, *Fashion: an Anthology* (exh. cat., Victoria and Albert Museum, London, 1971)

C. Gravelle LeCount, *Andean Folk Knitting* (Saint Paul, Minnesota, 1990)

S. Handley, *Nylon: the Story of a Fashion Revolution* (Baltimore, 1999)

N. Harte (ed.), *The New Draperies in the Low Countries and England, 1300–1800*, Pasold Studies in Textile History (Oxford, 1997)

M. Hartley and J. Ingleby, *The Old Handknitters of the Dales* [1951] (Ilkley, 2001)

M. Harvey, *Patons: A Story of Handknitting* (Ascot, 1985)

A.S. Henshall and S. Maxwell, 'Clothing and Other Articles Found in a Late Seventeenth-Century Grave at Gunnister, Shetland, *Proceedings of the Society of Antiquaries of Scotland* (1951–2), vol.86, pp.30–42

G. Henson, *History of the Framework Knitters* [1831] (Newton Abbot, 1970)

F. Hinchcliffe, *Knit One, Purl One: Historic and Contemporary Knitting from the V&A's Collection* (exh. cat., Victoria and Albert Museum, 1985)

C. Humphrey, *Quaker School Girl Samplers from Ackworth* (Britain, 2006)

G. Jaeger, *Health Culture*, trans. L. Tomalin (London, 1897)

M. Keighly, *A Fabric Huge: The Story of Listers* (London, 1989)

L. Koren, *New Fashion Japan* (Tokyo, 1984)

Leeds City Art Galleries, *Jean Muir* (exh. cat. 1980)

S.M. Levey, 'Illustrations of the History of Knitting Selected from the Collection of the Victoria and Albert Museum' *Textile History* (1969), vol.1, part 2, pp.183–205

S.M. Levey, 'Glove, Cap and Boothose', *Crafts* (July–Aug. 1982), pp.34–40

S. Levitt, *Victorians Unbuttoned: Registered Designs for Clothing, their Makers and Wearers, 1839–1900* (London, 1986)

P. Lewis, 'William Lee's Stocking Frame: Technical Evolution and Economic Viability 1589–1750', *Textile History* (1986), vol.17, no.2, pp.129–148

A.L. Macdonald, *No Idle Hands: A Social History of American Knitting* (New York, 1988)

S.A. Mason, *The History of the Worshipful Company of Framework Knitters* (Leicester, 2000)

S. McGregor, *The Complete Book of Traditional Scandinavian Knitting* (London, 1984)

M. Meikle, *Cowichan Indian Knitting* (Vancouver, 1987)

S. Menkes, *The Knitwear Revolution* (London, 1983)

J. Millington and S. Chapman (eds), *Four Centuries of Machine Knitting* (Leicester, 1989)

P. Noé (ed.), *Workshop Missoni: Daring to be Different* (Rome, 2009)

J. Norbury, *Traditional Knitting Patterns* (London, 1962)

O. Nordland, Primitive Scandinavian Textiles in Knotless Netting, *Studia Norvegica* no 10, (Oslo, 1961)

S. North and A. Hart, *Historical Fashion in Detail* (London, 1998)

L. O'Connell Edwards, 'Azores Lace', *Slipknot* (Summer 2010), no.128, p.21

L. O'Connell Edwards, 'Evidence for Hand-Knitting from Elizabethan England 1560–1600', *Text (Journal of the Textile Society)* (2007), vol.35, pp. 44–7

M. Palmer, *Framework Knitting* (Princes Risborough, Aylesbury, 1984)

E. Pasold, *Ladybird, Ladybird: A Story of Private Enterprise* (Manchester, 1977)

M. Pearson, *Traditional Knitting: Aran, Fair Isle and Fisher Ganseys* (London, 1984)

T. Rath, 'The Tewkesbury Hosiery Industry', *Textile History* (1976), vol.7, pp.140–53

C. Rew, *Bill Gibb: 'the Golden Boy of British Fashion'* (exh. cat., Aberdeen Art Gallery and Museums, 2003)

G. Riello and P. Parthasarathi, *The Spinning World*, Pasold Studies in Textile History, no.16 (Oxford, 2009)

M. Ringgaard, 'A Purple Knitted Silk Among Brown Rags. Excavated Textiles from an Eighteenth-Century Rubbish Dump in Copenhagen', in *Costume: Design and Decoration: Proceedings of the ICOM's Costume Committee* ed. Katia Johansen (Copenhagen and Lund, 2007), pp.93–7

R. Rutt, *A History of Hand-Knitting* (London, 1987)

E. Schiaparelli, *Shocking Life* (Dutton, 1954)

L. Sokalski, *Knitting Around the World* (Newtown, Connecticut, 1993)

N. Speiser, *The Manual of Braiding* (Basel, 1983)

D. Spencer, *Knitting Technology* [1983], 3rd ed. (Cambridge, 2001)

M. Stanley, 'Mil Anys de Punt', in *Mil Anys de Disseny en Punt* (exh. cat., Centre de Documentació i Museu Textil, Terrassa, 1997)

M. Stanley, 'Jumpers That Drive You Quite Insane', in *Disentangling Textiles*, eds M. Schoeser and C. Boydell (Middlesex, 2002)

A. Starmore, *Fair Isle Knitting Handbook* [1988] (London, 1990)

A. Starmore and A. Matheson, *Knitting from the British Islands* (London, 1983)

S. Stemp, *Jean Muir: Beyond Fashion* (Woodbridge, 2007)

A. Sundbø, *Setesdal Sweaters* (Kristiansand, 2001a)

A. Sundbø, *Everyday Knitting: Treasures from a Ragpile* [1994] (Kristiansand, 2001b)

A. Svenson and R. Warren, *Sock Monkeys (200 out of 1,863)* (New York, 2002)

L. Taylor, *Establishing Dress History* (Manchester, 2004)

F. Tellier-Loumagne, *The Art of Knitting*, trans. S. Black (London, 2005)

J. Thirsk, 'The Fantastical Folly of Fashion: the English Stocking Knitting Industry 1500–1700', in *Textile History and Economic History: Essays in Honour of Julia de Lacy Mann*, ed. N.B. Harte and K.B. Ponting (Manchester, 1973)

M. Thomas, *Knitting Book* [1938] (London, 1987)

G. Thompson, *Guernsey and Jersey Patterns* (London, 1955)

I. Turnau, 'The Diffusion of Knitting in Medieval Europe' in

N.B. Harte and K.G. Ponting (eds), *Cloth and Clothing in Medieval Europe* (London, 1983)

I. Turnau, *The History of Knitting Before Mass Production*, trans. by A. Szonert, (Warsaw, 1991)

I. Turnau and K.G. Ponting, 'Knitted Masterpieces', *Textile History* (1976) vol.7, pp.7–59

J. Turney, *The Culture of Knitting* (London, 2009)

I. Tutino Vercelloni (ed.), *Missonologia: The World of Missoni* (Milan, 1994)

G. Walker, *The Costume of Yorkshire* (London, 1814)

C. Weir, *As Poor as a Stockinger* (Nottingham, 1998)

F.A. Wells, *The British Hosiery and Knitwear Industry: its History and Organisation* (Newton Abbot, 1972)

E. Wilson and L. Taylor, *Through the Looking Glass* (London, 1989)

M. Wright, *Cornish Guernseys and Knit Frocks* (Penzance, 1979)

Glossary

beam Part of a warp-knitting machine around which the warp threads are wound and set horizontally in position.

bearded needle The original type of knitting element used on the earliest knitting machines developed by William Lee, and still used today on some straight bar and warp-knitting machines. It is made from one piece of sprung steel with its tip bent back to form a hook, and requires the use of a presser bar to form knitted loops.

braiding Process of diagonally interlacing three or more parallel threads to form one narrow fabric, known as a braid or plait.

chevening Hand-embroidered decoration worked on frame-knitted and industrially-knitted stockings in the nineteenth and early twentieth centuries. It is often in the form of a narrow line and arrowhead running from the foot to the calf.

circular knitting A type of knitting by hand- or weft-knitting on a circular or flat V-bed machine in which the direction of knitting is continuous, creating a seamless tube formed in a spiral. In hand-knitting, it is made on a set of four or five straight needles, or a modern circular needle. In industrial knitting, it refers to tubular knitting from machines that have circular needle beds.

combinations Name given to an all-in-one underwear garment, popular from the mid-nineteenth century to early twentieth century for men and, later, women, which combined a vest or undershirt with drawers or underpants in one piece.

compound needle The knitting element used on specialist machines, similar to a latch needle but with a sliding mechanism which opens and closes the hook of the needle.

crossed-loop technique In hand-knitting, a method of working knit and purl stitches into the back of the loop, which creates a crossed or twisted stitch, an effect also seen in **single-needle knitting** (**nalbinding**). See Thomas (1987), pp.50–7 for several variations.

cut-and-sew knitwear Fully cut from jersey fabrics or from **garment blanks**, which may have some trims included. Garment-length knitting sequences are produced on both circular and flat-bed machines, in continuous sequence, separated by draw threads. A typical sweater may have back and front cut from one piece and sleeves from another.

cut work Embroidery technique on finely woven fabric, where portions have been cut away and filled in with stitch work.

damask Term derived from woven cloth where a pattern is created on a monochrome fabric through the light and shade reflected by contrasting textures.

double bed Knitting machine with two needle beds.

double jacquard A patterned fabric based on rib structure which is created on a double bed flat knitting machine or circular rib machine. One needle bed knits the colour pattern on the face of the fabric and the other knits a backing from the yarns that would form floats in single-bed jacquard.

Dutch heel One of several methods of heel shaping in common use. The Dutch heel is square-shaped and made by knitting a rectangular heel flap, maintaining a fixed number of stitches in the centre when turning the heel.

felting Effect in woollen fabric (knitted or woven) in which the fibres are irreversibly enmeshed, from the deliberate action of washing and rubbing the fabric. See also **fulling**.

fleecy Machine-knitted single bed or circular knit fabric incorporating additional fleece yarn inlaid over the needles. During the finishing process, this is brushed to form an entangled surface to enhance insulation and warmth. Used historically in underwear and in outerwear.

floats Strands of yarn not knitted into the pattern which appear on the back of the knitted fabric until used again; particularly seen in coloured knitting.

float jacquard Created on a single needle bed machine, with floats of yarn across the back of the fabric between selected pattern stitches in that colour. In hand-knitting this fabric is often termed 'Fair Isle'.

fulling Term used in the medieval cap knitting trade to describe the deliberate enmeshing of the wool fibres through washing and agitation, closing the spaces in the knitted fabric. This allowed the knitting to be cut without it unravelling. See **felting**.

fully fashioned The shaping of individual garment pieces during knitting so that each edge is a **selvedge**. Shapings are often decorative, especially at the armholes, forming characteristic marks near the edge of the fabric and leaving a smooth edge for seaming. These fully fashioned increases and decreases are regarded as a mark of high quality knitwear. As there is no wastage, luxury knitwear in yarns such as cashmere are produced in this manner.

gansey Dialect term from Shetland, Yorkshire and Suffolk (*English Dialect Dictionary* 1900) for the knitted garment known as a **guernsey**.

garment blank Unshaped piece of machine-knitted fabric from which garment shapes are cut. These are created from a garment knitting programme sequence that usually incorporates a welt at the lower edge and other design features.

gauge A system of measuring the number of needles on a knitting machine needle bed. The larger the number of needles, the finer the gauge and the finer the resulting fabric. The English system is generally used for flat knitting machines, measured in needles per inch, denoted by the letter E, for example E 7 is a seven-gauge machine. Circular machines or Cotton machines often measure needles per 1.5 inches.

gores Triangular sections knitted into a garment (such as stockings or ladies' vests) which create additional three-dimensional shaping.

guernsey A jumper, both patterned and plain, originally worn by seamen and fishermen. The knitted, oiled-wool, close fitting sweaters with their distinctive textured and cable patterns were popular from the mid nineteenth century and fashionable for women in the 1880s. This style has become a classic garment of the twentieth century. The terms 'guernsey' and '**jersey**' originated in the Channel Islands of Guernsey and Jersey and were used to describe knitted fabric from the sixteenth century. The twentieth-century guernsey is generally (machine) knitted plain with a garter stitch welt left open at each side for ease of movement.

guide bar Component of a warp knitting machine which contains multiple yarn feeders. These are threaded with the warp threads from a beam and feed yarn to all the needles across the width of the machine simultaneously, one feeder per needle.

hosier A merchant trading in knitted stockings (hose) and other garments.

hosiery A term originally denoting knitted stockings, knitted by hand, hand frame or industrial machine. It also stands for the totality of products of the knitting industry, including legwear, underwear and outerwear, especially in the nineteenth and early twentieth centuries.

inlaid In machine-knitted construction a pattern made with additional yarn which is introduced to the surface of the fabric for decoration or texture, during the knitting process. Used in both warp- and weft-knitting.

intarsia Weft-knitted fabric with a pattern formed of solid areas of colour, each knitted from a separate yarn contained entirely within that area (i.e. not floated across the back). Originally worked using manual technique on single bed knitting machines, now mainly industrially knitted.

integral knitting Knitting of complete garments, often including finishing details such as edgings or pockets. Garments are based on tubular knitting, with all sections knitted together on the knitting machine, requiring no seaming operations. Produced on either circular or specialized flat V-bed machines.

jacquard Term originating from woven fabrics, based on the invention of Joseph Marie Jacquard for patterning on the loom. Applied to weft-knitted fabric in which needles are selected to knit different coloured yarns to create a pre-determined pattern in two or more colours; variations include use of contrast texture rather than colour. See **double jacquard** and **float jacquard**.

jersey 1) A knitted upper body garment with sleeves, knitted by hand or machine; first worn by men and boys for sports from the mid nineteenth century, later adopted by women. In the twentieth century, worn for sports or casual wear and also known as a jumper, pullover or sweater.
2) Stockinette fabric, such as was knitted in Jersey from the sixteenth century. Became a general term for fine weft-knitted fabric

(usually above gauge 16) made on circular machines as bulk fabric: either single jersey (one set of needles) or double jersey (two circular sets of needles) using various structures. Jersey fabric was fashionable in the late nineteenth century when jerseys for women were often made with front openings; again in the 1920s, when jersey fabric was used by Chanel for cardigan jackets, pullovers and skirts. In the 1960s and '70s synthetic double jersey dresses and suits became popular.

jumper Deriving from the loose upper garment or shirt worn by sailors and other workers, from the mid-nineteenth century used to describe a long-sleeved woollen sweater for sport and travel. In the USA a jumper was a woman's pinafore dress.

kneecaps Knitted tubular coverings for the knees, often shaped to the angle of the knee.

knitting up Picking up stitches with a knitting needle from the selvedge of a knitted section of a garment, in order to knit new sections such as collars and sleeves.

knotted work Late eighteenth-century term, used in knitting hosiery on the manual knitting frame. Stitches were transferred to adjacent needles by means of a tool with points, leaving the original loop in place across two needles, creating slanted double loops. When repeated for a number of rows right then left alternately, this produced a shaded rib effect. When the stocking was knitted sideways, this appeared as subtle vertical stripes down the leg.

latch needle Knitting element invented in the mid-nineteenth century, consisting of a hooked needle with a moveable latch. During the knitting process, the latch opens and closes over the hook holding a loop of yarn.

lisle Cotton yarn, also known as 'Scotch thread', tightly spun and given a mercerized finish to remove hairiness. Popular for quality hosiery in the mid nineteenth century to the early twentieth century.

merino Wool derived from the Spanish Merino sheep, which was imported into Australia in the late eighteenth century and since bred for its long, high-quality fibres. In the mid-nineteenth century, some manufacturers including I&R Morley used 'merino' as a term to describe a mix of wool and cotton fibres in hosiery and underwear.

muffattee A knitted wrist covering for warmth and protection, nineteenth century.

nalbinding/single needle knitting An ancient technique resembling knitting, but made using a threaded sewing needle and short lengths of yarn, passing the yarn through previous loops as in knotting. It does not unravel and no binding off is required. It is slower to produce than knitting with two needles; small items such as socks and bags were made. For details see Burnham (1972) and Nordland (1961).

needle bed Set of knitting elements of a knitting machine arranged either in linear or circular formation

plated A machine-knitting technique in which two colours are used together, one always remaining in front of the other, so an effect is created of one colour on each side of the fabric if knitted plain. In ribbed fabric, one colour appears on the outer surface (knit loops), the second colour being revealed when stretched (purl loops). In early eighteenth-century frame-knitting, plating was achieved in areas by the manual inlaying of the second yarn.

plush A type of pile fabric knitted on weft or warp machines with long loops created on one fabric surface, giving a textural surface imitating velvet.

pullover An early twentieth-century term for a knitted garment for the upper body, usually with sleeves, without fastenings, and therefore pulled over the head. The sleeveless form became popular in the 1920s and 1930s.

putting out system Practice of giving out work to knitters working in their own homes, also known as cottage workers or outworkers.

Raschel Name given to a highly developed type of warp-knitting machine, invented first in the late eighteenth century and taken further technically in the mid twentieth century, especially by Karl Mayer of Germany. The name also applies to fabrics produced on Raschel machines, such as figured lace and zig-zag colour patterns, said to be named after French celebrity Elisabeth Rachel Felix.

ribbing A knitted structure with great elasticity, in which knit and purl stitches occur in each row. However the stitches always maintain the same vertical alignment throughout so create vertical lines or 'ribs'.

selvedge The closed edge of a knitted or woven fabric resulting from the yarns changing direction at each side of the piece. In **fully fashioned** knitting the selvedges are also shaped.

sheath A tool used in hand-knitting to steady one needle and speed up the knitting process, worn tucked into a belt. It was commonly made of wood, with a straight or curved shape, and a hole at one end to insert the needle. Often intricately carved, sheaths were also made of metal or ivory. They were used widely in the hand-knitting industry of the seventeenth to the nineteenth centuries; leather pouches with holes, filled with horsehair and mounted on a belt are still used today in Shetland.

single bed A knitting machine with one (horizontal or 'flat') needle bed.

single-needle knitting See **nalbinding**

space-dyeing A method of hank-dyeing yarns in several colours, or shades, in which the colour changes along the length in a repeating sequence, giving a variegated appearance to the final fabric.

spencer In the nineteenth century, a close fitting bodice or jacket, often worn by women and children.

sprang A highly elastic structure produced by interlacing parallel threads which are fixed at both ends. The interlacing must be secured in some way to prevent unravelling.

stocking stitch/stockinette/stockinet Plain knitted fabric, knit face on one side, purl face on the other, originally used extensively for knitting stockings in the round.

straight bar frame General term for flat single bed knitting machines of the type derived from William Lee's original stocking frame, usually having **bearded needles**.

sweater American term used from the late nineteenth century for a jumper, jersey or gansey. Originally referred to a garment used in exercise training to absorb sweat.

Swiss (or German) darning Method of embroidering over knitted stocking stitch fabric to mimic the appearance of knitted stitches. Originally for reinforcing stocking heels, from the mid nineteenth century it was used decoratively in coloured yarns. See, for example, *Treasures in Needlework* (1855 p.337).

tablet weaving A method of weaving narrow fabrics in which warp yarns are threaded through 'tablets' or cards pierced with holes (e.g. a square tablet with four holes). The cards are repeatedly turned, creating a shed (space) for the weft thread to pass through.

tatting Fancy knotted work mimicking fine lace, made using a special tatting shuttle and fine thread. Popular in the nineteenth

century for collars, cuffs, trimmings and household items, it had a brief revival in the mid-twentieth century.

tuck stitch An incomplete machine knitting action which results in a loop or loops being held in the hook of a **latch needle**, or of a **bearded needle**, for one or more rows of knitting. It is used for decorative or textural effect, and tends to increase the width of the resulting fabric.

turn stitch In framework knitting, a manual technique for making textured patterns. A stitch loop was transferred to a pointed hand tool, physically turned and replaced on the knitting needle to create a reverse (purl) loop on the stocking stitch ground.

V-bed A flat knitting machine with two needle beds arranged in an inverted 'V' configuration, using latch needles. First developed in the mid-nineteenth century and used to make rib, interlock, double jacquard and circular fabrics.

warp Term applied to the set of vertical threads running the length of the fabric on a weaving loom or in woven cloth.

warp-knitting Process of machine knitting in which multiple threads running the length of a fabric are simultaneously worked into vertical chains of stitches interlinked to each other. Many varieties of warp-knitted fabric can be made, including meshes, crochet-style openwork and patterned lace fabrics. Uses include fashion, interior and technical fabrics.

weft Term applied to horizontal threads running across the width of a woven fabric; the thread used during weaving that intersects with the warp threads.

weft-knitting The process of hand- or machine-knitting in which the fabric is built up in horizontal rows of loops knitted sequentially by a single continuous thread (or a small number of threads) passing across the width. Also applies to circular knitting.

white work General term for a range of needlework and embroidery techniques using white thread on white cloth to create subtle textures and patterns.

worsted A method of spinning wool from long-staple fibres which are combed parallel to each other before spinning resulting in a smooth yarn; cloth woven or knitted from worsted-spun wool.

woollen Method of spinning wool from short-staple fibres which are roughly carded before spinning, resulting in a hairy yarn, suitable for **felting** or **fulling**; cloth woven or knitted from wool.

Acknowledgements

KNITTING HAS BEEN CENTRAL to my entire career whether as a craft maker, designer, businesswoman, lecturer or academic researcher. This book was inspired by the rich resources of the V&A's collection of knitted artefacts and knitwear, a collection that spans a wide historical time period from the fourth century to the present day. It serves not only to demonstrate the evolution of this humble domestic art, but also to illustrate and compare consummate craft skills and technological progression, knitting in everyday life and in industrial development. I am grateful for the support of V&A curator Susan North in researching the collection over a period of time and to Claire Wilcox for her helpful input. I would like to thank V&A Publishing, especially Mary Butler and Mark Eastment for their enthusiasm for this publication, and to the editor Frances Ambler and copy editor Philippa Baker for guiding the work to completion. I am grateful to Nigel Soper for the book's design and to Clare Davis for her work on its production. Thanks are due to Richard Davis for the photographs especially taken for the book and to picture researcher Kate Phillimore. Particular thanks go to the many external photographers, companies and contemporary designers, who have allowed their work to be reproduced, it has been impossible to include them all for reasons of space.

Many people have shared their knowledge and experiences during the research and preparation of the text. I am grateful to Frankie Salter and Janet Macintosh, and to members of the Knitting History Forum and the Knitting and Crochet Guild including Kirstie Buckland, Jane Malcolm-Davies, Ruth Gilbert and Mary Hawkins. Thanks must go to curators and staff of a number of specialist collections for providing images and information, including Mike Millward and Gail Marsh of the Rachel Kay-Shuttleworth collection at Gawthorpe Hall, Burnley; David Orton of the Leicester Arts and Museum Service and the Knitting Together project; Michael Schoedel of the German Hosiery Museum project; Audrey Winkler, Helen Brownett, Colin Moss and Milla at the Ruddington Framework Knitters Museum; Carol Christiansen of the Shetland Museum and Archive; Edwina Ehrman (now at the V&A) and Hilary Davidson of the Museum of London; Hilary North at The Knitting Reference Library, Winchester College of Art; and Katharine Baird at the London College of Fashion. Several people provided invaluable assistance in picture research including Lucy Fisher, Jen Sturrock, Zoe Beck and Kate Stewart, who deserves special mention for her excellent work in archival research. For their detailed comments on the text, thanks are particularly due to Mary Schoeser, Susan North, and Anne Gibson, and to Diana Coben for reading early drafts. Thanks also to Reiner Rockel for his helpful suggestions. Lastly, the book would not have appeared at all without the support of family and friends, especially my husband Morris.

SANDY BLACK
March 2012

Picture Credits

All images are © Victoria and Albert Museum, London, except: **p.2** Rijksmuseum, Amsterdam; **p.15** Hamburger Kunsthalle, Hamburg, Germany/The Bridgeman Art Library; **p.18** The Royal Collection © 2012 Her Majesty Queen Elizabeth II; **p.27** © 2012 Image copyright The Metropolitan Museum of Art/Art Resource/Scala, Florence; **p.29** EMap Archive, London College of Fashion, courtesy of *Drapers*; **p.31** © Museum of London; **p.50** © Estate of Stanley Cursiter 2012. All Rights Reserved, DACS/City of Edinburgh Museums and Art Galleries, Scotland/The Bridgeman Art Library; **p.52** Shetland Museum and Archive; **p.57** Shetland Museum and Archive; **p.58** Shetland Museum and Archive; **p.61** Lorenzo Agius @ Orchard Represents. Courtesy Marks and Spencer; **p.62** Ruddington Framework Knitters' Museum, Nottingham; **p.71 top** Mary Evans/Roger Worsley Archive; **p.71 bottom** City of Westminster Archives Centre; **p.74** The National Archives; **p.75** EMap Archive, London College of Fashion, courtesy of *Drapers*; **p.76** Photo by Sotha Bourne. © Powerhouse Museum, Sydney/Yoshiki Hishinuma; **p.77** Used with the permission by Rowlinson Knitwear Ltd; **p.80** Fashion Museum, Bath and North East Somerset Council/The Bridgeman Art Library; **p.84 left** Photo by Lutz Bongarts/Bongarts/Getty Images; **p.84 right** Speedo trade mark logo and Fastskin fabric used with the permission of Speedo; **p.85** Chaloner Woods/Hulton Archive; **p.86** Courtesy Ugg Australia; **p.87** Courtesy Pringle; **p.88** United Artists/The Kobal Collection; **p.89** Courtesy John Smedley; **p.98** Brian Duffy/*Vogue* © The Condé Nast Publications Ltd; **p.99** David Bailey/*Vogue* © The Condé Nast Publications Ltd; **p.100** Copyright Norman Parkinson Ltd/Courtesy of the Norman Parkinson Archive; **p.107** Shetland Museum and Archive; **p.108** Photograph reproduced with the kind permission of the Royal Pavilion & Museums (Brighton & Hove); **p.110** Shetland Museum and Archive; **p.130** Photo by Patrick Jackson; **p.132** Ruddington Framework Knitters' Museum, Nottingham; **p.135** Courtesy of Jaeger; **p.144** Courtesy Celia Pym; **p.145** Photo by Daily Herald Archive/SSPL/Getty Images; **p.148** Courtesy D.C.Thomson & Co., Ltd.; **p.151** Courtesy of Jaeger; **p.152** Courtesy Alison Murray; **p.154** bottom Courtesy MQ Publications Ltd; **p.155** Courtesy Amy Twigger Holroyd; **p.164** Photo by Sasha/Getty Images; **p.165** 20th Century Fox/The Kobal Collection; **p.167** Photo by Keystone/Getty Images; **p.166** Photo by Claire Davis at Clements Ribeiro; **p.169** Catwalking; **p.171** Photograph by Carrie Branovan © 2012; **p.172** Albert Watson/*Vogue* © The Condé Nast Publications Ltd.; **p.173 right** Photo by Rolph Gobits. Courtesy Patricia Roberts; **p.174 top** © Guardian News & Media Ltd 1984; **p.177** Photo by Clive Arrowsmith; **p.182** Courtesy Peter Pilotto; **p.183** Courtesy Crea Concept; **p.184** Photo by Ben Gold. Courtesy Sarah Ratty; **p.185** Catwalking; **pp.186–7** Courtesy of Issey Miyake Inc.; **p.188** Peter Lindbergh/*Vogue* © The Condé Nast Publications Ltd; **p.191** Courtesy Yohji Yamamoto; **p.193** Courtesy Barbara Hulanicki Design; **p.194** David Montgomery/*Vogue* © The Condé Nast Publications Ltd; **p.195 left** Photo by Clive Arrowsmith. Courtesy Shi Cashmere; **p.195 right** © 2012 Woolmark Archive (Australian Wool Innovation Ltd) and the London College of Fashion; **p.197** David Bailey/*Vogue* © The Condé Nast Publications Ltd; **p.198** Terence Donavan/*Vogue* © The Condé Nast Publications Ltd; **p.199 right** Courtesy Missoni; **p.203** © Norman Parkinson Ltd courtesy Norman Parkinson Archive; **p.204** © The Trustees of the National Museums of Scotland; **p.206** Eric Boman/*Vogue* © The Condé Nast Publications Ltd; **p.210** Photography by Peter Gehrke; **p.211** Catwalking; **p.212** Photography by Fiona Garden; **p.213** Photo by Rob Meyers. Courtesy Sibling; **pp.214–5** All images Catwalking; **p.216** Photographed by Carl Bengtsson; **p.217** Courtesy Yoshiki Hishinuma; **p.220 top second from right** Courtesy Juliana Sissons; **p.220 top right** © Science Museum/Science & Society; **p.221 left** © Science Museum/Science & Society; **p.222 top second left** © Science Museum/Science & Society; **p.222 top second right** © NMeM/Daily Herald Archive/Science & Society; **p.222 bottom left** Courtesy Michael Schoedel, German Hosiery Museum; **p.223 top left** Courtesy Stoll Knitting; **p.223 second left** Daily Herald Archive/NMeM/Science & Society Picture Library; **top second right** Courtesy Missoni; **p.223 top right** Catwalking.com; **p.223 bottom left** Courtesy Missoni; **p.223 bottom second from left** Courtesy Barbara Hulanicki Design; **p.223 bottom right** Photo by Sotha Bourne. © Powerhouse Museum, Sydney/Yoshiki Hishinuma; **Back jacket illustration** Photography by Peter Gehrke

Index

Page numbers in *italic* refer to the captions